TRADITIONS AND VALUES

American Diplomacy, 1865-1945

Edited by
Norman A. Graebner

Series Editor
Kenneth W. Thompson

UNIVERSITY PRESS OF AMERICA

LANHAM • NEW YORK • LONDON

University Press of America,® Inc.

4720 Boston Way
Lanham, MD 20706

3 Henrietta Street
London WC2E 8LU England

Printed in the United States of America

Co-published by arrangement with
The White Burkett Miller Center of Public Affairs,
University of Virginia

Library of Congress Cataloging in Publication Data
Main entry under title:

Traditions and values.

(American values projected abroad ; v. 8)
Bibliography: p.
1. United States—Foreign relations—1865-
I. Graebner, Norman A. II. Series.
JX1417.A74 1982 vol. 8 [E661.7] 303.4'8273 s 85-5396
ISBN 0-8191-4650-1 (alk. paper) [327.73]
ISBN 0-8191-4651-X (pbk. : alk. paper)

AMERICAN VALUES PROJECTED ABROAD

VOLUME VIII

A SERIES FUNDED BY THE
EXXON EDUCATION FOUNDATION

FOUNDATIONS OF AMERICAN VALUES

Vol. I Western Heritage and American Values: Law, Theology and History, *By Alberto Coll*
Vol. II Political Traditions and Contemporary Problems, *Edited by Kenneth W. Thompson*
Vol. III Institutions for Projecting American Values Abroad, *Edited by Kenneth W. Thompson*
Vol. IV Essays on Lincoln's Faith and Politics, *By Hans J. Morgenthau and David Hein*
Vol. V The Predicament of Human Rights: The Carter and Reagan Policies, *By Nicolai N. Petro*
Vol. VI Writing History and Making Policy: The Cold War, Vietnam, and Revisionism, *By Richard A. Melanson*
Vol. VII Traditions and Values: American Diplomacy, 1790 to 1865, *Edited by Norman Graebner*
Vol. VIII Traditions and Values: American Diplomacy, 1865 to 1945, *Edited by Norman Graebner*
Vol. IX Traditions and Values: American Diplomacy, 1945 to the Present, *Edited by Kenneth W. Thompson*

AMERICAN VALUES VIEWED THROUGH OTHER CULTURES

Vol. X The Elements of International Strategy: A Primer for the Nuclear Age, *By Louis J. Halle*
Vol. XI Nationalism and Internationalism: European and American Perspectives, *By Erich Hula*
Vol. XII Diplomacy and Values: The Life and Works of Stephen Kertesz in Europe and America, *Edited by Kenneth W. Thompson*
Vol. XIII Islamic Values and World View: Khomeyni on Man, the State and International Politics, *By Farhang Rajaee*
Vol. XIV Culture & Democracy: Anthropological Reflections on Modern India, *By R.S. Khare*
Vol. XV An Ambassador's Journey: An Exploration of People and Culture, *By Charles Baldwin*
Vol. XVI Selections From *The New American Commonwealth*, *By Louis Heren*
Vol. XVII African and American Values: Liberia and West Africa, *By Katherine Harris*
Vol. XVIII United States Foreign Policy Towards Sub-Saharan Africa: Change, Continuity, and Constraint, *By David A. Dickson II*
Vol. XIX Latin American Values: Their Influence on Political Decisions and Processes, *By Julie Bunck*
Vol. XX The Primacy of Freedom in Development, *By Ambassador Soedjatmoko*

TABLE OF CONTENTS

AUTHORS

Clifford Haury, a graduate of the University of Virginia, has taught American history at Piedmont Virginia Community College, Charlottesville, for the past half dozen years. His scholarly work has focused on American relations with Bismarck's Europe in the late nineteenth century.

Richard E. Welch, Jr. is professor of history at Lafayette College, Easton, Pennsylvania. His many writings on the foreign policies of the United States at the turn of the century include a biography of Senator George Frisbie Hoar, an ardent anti-imperialist, and the more general study, *Response to Imperialism: The United States and the Philippine-American War, 1899–1902.*

Frederick W. Marks III resides at Forest Hills, New York. His perceptive studies on the external relations of the United States include *Independence on Trial: Foreign Affairs and the Making of the Constitution,* and a realist analysis of Theodore Roosevelt, *Velvet on Iron.*

Lloyd Ambrosius, professor of history at the University of Nebraska, has focused his scholarly endeavors on United States relations with Germany's Weimar Republic. His research has developed two themes: the German question at the Versailles Conference in 1919 and United States-German relations in the 1920s.

Betty Glad is professor of political science at the University of Illinois. Her major work on American foreign relations is *Charles Evans Hughes and the Illusion of Innocence: A Study of American Diplomacy.* More recently she has published a major work on the presidency of Jimmy Carter.

Richard Dean Burns is professor of history at California State University, Los Angeles. His work on Cordell Hull began as a graduate student at the University of Illinois. His chief effort as a historian has been in the field of bibliography. His writings include the massive *Guide to American Foreign Relations since 1700.*

Whittle Johnston is professor of political science at the University of Virginia. His major interest is United States foreign relations during the past half century, with major focus on Woodrow Wilson and American-Soviet relations since the 1930s.

PREFACE

The period from 1865 through World War II foreshadows the era of American supremacy in world politics. The Civil War revealed the capacity of the United States to survive conflict which in resources and casualties exceeded international conflicts from Waterloo to the Battle of the Marne.

Professor Norman A. Graebner is one of the nation's most respected diplomatic historians. Over the past two decades, his courses in diplomatic history at the University of Virginia have been immensely popular and well-subscribed. In contrast to many historians, Graebner is profoundly interested in the influence of traditions and ideas on diplomacy. Indeed he has written an important book on precisely that subject.

For this reason, it was natural in planning a series on American Values to turn to him for writing and editing two volumes on the American Diplomatic Tradition. Not only has he continued throughout his career to be concerned with ideas and traditions but his knowledge of the broad sweep of diplomatic history is unsurpassed.

The present volume, conceived and organized by Professor Graebner, contains essays on key American statesmen and diplomatists. It provides insights into the period by exploring the leaders who placed their imprints on its unfolding history. Graebner has enjoyed close intellectual ties with the contributors. Some are his students or colleagues and others are scholars with whom he has been associated in other projects.

Traditions and values undergird policies and actions. We can better understand the nation's course if we comprehend the operative values of those responsible for the decisions that shaped history. By throwing the spotlight on such traditions, Graebner and his contributors help explain American diplomacy.

Kenneth Thompson

INTRODUCTION

In 1865 the United States emerged from four years of total war as potentially the most powerful nation in the world. Few wars of modern times had involved more men or created more death and destruction. The American economy had demonstrated the capacity to sustain a massive military effort, to supply large armies with food and clothing as well as the best in military equipment, without demanding drastic sacrifices from the civilian population. Moreover, the American Civil War had increased the power of business and government to harness the nation's vast wealth and energy and direct them toward the achievement of national purposes. At the threshold of a totally unprecedented agricultural, industrial, and commercial expansion, the United States in time would project its growing power into the external world. Still unpredictable were the occasions for making that power effective and the ultimate nature and quality of the country's international role.

Protected by two oceans, both secured by the British Navy, post-Civil War Americans had long deserted the Founding Fathers' intellectual concern for the European balance of power. American involvement in the politics of Europe and Asia had become a matter of choice, one which the government of the United States, in the absence of any direct threats to American economic and security interests, had generally refused to exercise. Avoiding an active diplomacy in the affairs of the world, American too readily viewed the competitive, often cynical, mode of European politics as something to be shunned, even condemned. For them isolationism from world politics had come to reflect, not a favorable geographic position and the presence of the required European equilibrium, but a superior morality. Lord Bryce, the brilliant English critic of American life, attributed America's strange aversion to power politics to special geographic and political advantages that would one day disappear:

> America lives in a world of her own. . . . Safe from attack, safe even from menace, she hears from afar the warring

> cries of European races and faiths, as the gods of Epicurus listened to the murmurs of the unhappy earth spread out beneath their golden dwellings. . . . Had Canada or Mexico grown to be a great power, had France not sold Louisiana, or had England, rooted on the American continent, become a military despotism, the United States could not indulge the easy optimism which makes them tolerate the faults of their government. . . . Since the War of Secession ended, no serious danger has arisen either from within or from without to alarm transatlantic statesmen. Social convulsions from within, warlike assaults from without, seen now as unlikely to try the fabric of the American Constitution, as an earthquake to rend the walls of the Capitol.

Latin America, where United States power was predominant, was a special case. Still even in this arena the United States government after the Civil War was careful to obey the precepts of the Founding Fathers not to interfere in the internal affairs of other nations or empires. The Monroe administration had postponed the recognition of the Latin American republics until it was certain that Spain could not reconquer them; as a result recognition itself did not produce any break with the Spanish government in Madrid. The experience of the Civil War reaffirmed the American devotion to the principle of nonintervention as secretary of state William H. Seward reminded the European powers that they had no right to interfere in the American struggle, that the government of the United States had the obligation to put down any internal rebellion against its authority. It was not strange, therefore, that Hamilton Fish, President U. S. Grant's secretary of state, refused to support the Cuban people in their struggle against Spanish misrule despite the power of the United States to do so effectively. Fish recognized the Spanish-Cuban conflict as an imperial affair, and thus outside the legitimate concerns of American policy.

Thereafter the growing power of the United States, when contrasted to the political chaos, economic backwardness, and military impotence of the Latin American states, would encourage United States involvement in purely Latin American affairs. In the late nineteenth century the United States interfered in the struggle between Chile and Peru over control of the deserts that separated them, the British-Venezuelan boundary dispute in British

Guiana, and the renewal of the Cuban insurgency against Spanish rule. The American military involvement in the Cuban struggle for independence in 1898 was such a massive break from the tradition of nonintervention in other nations' affairs that Europe's general silence seems remarkable. Behind the intervention in Spain's imperial troubles was the capacity of the Cuban Junta in New York and its accomplices in the American press to arouse a high degree of anti-Spanish sentiment in the country and, more important, the knowledge that a decrepit Spanish monarchy could offer little resistance to American power in the Western Hemisphere and the Pacific. All of this influenced William McKinley's decision for war. There was nothing unique in the American crusade for humanity which focused on Spanish repression in Cuba—there had been verbal crusades for humanity toward the oppressed of Europe as well—but this one carried the assurance that its triumph would be swift and impressive. Had Cuba lain off the coast of Asia Minor there would have been no war of liberation in 1898. The experience of easy success in Cuba encouraged the subsequent American interventions in Caribbean affairs, toppling local governments with such facility that the role of force was scarcely apparent at all.

Having disposed of Spanish resistance in its quest for the Philippines, Guam, and Puerto Rico, the United States mounted the world stage as a major force, with commitments extending at last into the Eastern Hemisphere. What quickly determined the nature of the country's burgeoning international role, and rendered it totally unique, was the essential fact that the United States, with its vast territories and ample resources, entered the twentieth century not only with latent feelings of moral superiority, but also as a satiated power, determined to maintain its special advantages at the least possible cost to the American people. Lacking any further territorial ambitions, the United States no longer had any use for war. To prevent future conflicts that could not serve their country's interests American leaders searched for non-power devices to govern international affairs. The elimination of aggression and war would preserve the status quo and, with it, the dominance of the established powers, most notably Britain, France, and the United States. The assumption of a new rationality in world affairs, added to the peculiar attractiveness of the status quo, extended American purposes to include the general peace. Any breakdown of the peace might threaten the existing international order and, in the process, the special economic and security position of the United States. At the same time the new American leadership, assuming a new rationality in world affairs, denied the legitimacy, even the need, of employing force. Traditionally the reliance on national interest and the balance of power as guides to national policy had compelled governments to consider the interests and power of other states. Such necessities set limits to national goals. But the assumption of a new rationality among nations rendered United States concerns coterminous with such universal ideals as peace, order, and justice. America's self-assigned role in world affairs as the special advocate of international peace and stability, if successful, would serve American interests admirably. Such universal objectives, however, ignored the historic rule that the ends of policy always be governed by the means available. The very reasonableness of the nation's purposes seemed sufficient to assure their triumph.

It was left for Woodrow Wilson to embody such notions of an American-led international order in the external policies of the United States. What encouraged the conviction that the United States dared do no less and still be true to its special morality and its mission to humankind was the sheer destructiveness of the Great War of 1914–1918. Hopefully American influence would bring the postwar world under the influence of a more wholesome approach to foreign affairs, eliminating at last the secret and undemocratic practices that had saddled Europe with the most dreadful of wars. Wilson placed his hopes for lasting peace in the League of Nations, a universal collective security system in which the peace-loving nations, without any regard for their own national interests, would combine their strength to deter aggression. To protect the world against the possible recurrence of the recent European catastrophe, Wilsonian internationalists, no less than the President himself, simply ignored the persistence of power politics in history and in the world around them. Wishing and generalization soon prevailed over any analysis of the ongoing realities of international life. The end of lasting and universal peace overwhelmed the problem of means. Wilson once quieted the doubts of his adversaries who questioned the effectiveness of the League of Nations with the assurance: "If it won't work, it must be made to work." Schemes for rendering the League effective did not require explanations of how they would work; the consequences of failure were too disastrous to contemplate.

In the seemingly rational world of Woodrow Wilson and his successors of the interwar years, especially Charles Evans Hughes and Cordell Hull (both subjects of this volume), any changes in the Versailles settlement, to be legitimate, had also to be peaceful. In a world allegedly governed by principle and law, no country had the right to bargain with aggressors over changes in established treaties, especially since such bargaining would merely stimulate the appetite for further aggression. This approach to international conflict denied diplomacy its traditional role of seeking political accommodation among antagonists. For Hughes the assumption of a harmony of interests among nations, permitting peaceful solutions to international conflicts, faced no challenge simply because the world of the 1920s remained fundamentally stable. The dissatisfied countries—Germany, Japan, and Russia—were not yet prepared to challenge the Western powers. In an environment without apparent aggressors Hughes's achievements appeared substantial enough. Yet his major triumph, the Washington Treaties of 1922, in no way prepared the United States either to limit or to come to terms with future Japanese expansion in the Pacific.

Cordell Hull was confronted with the realities of German, Italian, and Japanese aggression after 1934. Still his responses consisted of little but appeals to the aggressors that they, like the United States, abide by the provisions and spirit of the Washington Treaties and the Kellogg-Briand Peace Pact of 1928, and thus seek no changes in the international order not achieveable through mutual agreement alone. Both Hull and President Franklin D. Roosevelt shunned all forms of diplomacy designed to gain some accommodation with the expansionist states; they shunned as well every threat to use force. Concessions to aggressors might indeed be repugnant and politically damaging, but the mere refusal to negotiate with Germany and Japan did not control their behavior. At the end the American determination to avoid accommodation gave the aggressors the choice of capitulation or war. This limited the American choice to the acceptance of unwanted change, unmodified by mutual agreement, or war. Having avoided diplomacy with Germany and Japan which in some measure reflected the desires of those two countries, the United States, following Pearl Harbor, found itself at war with both.

Peace in the 1930s required no less than full British-American cooperation either in defense of the Versailles settlement or in its modification. It was largely Anglo-American power that had created the international order now under attack. Earlier in the century Theodore Roosevelt, joined by his English and American friends, had advocated strong British-American ties as the surest guarantee of international stability. That assumption of a special relationship between the two countries did not survive the Great War. Thereafter some London officials still hoped that the United States would follow the British lead in upholding Versailles and the European equilibrium, recognizing in the process the importance of the British Empire to international stability. Instead they discovered an America determined to pursue its own course or no course at all. British foreign policy elites found the Roosevelt administration incomprehensible, its policies irrelevant. Sir Ronald Lindsay, the British ambassador, reported from Washington in 1934:

> In all major claims of policy, the devaluation of the dollar, the experimentation of the New Deal, the silver policy, no regard has been paid to foreign interests. . . . Nevertheless the real grievance of the world against America is not that she has been selfish, for that might be forgiven by governments that are themselves not entirely altruistic; and not even that she has supplied insults in the place of collaboration for to that we are all accustomed; but that the measures which she has adopted should have produced such very modest results to her own benefit; for the comparative failure of the New Deal induces danger and uncertainty everywhere, and retards or imperils the success that others may hope for or achieve.

When the Axis powers, over the next three years, opened their assault on the Versailles structure, the Roosevelt policies remained unchanged. The American drift amid the growing international chaos, marked by Hull's preachments to the aggressors in behalf of the principles of peaceful change and self-determination of peoples, sustained the British disillusionment.

Meanwhile Washington revealed little appreciation for Britain or British leadership. It viewed the British Empire, not as a source of stability in Asia and Africa, but as an immoral anachronism that had no right to exist. American officials attributed Britain's failure to stand up to Hitler's open defiance of the Versailles Treaty as evidence, not of Britain's economic decline, but of British irresponsibility. In time United States military officers developed a profound disrespect toward Great Britain, believing the problem one of nerve rather than military weakness—a weakness especially evident when contrasted to Germany's economic and military power. Roosevelt agreed with that judgment, rejecting the view that Britain was less than opulent. As late as August, 1944, he wrote to secretary of the treasury Henry Morgenthau: "This is very interesting. I had no idea England was broke."

Beyond the defeat of the Axis powers in the years following Pearl Harbor, Roosevelt and his advisers anticipated the reestablishment of the lost world of Versailles. The Atlantic Charter of August, 1941, promised self-determination to all areas occupied by Nazi forces, especially the states of Eastern Europe. Unfortunately, the more thorough the defeat of Germany and Italy, the more pervading would be the destruction of the continental balance of power, the more complete the Russian dominance of the German-occupied lands of Eastern Europe. For Stalin the only emoluments of victory commensurate with the price that Russia would ultimately pay for its narrow victory over Germany would lay in its political and military control of those countries that had fallen so easily to the Nazis. For Roosevelt this created a cruel dilemma, giving him the choice of accepting wartime territorial arrangements for Eastern Europe or simply avoiding such decisions with the prospect that at the end the United States would either have another war or would accept unwanted infringements on the promise of self-determination that it could not prevent. For Roosevelt, Stalin's designs on the regions bordering Russia were politically embarrassing. As the final essay in this book reveals, he could find no answer in force or accommodation. For that reason Winston Churchill's efforts to deal directly with Russia's wartime expansionism scarcely endeared him to the President. During the war Roosevelt harbored doubts about colonialist, balance-of-power Britain as well as expansionist Russia. If power politics should return to the world, Roosevelt hoped that the United States could play the role of arbiter, casting judgment but avoiding direct involvement.

World War II confirmed America's rise to a dominant position in world affairs, overshadowing that of Great Britain and the other Western democracies. But victory was not commensurate with the triumph of a Wilsonian world order; it would not usher in the American Century. Russia had carried the major burden of the war. Still the Kremlin had long rejected America's liberal-democratic principles for the postwar reconstruction of Europe. It was not clear at the war's end how the two great powers could protect their economic and security interests amid the pressures to disentangle their forces from the heart of Europe. Therein lay the tragedy of the war. Victory itself raised issues among the allies as troublesome, inescapable, and divisive as those which had earlier separated the allies from their Axis enemies. Successful allies might agree in wartime on the need of victory; they never agree for long on the design of the ensuing peace. Victory, no matter how complete, never eliminated the need of governments to come to terms with the demands and ambitions of others, be they allies or enemies. It is not strange, therefore, that this country's major triumphs in the two great wars of this century failed to achieve the promised triumphs of a new international order in which all people, enjoying governments of their own choice, would cooperate in the maintenance of peace. That long-standing ambition could never transcend the dreams of the American people themselves.

1

HAMILTON FISH AND THE CONSERVATIVE TRADITION

Clifford W. Haury

In his *Education,* Henry Adams wrote of Hamilton Fish, secretary of state in the administration of President U.S. Grant, that he "felt no prejudice whatever in his favor, and he had nothing in mind or person to attract regard; his social gifts were not remarkable; he was not in the least magnetic; he was far from young, but he won confidence from the start and remained a friend to the finish." Contemporaries and historians agree that Fish was not quick witted or an original thinker. He lacked both a sense of humor and a brilliant intellect. In fact, his appointment as secretary of state in March, 1869, came as a surprise that he politely declined, but since the Senate had by then approved his nomination, he reluctantly accepted the office. To Charles Sumner, Chairman of the Senate Foreign Relations Committee and a friend, he wrote: "Very much against my wishes, and after a very positive refusal, I am going to Washington to undertake duties for which I have little taste, and less fitness."

Yet even with these apparent handicaps, Hamilton Fish carved a record as secretary of state that marked him a worthy successor to William H. Seward. As a crisis manager and diplomatist, his instinctive caution, discipline, and sound judgement served him well. His fluency in French and his command of German and Italian made his dealings with the Washington diplomatic corps remarkably effective. Finally, although he was an incrementalist, taking one step at a time, "plodding rather than brilliant," as Allan Nevins notes, that trait allowed him to judge and handle a plethora of complicated diplomatic problems—the Alabama claims controversy with Great Britain, the Franco-Prussian War, the tensions with Spain over the Cuban revolt, Russian difficulties with Turkey and the Great Powers over the Black Sea, American interests in the Pacific and in Central America, and finally America's chief concrete interest in the world balance of power, the preservation of peace.

II

The Franco-Prussian War arrived in July, 1870, with such celerity that it astonished President Grant despite ample documentation of its coming both in the American press and in the diplomatic correspondence. Grant nursed a deep-seated hostility toward France. He had despised Napoleon's intrigues in Mexico with Maximillian and had ordered Union troops to the Rio Grande in 1865 during the Mexican crisis. He was not averse to Prussian punishment of the French. He instructed assistant secretary of state J. C. Bancroft Davis to inform the French minister in Washington, Jules Berthemy, that although the American government would officially observe a strict neutrality, he should not be surprised if the American people revealed themselves to be pro-Prussian, because while Germans had sympathized with the Union government, volunteered in the Union army, and bought bonds, the French government had exhibited little sympathy for the Union, had negotiated a loan for the Confederacy, and had sent a military expedition into Mexico "construed by the people as an act hostile to this country."[1]

Although Grant and the Cabinet appeared pro-German in sentiment, secretary of state Hamilton Fish, despite alleged unofficial statements condemning France, on balance appeared most judicious toward both sides. He hoped the "unnecessary war" would remain localized. To the American minister resident in Turkey, E. Joy Morris, Fish recalled that "the French nation was our early ally and we are not ungrateful nor forgetful. Prussia gave us her sympathy during the late struggle, and her people have contributed much to our increase. The *people* of both nations are our friends. . . . "[2] Fish thereafter attempted to be equitable toward both powers and use his influence to end the war on terms that would provide a lasting peace.

The first pressing matter for the State Department was the Prussian request that the American government assume the protection of German citizens in France. Fish instructed secretary of the Paris legation Wickham Hoffman to seek French consent for this request, which he did. At the same time, two American ministers, the writer and poet John Lothrop Motley in London and the historian George Bancroft in Berlin, advised Fish that the underlying cause of the war was French unwillingness to accede to the unification of Germany and the disturbance of the balance of power in central Europe after the Prussian defeat of Austria in 1866.[3]

By early August, 1870, the major powers in Europe—Great Britain, Austria-Hungary, and Russia—seemed determined to remain neutral in the war. As the month proceeded, the Grant administration formulated American policy toward the war. On August 22, 1870, President Grant issued the American proclamation of neutrality.[4] The course of events in early September provoked a peculiar and significant expansion of the original policy of strict and impartial neutrality. At Sedan, Prussia won a stunning victory and captured Napoleon III and his army. In Paris, Leon Gambetta proclaimed a French republic. The State Department counseled Minister Elihu Washburne to recognize the republic if it was the *de facto* government. This he did on September 7, 1870, in an interview with Jules Favre, acting French Foreign Minister. During the meeting Favre requested American intervention together with other neutral European powers to reestablish peace. Hamilton Fish replied with two concurrent telegrams. One requested that Bancroft ascertain whether the North German Confederation would accept such intervention; the other informed Washburne that it was not the policy of the United States to act jointly with the European powers in such matters, but that the United States would offer its good offices unilaterally if both sides accepted. Bismarck rejected the American inquiry, but for Fish the American interest in the restoration of peace on the continent proved more compelling than the interest in noninvolvement in European affairs. In his annual message to Congress in December, President Grant summarized the intervention question, and noted that if in the future unilateral American mediation could expedite the "return of peace," the United States would take that action.[5]

As soon as the news of the French disaster at Sedan arrived at the State Department by cable telegram, officials in Washington contemplated the future of Europe in the wake of the German victory over France. American diplomatists recognized that Germany, after Sedan, had displaced France as the most powerful nation on the continent, but were equivocal on the question of German territorial acquisition from France as a result of the war. Reflecting this ambivalence, Fish outlined the American position on the peace terms to Bancroft. The war, he wrote, "should find an early end," but the government would not "express any opinion as to the terms or conditions" except that they not contain "extreme demands" which might be "humiliating or derogatory to the pride of the great people who were our earliest and fast ally." Fish realized that embittered feelings in France would render peace tenuous and that any territorial dismemberment would likely sow the seeds of future conflict.[6]

During October, 1870, French pressure mounted for an official American statement disapproving German territorial acquisitions, but Fish resisted these overtures and became annoyed with French Minister Jules Berthemy's persistence. When the preliminary peace treaty was signed late in February 1871, France lost all Alsace—with the exception of the fortress Belfort—and a substantial portion of Lorraine, including Metz, and agreed to an indemnity of two hundred million pounds. Noting the lively French hatred of Germany, Fish expressed the official opinion of the American government when he wrote: "It is hoped that the terms upon which it has been brought to a close may not leave a feeling which time will not efface and that peace may be sincere and lasting."[7] Both Fish and his assistant, J. C. Bancroft Davis, drawing upon the American diplomatic correspondence concerning the war and the peace treaty, had substantial reason to doubt the durability of the peace in Europe.

III

The Franco-Prussian War allowed the United States and Russia to press the British concerning matters of grave importance to each, the *Alabama* claims, and the neutralization of the Black Sea, respectively. For Hamilton Fish, the Russian denunciation of the Black Sea clauses of the Treaty of Paris of 1856 and the consequent Anglo-Russian war scare, when combined with the British preoccupation with changes in the European balance of power on the continent caused by the German victory over France, offered the most opportune moment to press the British for a solution of all outstanding issues—the *Alabama* claims, the Canadian fisheries question, and the San Juan boundary dispute in the Pacific. In the pattern of his predecessors, Fish derived American advantage from disruption in the European balance of power. The measure of success for both Russia and America became patent in the Treaty of London, on the one hand, and the Treaty of Washington, on the other.

As early as the summer of 1869, secretary Fish was advised

that Russia would seize the first opportunity to abrogate the restrictions on the Black Sea, sanctioned in the Treaty of Paris of 1856 ending the Crimean War. The Black Sea clauses neutralized the area by forbidding the construction or maintenance of a navy or naval fortifications. Minister resident in Turkey Morris, a veteran of nine years service, reaffirmed Russian intentions in the summer of 1870. "Russia," he wrote " . . . will try to take advantage of the crisis and provoke a revision of the treaties of 1856, by which the Black Sea was neutralized, and the Bosphorous and Dardanelles were closed to the passage of her vessels of war."[8]

On October 31, 1870, Russian Foreign Minister Gorchakov issued a circular note to the powers announcing unilateral Russian renunciation of the Black Sea clauses. John Jay, minister to Austria-Hungary, telegraphed the news to the State Department. In England, John Lothrop Motley reported that the British denunciation produced a "very great anxiety" and fear of general war. British foreign secretary Granville answered the Gorchakov circular with a declaration that Britain could not sanction Russian revision of the Treaty. Prince Bismarck, the Prussian chancellor, suggested a conference to settle the matter. In early December 1870, Britain, Russia, Prussia, Turkey, Italy, and Austria-Hungary accepted the conference proposal, and the crisis waned considerably.[9]

From the outset of the Anglo-Russian war scare, European opinion calculated a rising American interest by calling attention to Russian-American amity extending from the Civil War era and by dwelling on the unsettled Anglo-American *Alabama* claims dispute. In fact, in November, 1870, the Russian Minister in Washington, Constantine Catacazy, hinted to Hamilton Fish that the time was opportune to settle the *Alabama* claims.[10] Discussions in Washington gave credence to European speculation of a Russian-American entente. Just as Russia sought to turn the Franco-Prussian war to its advantage and abrogate the Black Sea clauses, the United States, went the rumors, sought to press a settlement of the *Alabama* claims in the midst of the Anglo-Russian crisis. At the least, Secretary of State Fish wished that the British see such a course as feasible. He alluded to Catacazy's suggestion in conversation with British Minister Sir Edward Thornton. Thornton needed no reminder that the United States could complicate the Anglo-Russian crisis not only by pressing the claims, but by allowing, in the event of war, the fitting out of Russian commerce destroyers in American ports in the fashion of the *Alabama*. Early in December, 1870, Fish removed any doubts of his willingness to manipulate the Anglo-Russian crisis to American advantage in an instruction to John Jay in Vienna. Jay had reported a casual conversation with Baron Rothschild, British financial magnate, concerning possible Anglo-Russian war. Jay had commented that the United States would remain neutral. Fish answered that it was "probably quite true" that America would remain neutral, but advised Jay to exercise caution in predicting American actions and "especially to avoid a reply which either by admission or omission should imply that this Government would not avail itself of the occasion which may seem most opportune for pressing the settlement of any questions between it and any other Government."[11]

Fish's timing was crucial. The Gladston-Granville ministry, perceiving British isolation in the crisis with Russia, began to work with solicitude on the unsettled relations with America. Moreover, the Secretary of State employed excellent "carrot and stick" diplomacy. At the same meeting with Sir Edward Thornton in which he referred to the Russian suggestions of action against England, Fish dropped any reference to Canadian independence as related to the claims, and instead suggested an official British expression of regret in the *Alabama* case. This step was undoubtedly connected with the impending break in relations between Grant, Fish, and Senator Charles Summer, the foremost advocate of the so-called indirect claims, but was also related to Fish's appreciation of the conservative tradition in American foreign policy which expoloited the disruptions in the European balance of power, in this case to turn British distress to American success. Also, by this time Fish was aware that pro-American annexationist sentiment in parts of Canada had waned, and that some New Englanders were ready to employ arms to settle the Canadian fisheries question. Therefore, he chose this moment to soften the American position.[12] President Grant's State of the Union message in December, 1870, mirrored Fish's new position. It contained no reference to indirect claims or Canadian independence and expressed American willingness to negotiate. By the end of 1870, Fish had anchored the American position on the *Alabama* claims to two objectives—the possible and the peaceable.

In February, 1871, the United States and Great Britain announced the formation of a Joint High Commission in Washington to discuss the Alabama claims, the Canadian fisheries, and all other questions. Just weeks earlier, Great Britain, Russia, and all other interested nations convened the London Conference on the Anglo-

Russian dispute over the Black Sea. All three nations—America, Russia, and Great Britain—perceived their national interest to be the preservation of peace. The Treaties of London and Washington, signed in March and May, 1871, respectively, were the products of their endeavors.

The Treaty of Washington was, as Charles Campell has noted, a "quasi-settlement," and therefore the beginning of a process of Anglo-American arbitration and negotiation. The most explosive issue, the *Alabama* claims, went to a Geneva tribunal composed of the United States, Great Britain, Italy, Switzerland, and Brazil for adjucation on the principle of "due diligence" as defined by the treaty; the British also expressed officially their regret for the escape and damages the Confederate vessels had inflicted. Second, the San Juan boundary dispute was sent to arbitration under the Emperor of Germany. Third, on the question of the North American fisheries, both Canada and the United States were accorded reciprocal inshore fishing rights for ten years, with an arbitration commission in Halifax, Nova Scotia, to set the sum America would pay for this supposedly unequal reciprocity. Fourth, routine Civil War claims were assigned to a joint commission meeting in Washington. Fifth, the treaty exchanged free navigation rights for Americans and Canadians on a number of rivers and lakes, most notably the St. Lawrence River.[13]

The complex negotiations and arbitrations that commenced with the Treaty of Washington outlived Fish's tenure as secretary of state, but the document was the capstone of his diplomatic career. Although he had no prior experience, Fish, like his predecessor William Seward, mastered quickly the intricacies of diplomacy. He successfully followed in the historic American diplomatic practice of exploiting the disruptions in the European balance of power, but he carefully defined United States claims so that they were reasonable and in the long-term interest of peace. No level of international pressure would force Britain to capitulate. Moreover, when the Treaty of Washington is linked with the Treaty of London of that same year, it represents British recognition of the United States as a major component in the world balance of power and contributor to the preservation of peace.[14]

IV

Hamilton Fish inherited a rebellion in Cuba against Spanish rule. He related this revolt to the source of friction and bitterness in the *Alabama* claims—the British recognition of Confederate belligerency in 1861. President Grant and some advisors sought an American recognition of Cuban belligerency early in the administration, but Fish recognized the inconsistency of claiming such a right in the case of Cuba, while denying Britain that right in the case of the Confederate states. On the other hand, Fish was not willing to renounce recognition, as Senator Charles Sumner desired, as a possible alternative. In the end, the secretary of state embraced the conservative American diplomatic tradition—examine the case, determine whether the Cuban insurgents or the Spanish qualified as the *de facto* government, and make the decision on that basis.

Fish applied a number of diplomatic techniques to move Spain to reforms in Cuba. He threatened the recognition of belligerency. He suggested possible American intervention. Several times he offered the Spanish the good offices of the President as mediator. At least twice Fish instructed the American minister in Madrid to request his passports when there was no movement on the Cuban issues. Finally, when the most serious diplomatic crisis came in 1873 with the seizure of the *Virginius* and the execution of fifty-three of its passengers and crew, Fish used the crisis to redefine American interests in Cuba as well as to demand Spanish reform of its administration of Cuba and punishment of those responsible for the *Virginius* executions. He entrusted Caleb Cushing, one of America's foremost diplomats, with the task of negotiating a general settlement.

All efforts notwithstanding, Fish produced no Spanish equivalent to the Treaty of Washington; nor was he any more successful at convincing the Spanish government to grant independence to Cuba than he was at getting the British to sever all ties to Canada. Yet to gauge American diplomacy toward Cuba a failure is an oversimplification. No problem—European, Asian, or American—elicited more of his personal attention than the Ten Year's War. Despite belligerent talk from Congress, the President, and minister to Spain Daniel Sickles, as well as a war scare created by the *Virginius* affair, Fish consistently defined the American interest to be that of preserving peace with Spain. Although he felt the proper status for Cuba was independence, the Secretary did not risk war with Spain at a time when the United States Navy was in decline, the army reduced, the national debt sizable, and the delicate arbitration with the British underway as a manifest example of diplomatic means other than force.[15] By 1877 the same process of negotiation, so successful in reducing Anglo-American frictions, had produced little result. Moreover, his ultimate objective, though not accomplished during his tenure, was laudable: the independence of Cuba to be achieved by Spanish volition without American intervention or a Spanish-American War. Fish did not achieve this end, but his persistence and energy in its behalf were noteworthy. Finally, to measure Fish's Cuban diplomacy as a failure in the light of the Treaty of Washington obscures the continuity in approach in both cases: arbitration, negotiation, and peace as the proper national interests.

In the fall of 1868, Cuban nationalists rebelled against Spain. The United States suffered serious consequences from the revolt: commerce shrank, investment diminished, Americans were killed and wounded. In April, 1869, the rebels declared a republic and named Manuel de Cespedes President. Although they controlled little territory and lacked organization, the Cubans demanded independence. Spain offered no concessions without the precondition that the rebels lay down their arms.

In Spain the Liberals were in power. Although they had favored reforms in Cuba, they refused compromise. The insurgents, on the other hand, would not cease the rebellion. Into this situation, Hamilton Fish thrust a new American diplomat, General Daniel E. Sickles. American sympathies were clearly evident in his instructions. President Grant offered his good offices on the bases that Spain grant independence to Cuba, with compensation for "property and domain" paid by the Cubans, the abolition of slavery in Cuba and Puerto Rico, and an armistice, but not as a precondition. Fish added that if Spain refused, "an early recognition of belligerency [was] the logical deduction."[16]

In August, 1869, with no movement apparent, President Grant, influenced by the propaganda of the Cuban exiles in the United States, the sympathy of friends and Congressmen for the revolutionaries, and the atrocity stories emanating from Cuba, signed a decree recognizing Cuban belligerency. Although the secretary of state signed the proclamation, he never published it. Fish argued that recognition of belligerency in Cuba imperiled the American case against Britain in the *Alabama* claims, and was unwarranted because the Cuban nationalists neither controlled territory nor had civilian jurisdiction enough to constitute a *de facto* government. Grant acquiesced to Fish's arguments Fish denied officially that recognition of belligerency had been considered. But Spanish delay in answering the American proposal prompted Grant to ask Fish to place a time limit of October 1, 1869, on his proposal.[17] Spain refused the American initiative by asking for an insurgent cease fire prior to discussions and a plebiscite in Cuba concerning the matter of independence. Fish viewed these demands as impractical. When the time limit expired, he withdrew the offer.

During the first months of 1870, Fish set his sights considerably lower: the abolition of slavery in Cuba and Puerto Rico, which he described as the *"sine qua non"* of any settlement over Cuba. The Spanish promulgated a plan of abolition, limited in scope so much so it fell short of American desires. Moreover, Spanish authorities in Cuba failed to carry out its provisions. Fish asked Spain to execute the emancipation plan without further delay.[18] Early in 1871 Fish hoped a new Spanish government and monarch could grapple with the Cuban insurrection, but was no more successful in prodding it into action.[19] The Madrid government chose to do the minimum necessary to keep the United States from intervening in Cuba, while it tried to crush the insurgency in a pattern that was a harbinger of Spanish strategy after 1895. Fish found this policy frustrating enough to replace, in April, 1872, the American position and experiment with a new tactic. America had pleaded in vain for a "more humane and Christian mode of warfare in Cuba." No Spanish statesman denied atrocities, but neither were they stopped. Also, the United States had urged Spain "to grant some amelioration of the severely despotic rule practiced in Cuba," once again without results. As for the abolition of slavery in Cuba and Puerto Rico, the decree was a dead letter. Despite public opinion in sympathy with the Cubans, the Grant administration had observed neutrality by repressing American-based filibusterers. Yet the Spanish had seized the estates of American citizens and embargoed their proceeds. In sum, the relations between the two countries were unsatisfactory. Although the President did not wish to "foment a rupture" with Spain, Fish ordered Sickles recalled. There would be no replacement, he added, until there was greater hope of resolution of the outstanding issues.[20]

Sickles remained in Madrid, however, because the Spanish offered some changes. Spain issued a decree implementing the July, 1870, emancipation plan. Fish doubted the sincerity of the action because by October, 1872, the Spanish government had failed to execute the abolition decree in Cuba. Also, after four years, the Cuban rebellion still raged on. Unless Spain supressed the revolt, Fish hinted, it might become the "duty" of the Grant administration to change its policy toward Cuba. He concluded:

> A nation gives justification to resistance, while admitted wrongs remain unredressed. Resistance ceases to be justifiable when no wrongs are either admitted or alleged. Redress wrongs and resistance will cease. . . . Spain must not be surprised to find as the inevitable result of the delay, a marked change in the feeling and in the temper of the People and of the Government of the United States.

Before Sickles communicated Fish's message, the Spanish offered additional proposals on Cuba. Spain wished to ascertain whether President Grant would mediate the Cuban affair on the bases of municipal franchise for freemen, the gradual abolition of slavery, and provincial autonomy, but with the condition that the rebels lay down their arms. Fish replied that considering the bloodshed on both sides, there was no possibility of a rebel armistice without assurances from Spain regarding the reforms. He reminded the Spanish that the President had offered his good offices three years earlier with no result. Any mediation effort was to no avail unless both parties were disposed to accept it, there were no conditions, and the specifics of the reforms were spelled out. If Spain asked mediation, and designated reforms, among them a provincial legislature, the abolition of slavery in all forms, municipal government, self taxation, guaranteed personal and property rights, exemption from standing armies, and control of the internal affairs of the island, then the President would be willing to mediate. Fish concluded by stating that if no practical result was obtained it was "of little avail to continue an Envoy Extraordinary at Madrid."[22] Interestingly enough, Fish discussed the proposal in the cabinet on November 12, six days after he had written the reply. Although Grant expressed willingness to mediate, Fish remined him that the mediation offer in 1869 bore no fruit. He suggested that the United States could, as he already had, ask Spain to indicate specific reforms for Cuba and to make a formal request for presidential good offices or face the possibility of the recall of the American minister.[23]

Sickles' recall appeared a possible prelude to American intervention and a declaration of war, but the Secretary of State wished to prod Spain to reform and preserve the peace. In lieu of the recall, Fish devised a scheme, in anticipation of Grant's annual message, to ask Congress for high discriminatory duties on goods from all slaveholding countries. Since the United States was the market for three quarters of Cuban sugar production, this move would strike and economic blow against Spain. Grant grudgingly accepted this plan, and Fish prepared a statement for his message. The news quickly reached Spanish minister Don Josè Polo de Bernabe, who communicated hastily with Madrid. The home government cabled Polo the executive decrees concerning Puerto Rico: separation of civil and military power, the extension of Spanish provincial law, election of municipal governments, and the introduction of a bill for Puerto Rican emancipation in the *Cortes*. The concessions on Puerto Rico, Polo told Fish, were evidence of Spain's intent toward Cuba. A pleased Fish confidentially informed Polo that the discriminatory tariff request would be held for further consideration. Thereafter the Spanish Government issued the executive decrees on Puerto Rico, and by March, 1873, a law for immediate emancipation passed the *Cortes*.[24]

What was possible for Puerto Rico was impossible for Cuba. The Spanish were even unwilling to go beyond limited gradual abolition of slavery. Moreover, revolution shook Spain in February, 1873, when a republican government took power. Although Fish hoped this change in government would soften the Spanish position on Cuba, there was little change. His disappointment with the new Spanish republican government was apparent when he wrote of an interview between Sickles and the Spanish minister of foreign affairs, "the general results . . . may be said to be that the causes of our complaint 'will receive consideration'—Tomorrow! and tomorrow!"[25] Fish noted that there was "remarkable similarity" in the outrages and cruelties charged against the insurgents in Spain by the republican government and those charged against the Spanish authorities in Cuba by the Cuban *insurrectos*—the destruction of communications, burning of crops, forced tribute and taxation, the burning of towns, robbery, immolation of civilians, and the shooting of prisoners of war.[26]

All of this Fish had heard from still another source. From the mountains of Oriente province in Cuba, Carlos Manuel de Cespedes, the President of the Cuban "republic," wrote Grant in March, 1873, to ask American intervention. Cespedes noted that the republicans in Spain were as intent as the old government on crushing the Cuban revolt. Fish suspected as much himself.[27]

In the summer of 1873, Fish reviewed the diplomatic impasse over Cuba when he wrote that President Grant had heard with regret the Madrid Ministry's announcement that no reforms would come in Cuba without a rebel armistice. The Spanish had retreated to the original position of 1869; Fish did likewise. This announcement "amounts practically to a declaration of perpetual war," the Secretary wrote Sickles, which will make other powers consider "its bearing and its effect with reference to their own interests and duties." He concluded that it might become the duty of other powers to take notice of the prolongation of the "conflict without results." The President hoped that the United States would not be "first of the nations" to recognize these facts. Once again Fish resurrected the implied threat of recognition of belligerency and intervention.[28]

This more strident tone in American diplomacy came in advance of the *Virginius* affair in November, 1873. More than two weeks before the ship's seizure, Fish specified certain American demands for Cuba: the release of embargoed estates and their proceeds, the abolition of slavery, and other reforms. Successive governments had tendered assurances but produced no action. In words that rank among Fish's most threatening, the Secretary observed that Cuba groaned under a "martial law." If Spain was powerless in Cuba, each country had to determine the steps necessary to protect its own interests. President Grant might thus be forced to elect between recognizing the pro-slavery clubs of Havana as the actual *de facto* rulers of Cuba and recognizing the right of anti-slavery republicans to carry on war for the dominion of a territory which was "practically abandoned" by Spain. "I need not intimate to you," he told Sickles, "in which direction the option would be exercised."[29]

V

The *Virginius* affair burst on the diplomatic horizon on November 5, 1873, when American consul Henry C. Hall telegraphed Fish that the Spanish had captured the vessel. The *Virginius,* flying the American flag and ostensibly in American registry, had often served the Cuban junta by carrying arms, ammunition, and men to Cuba, as Fish already knew. The most alarming news, however, came on November 2 and concerned not the ship but the fate of those aboard. Despite a telegram from Madrid not to inflict penalties without referring them to the ministry at home, Spanish authorities had, with "indecent and barbarous haste . . . precipitated in cold blood and vindictiveness" executed fifty-three of the crew and passengers. "Such wholesale butchery and murder," Fish wrote to Sickles, "is almost incredible. . . . No government deserves to exist which can tolerate such crimes." Yet Fish recognized a pattern in this crisis. He observed that "this is but another instance in the long catalogue of the defiance of the Home Government by those entrusted with authority in Cuba and adds another page to the dark history of bloody vengeance and cruel disregard of the rules of civilized war, and of common humanity. . . . " Fish noted that the prompt Spanish reaction of revulsion at the deed was welcome, but he expected condemnation and punishment for the perpetrators. Failure to act would denote approval of the outrage and a sign of Spain's inability to govern."[30]

That the crisis threatened war was clearly evident in the Grant administration's excited discussions of naval and military readiness and its preliminary preparations. Moreover, the Cabinet on November 14 took up the question of demands upon the Spanish government. This debate produced a telegram to Sickles to seek restoration of the *Virginius,* the release and delivery of the prisoners therefrom, a salute to the flag, and punishment of those officials responsible. The ultimatum carried a twelve day time limit. Sickles was to close the legation and request his passports if no Spanish reply was forthcoming.[31]

Spain, impressed by the popular feelings for war on both sides of the Atlantic and by the apparent rancor between Minister Sickles and foreign minister Josè de Carvajal over the matter, requested a transfer of the *Virginius* negotiations to Washington and asked for time to gather facts. The Spanish government assured Fish that it would punish those guilty and make full reparations. On his part, Fish ordered Sickles to remain at his post and await instructions. The Spanish sought, however, to delay a solution beyond the deadline of November 26. President Grant intervened and instructed Fish to have Sickles leave Madrid unless a satisfactory proposition was tendered by the end of that day.[32]

The war scare abated when the Spanish dispatched a proposition on November 26 that Grant and Fish approved. Formalized in a protocol on November 29, 1873, the proposition provided that the *Virginius* and its survivors, both passengers and crew, be restored to American custody; that the American flag be saluted on December 25 unless Spain proved the *Virginius* had no right to fly it; that Spain would proceed against the officials of Santiago through the courts and inflict punishment if laws or treaty rights were violated, and that the United States would institute an inquiry and legal proceedings against any person who had violated American laws if the ship were not entitled to fly the

American flag.[33] During the month of December, the ship and its survivors were surrendered to the American Navy in Cuba. Also, the Attorney General decided that the *Virginius* was not "rightfully" carrying the American flag, and consequently the salute was "spontaneously dispensed with."[34]

The issue that eluded resolution was punishment of those responsible for the *Virginius* executions, most notably General Juan Burriel, the Governor General of Santiago. Yet in December, 1873, the Spanish promised to proceed with that task. Moreover, in December Fish assigned a new minister to Spain, Caleb Cushing, a veteran of diplomatic service, a scholar of Spain, its literature and customs, and friend to many Spanish authorities. The Cushing mission commenced with the secretary's grand review of Spanish-American relations. Fish defined United States interest as the independence of Cuba. He wrote: "And while such independence is the manifest exigency of the political interests of the Cubans themselves, it is equally so that of the rest of America, including the United States." Short of independence was autonomy for Cuba along the model of Canada. Fish instructed Cushing to "support it as the next best thing to the absolute independence of Cuba." As for annexation by the United States, Fish was clear: "The President does not meditate or desire the annexation of Cuba . . . but its elevation into an independent republic of freeman. . . . "[35]

During 1874, the two immediate problems of Spanish-American relations were the question of trial and punishment of the perpetrators of the *Virginius* outrage, most notably General Juan Burriel, the Governor General of Santiago, and an indemnity for those who were detained or killed.[36] Fish found only frustration as the Spanish refused to move on either count. Of the two problems, his feeling of urgency was greater in the case of the indemnity. President Grant wanted to announce a settlement in his annual message to the Congress in December. The pressure finally paid dividends when Spain agreed to pay the indemnity for all passengers and crew who were not also claimed by the British, who had negotiated a settlement earlier. Progress halted on setting the amount when a revolution once again shook Madrid. Grant and Fish decided to utilize the situation to accelerate Spanish action. Fish dispatched a letter from Grant accrediting Cushing to the new monarch, Alfonso XII, but instructed him not to deliver his credentials until the Spanish agreed to the terms of the indemnity. Although Grant had no document to transmit to the Congress in December, the American tactics produced an agreement in time for a Special Session of

Congress in March. Cushing secured an $80,000 indemnity. The Spanish government paid the full amount in May, 1875.[37]

Grant and Fish appeared quite pleased with Cushing's work, so much so that Fish in early June sent him congratulations on a year of good work in Spain. Ever persistent, the secretary reminded Cushing to "seek satisfaction" on the question of punishment for General Burriel and his company. Although the General had been recalled from Cuba and had retired, he was not brought to trial. To Fish's alarm, he was instead promoted in August, 1875. The Secretary protested vehemently that this act violated the protocol of November 29, 1873, on the *Virginius* affair, but Madrid failed to respond.[38]

Because of the Burriel matter, the instability of the Spanish Ministry and country, the continuing war in Cuba, and public and congressional clamor for intervention which appeared to attract President Grant, Fish undertook a massive restatement of American objectives for Cuba during 1875. Affairs in Cuba were unsatisfactory, wrote Fish. Spain had failed to suppress the revolution. The most prominent consequences for Americans involved the embargo and confiscation of American estates and property in Cuba, as yet unrestored, the continuing trial of American citizens in violation of the treaty of 1795, the lack of action to try and punish General Burriel and his cohorts. As for the revolt, Fish had no doubt that the "final issue" was to "break the bonds which attached Cuba as a colony to Spain." Also, it was impossible to conceal American sympathy for the movement, more so since it involved the question of slavery as well. Therefore, the Grant administration sought the return of embargoed estates and property, trial under treaty rights for its citizens, Spanish enforcement of its orders and decrees in Cuba, and an end to the war. Britain had relaxed its old system of colonial dependence for Canada, but not Spain for Cuba. Indeed America had received numerous requests from the Cuban insurgents for aid and for seven years had attempted to supress filibustering activities from its waters in the hope Spain would pacify Cuba. That day had not come. President Grant considered a change in American policy toward Cuba. The President, offering again his good offices, felt "that the time is at hand when it may be the duty of other governments to intervene, solely with the view of bringing to an end a disastrous and destructive conflict, and of restoring peace, in the Island of Cuba." Grant would submit the subject, with his views, "for the consideration of the Congress." Fish transmitted this same message to minister Robert C. Schenck in London to seek support from Prime Minister Derby. Cushing was instructed to defer his presentation until the United States determined whether joint action with Great Britain was possible.[39]

Fish wished to accomplish three things with the famous "No. 266," as the message was called. First, he wanted to steer the Congress and President away from a policy of recognition of belligerency or independence because he felt those moves unwarranted. No *de facto* government in Cuba, worthy of recognition, had supplanted the Spanish. Second, he intended to threaten Spain with intervention if the war in Cuba continued. Third, he sought to court support in Europe for the policy. The Spanish parried "No. 266" even before it was presented in Madrid. Cushing telegraphed Fish on November 16 a summary of a note from the Spanish government which answered nearly point by point all of Fish's arguments on Cuba. This gave Fish pause, but after concluding that the Spanish note did not substantially affect his own, he cabled Cushing to read it in Madrid on November 27, 1875. Thereafter on December 6, Fish informed Cushing that the President's annual message would mirror the position taken in "No. 266"—the President would condemn recognition of belligerency or independence in strong terms, but suggest mediation and intervention "by other powers" as a contingency if the war in Cuba continued.[40]

Fish's initiative was a precursor of John Hay's Open Door notes of 1899 and 1900. During December "No. 266" went as a circular letter to all major European governments to court support. In turn the British, German, French, Austrian, and Russian governments heard "No. 266", as well as did Lisbon and Rome. Fish did not ask these governments to join America in intervention, but rather to exert pressure on the Spanish government to terminate the war in Cuba and pacify the island "to avoid the necessity of intervention." Like Hay's Open Door notes, "No. 266" brought little concrete response in Europe. First, the Spanish were quick to point out that the Cuban rebellion was a domestic or internal problem, the same position the Union government had utilized during the Civil War. Second, the European powers were preoccupied with a similar diplomatic initiative by Austria-Hungary, proposing reform for the Ottoman Empire to quell a Balkans revolt, the so-called Andrassy Note. Like Spain, Turkey attempted to forestall the initiative by proposing its own set of reforms. In much the same fashion as Hamilton Fish, Andrassy sent his own set of reforms to the European powers late in 1875. The European powers, as well as Turkey, accepted the Andrassy reforms, but in Cuba the insurgents rejected the Fish proposals on the grounds that they were inadequate without a great power guarantee.[41]

The new Cuban iniative came to little. Although Fish had dramatically restated the American position on Cuba, Spain did not alter its means or its objectives in Cuba. The circular letter to the European capitals did throw the Spanish government on the defensive by forcing it to justify and explain its position on Cuba, but the major powers exerted no pressure on Spain to reform. Moreover, when this European initiative came to public knowledge early in 1876, a portion of the American press roundly criticized Fish for violating the spirit of the Monroe Doctrine by approaching the European powers with a joint intervention scheme.[42]

Early in 1876 the Spanish requested, during a frank interview between Calderon y Collantes, Spanish foreign minister, and Cushing, that Fish specify "the precise thing" which the United States would advise Spain to do about Cuba. Fish answered, first, that the United States had no desire "for the acquisition of Cuba, or for its annexation directly or indirectly . . . there are at this time no considerations, moral, social, political or financial, which are regarded by the President as making the acquisition of Cuba by the United States either desirable or convenient." Second, the President wished to maintain peace. With these premises, Fish asked four reforms: the observance of treaty obligation for persons and property; the restoration of peace, with an amnesty and self government for Cuba; gradual but effective emancipation of slavery; and, finally, improvement of commercial facilities and the removal of obstructions to trade and commerce. Fish concluded that if Spain agreed with the President on these means to the restoration of order in Cuba, and if Spain requested it, he would use his good offices to that end.[43]

Spain employed the technique it had mastered—the incremental approach—to answer the American suggestions. On the one hand, the government removed many of the grievances concerning American treaty rights in Cuba with regard to person, property, estates, taxation, military and commercial jurisdiction. On the other hand, the Spanish made the reforms in Cuba contingent on cessation of the revolt, and made no move to introduce an emancipation plan for Cuba in the Spanish *Cortes*. Fish valued the little victories, but became pessimistic about the plight of Cuba, and commented that there was little hope for the cause of good government in Cuba. In a reflective moment, he even detected the Spanish gradualist approach. Cushing too, despairing of a solution, had commented on it. "It is true," Fish mused, "that the promises of an early termination of the trouble in Cuba and the professions of great things await to be done, always followed by the smallest amount of realization, have become as you say 'a thrice-told tale.' "[44]

By late 1876, both the Cuban insurgents and the Spanish government had come to a similar conclusion: that the war in Cuba was unwinable for both. Negotiations began between the two. Without American mediation, Spain set out to restore peace. A further signal of that intention appeared in late 1876 when Arsenio Martinez Campos arrived in Cuba as the new Captain General, with orders to end the Ten Years' War. Although resistance persisted, many rebel leaders laid down their arms.[45] Campos employed a clever combination of sword and olive branch which led to the Pact of Zanjon, signed February, 1878. This treaty granted a general amnesty, freedom for slaves who were insurgents, freedom to emigrate from Cuba, and the establishment of the political, organizational, and administrative laws of Puerto Rico in Cuba, in return for rebel capitulation and allegiance to Spain.[46]

When Fish left office in March, 1877, he kept abreast of the Cuban situation through Henry C. Hall, American consul in Havana. In August, 1877, he wrote to Hall that the end of the Cuban rebellion was approaching.[47] Although both Fish and the Cuban patriots saw their two central objectives, independence for Cuba and emancipation of all Cuban slaves, thwarted, the Pact of Zanjon restored a nominal peace to the island and ended the Ten Years' War. Hamilton Fish could take solace in the fact that he had steadfastly remained true to two major concerns of American diplomacy: the preservation of the peace with Spain and the policy of non-intervention on behalf of a rebel government that did not deserve recognition as *de facto* ruler of Cuba.

VI

Completion of the Suez Canal in 1869 engendered a genuine American interest in a Central American canal. An isthmian canal would serve two purposes, strategic and commercial. The waterway would diminish transit time between the oceans for purposes of both national defense and trade. Grant and Fish inherited negotiations with Columbia concerning a canal through Panama. The Columbian Senate had rejected Seward's treaty of January, 1869, but had indicated its desire to continue discussions. Grant appointed General Stephen A. Hurlbut as minister to Columbia, and little more than a year later he concluded a new treaty. The Columbian Senate amended this treaty to close the canal in the case of war with one of the contracting parties to warships of both belligerents. Fish found that this change obliterated the strategic importance of the waterway, and did not press for the ratification of the Hurlbut Treaty.[48]

The administration also considered the Nicaraguan route. Seward had secured transit rights in 1867 in the Dickinson-Ayon treaty. President Grant appointed an Interoceanic Canal Commission to investigate all site possibilities, and the Commission in 1876 recommended the Nicaraguan route. Fish thereupon negotiated with Dr. Adan Cardenas of Nicaragua, and suspecting that British influence had bolstered Columbian resistance in the prior case, simply attempted to secure a neutralized canal guaranteed by the principal maritime powers. The Nicaraguan talks displayed Fish's sensitivity to the American obligations under the Clayton-Bulwer Treaty of 1850, and his willingness to retreat to its strict interpretation in order to see the start of a canal. Yet Nicaraguan objections to this treaty ended all hope of an agreement. The failure represented one of Fish's Caribbean frustrations, like that of Cuba. By the year 1877, the United States was no nearer to isthmian canal, although interest in the project had blossomed anew and would persist for the rest of the century.[49]

Beyond a canal lay the Pacific Ocean. There the nation's objectives were varied: a strategic interest in ports and coaling stations, a commercial interest in trade, the desirability of island possessions or at the least privileges adjacent to the Far East, and the fear that European powers would seize and dominate these areas. To some degree all these factors were related to the question of Hawaii.[50]

Seward had submitted a reciprocity treaty with Hawaii to the Senate before he left office. Fish had been in the state department little more than a year when the Senate defeated the treaty. Yet at precisely that moment, Fish's Minister to Hawaii, the energetic Henry A. Peirce, became an ardent advocate of annexation. More important than reciprocity, thought Peirce, was American control of the islands.[51] Fish was impressed enough to read Peirce's views to the cabinet on three different occasions, adding that since the King was the last of his dynasty, the islands might soon change their government. If America showed no interest, Hawaii might gravitate to another power.[52] Yet to Fish's chagrin the cabinet, the President, and the Congress took little interest. The death of the Hawaiian monarch rekindled American interest during 1873. Fish outlined American objectives to Peirce after discussions with the President and the cabinet. Noting that the acquisition of territory "beyond the sea" met the opposition of "many discreet men," it could only result from long deliberation and calculation of advantages and disadvantages. The position of the Sandwich islands, Fish wrote, "fronting and commanding" our Pacific coast, gave America "a peculiar interest" in their future. The United States could not assent to their transfer to "any powerful maritime or commercial nation." Moreover, since there was pro-annexationist sentiment both in Hawaii and in America, Fish ordered Peirce "not to discourage the feeling that may exist in favor of annexation to the United States," and to sound out Hawaiian authorities who were disposed to annexation on the "manner and the terms and conditions" of such a transfer.[53]

The Hawaiian government did respond, short of annexation, with an offer of reciprocity linked with the cession of Pearl Harbor, a coveted naval port. Peirce, believing that such an agreement was a prelude to annexation, endorsed this proposition.[54] Opposition from native born Hawaiian politicians caused the government to withdraw this offer. In the succession crisis that soon followed, Kalakua gained the throne. His interest in reciprocity was directly related to American support for his regime. By November, 1874, Hawaii was once again ready to negotiate reciprocity, but without the cession of Pearl Harbor. Fish suggested this addition to the draft treaty, but the Hawaiian diplomat, Henry Carter, pleaded that it was now unacceptable and might imperil the treaty both in Hawaii and in the Senate. With cabinet assent, the reciprocity treaty, without the cession of Pearl Harbor, was signed on January 30, 1875. Most importantly, unrefined sugar was admitted duty-free for seven years in return for the admission of American goods and manufactured items.[55]

As in 1855 and 1867, the Senate was the major barrier. Fish added an amendment to deny other nations what America did not secure—a naval base. The amended treaty, urged by Grant, Fish, and the tireless Peirce, passed in March, 1875. The treaty required enabling legislation from the Congress, but it did not come before the House until 1876. Fish transmitted the treaty with his set of justifications. He made a historical case by noting that he was following the tradition not only of Seward, but also of Webster. Hawaii would, in the future, come under American control. As Seward had believed, the United States would secure a naval station on the way to China. The twin themes of strategy and commerce were also visible: Hawaii was strategic to the defense of the West Coast, and a way station for commerce with Asia. In may, 1876, the treaty proponents prevailed in the House, and the Senate approved in August.

The Hawaiian Reciprocity Treaty was not annexation, yet James Chapin labels it "the greatest expanionist triumph of the Grant Administration,"[56] and sees Fish as its architect. Although the treaty had its roots in the 1850's and to some extent laid the foundation for annexation in the 1890's, once again the secretary actually settled for a compromise. Rather than expanding the American empire and gaining all of America's objectives, the Hawaiian episode continued the pattern that bedeviled Fish in the cases of Cuba and the isthmian canal: the attainment of less than desirable. The treaty was at best a qualified success for Fish. The United States had not annexed the islands, nor had it acquired a base at Pearl Harbor.

VII

A one-term Governor, Representative, and Senator from New York, Hamilton Fish was a two-term secretary of state. What combination of character, circumstance, personality and policies made his second career in government so noteworthy while the first was so ostensibly a failure? What were the taproots of his diplomacy? First, Fish saw the preservation of peace as America's primary national interest. He sought not only to keep the peace with Spain during the Ten Years' War in Cuba, but also recognized the American stake in the disruption of the European balance of power during the Franco-Prussian war and offered unilateral mediation to the belligerents. With regard to Great Britain, his diplomacy produced the Treaty of Washington, landmark in the evolution of Anglo-American diplomacy from the confrontation and antagonism of the Civil War era to later arbitration and peaceful resolution of problems.

Second, Fish championed calculated peaceful expansion. He resisted three major temptations to engage the United States in territorial expansion: the annexation of Santo Domingo, the possibilities that American support for the Cuban revolt and independence might open new expansionist opportunities, and the lure of Canadian annexation. He never wholeheartedly supported Grant's efforts on behalf of Dominican annexation, arrayed himself openly against Cuban acquisition, and employed the Canadian issue as the extreme American diplomatic position on the road to a compromise that eliminated the issue. On the other hand, he actively pursued the acquisition of Hawaii, investigated American interests in Samoa, and sought the construction of a canal in Central America. Fish deserves neither the label "expansionist" or "anti-expansionist." He was not interested in acquiring territories without an economic, political, or strategic interest and without assessing potential problems. The case of Hawaii documents his beliefs very well. It is proper to note that American territorial expansion in fact ceased during his tenure. The expansion he did secure was strategic and commercial.

Third, he cultivated a policy of non-intervention in the internal affairs of nations, so dominant a theme of his predecessor and fellow New Yorker, William H. Seward. In the case that parallels the Union government's situation during the Civil War, Fish treated the Cuban revolt as a Spanish problem and sought a solution on that basis. He employed the diplomatic technique of threatening intervention to gain concessions from Spain, but never seriously considered forceful intervention as a proper policy. Any such action was the antithesis of the American position regarding British recognition of Confederate belligerency in the Civil War. Moreover, according to conservative tradition that had existed since the time of Washington, no *de facto* government worthy of recognition had established itself in Cuba. The cost of such a course could be war. Fish never took a pro-Spanish position on Cuba.[57] He simply honored the precedents in American diplomacy for non-intervention: the behavior of the United States in the Latin American revolutions of the Monroe-Adams years, the revolutions in central Europe in the late 1840's, and the Polish revolt and Confederate rebellion in the 1860's.

Fourth, along with the President, Fish was an adherent to the no transfer clause of the Monroe Doctrine. Although the President first stated the no transfer clause in relation to the Danish West Indies, the most dramatic application came in the case of Hawaii. Because of the commercial and strategic importance of the Sandwich Islands, Fish felt compelled to state that there were only two acceptable solutions for Hawaii: native control, or American control.

Fish alone served Grant nearly eight years. Central to that fact was an attribute that links the secretary to his predecessor. Like Seward, Fish profited immensely from on-the-job experience. His prior preparation in foreign relations consisted of two years service on the Senate Foreign Relations Committee and two years abroad in Europe, all in the 1850's. His capacity to learn the essentials of proper diplomatic behavior, his doggedness, his good judgement, and his lawyer-like attention to detail and precedent elevated him quickly from novice to seasoned diplomatist, and by the reckoning of historians, to a successful career as secretary of state. Yet Fish manifested little tendency to establish general American policy. Rather, he negotiated case by case. Although American policy on Cuba and the *Alabama* claims employed linkage, this was the exception rather than the rule. American diplomacy toward Europe, the Caribbean, Asia, and the Pacific, and even Central and South America, was at times inconsistent and contradictory. Grant deserves much of the blame, but Fish, master of his department most certainly after 1871, qualifies for criticism as well.

Hamilton Fish was a magnificent monument of the past—the conservative tradition of American diplomacy. As the *New York Times* commented on the occasion of his death in September, 1893, he retired justified in believing that he had been of great service to his country. His official life was without taint of personal or political ambition in an era whose hallmark was the contrary. Hamilton Fish, wrote the *New York Times,* "may be regarded as practically the last of the statesmen bred and trained in the school of the early Whigs who brought to the Republican Party a rare combination of conservatism and of force."[58] More conservative than forceful, Hamilton Fish managed American diplomacy with the restraint and circumspection that clearly delineates him from many of the secretaries who followed him. In many respects, his record distinguishes him from William H. Seward as well. He was not the expansionist Seward sought to be, nor did he share Seward's world vision. Undoubtedly unique, Hamilton Fish was a transitional figure in the change from the an older, traditional diplomacy to a new mode rather less restrained.[59]

NOTES

1. Otto zu Stolberg-Wernigerode, *Germany and the United States during the Era of Bismarck* (Reading, Pa. The Janssen Foundation, 1937), p. 111; Allan Nevins, *Hamilton Fish: The Inner History of the Grant Administration* (New York:Ungar Publishing Company, 1957), I, 400–02.
2. National Archives, Records of the Department of State, Instructions,

Turkey, vol. 2, Fish to Morris, 13 August 1870. Hereafter cited as Instructions.

3. National Archives, Records of the Department of State, Despatches, Britain, vol. 104, Motley to Fish, nos. 403, 404, 28 July 1870; Despatches, Prussia, vol. 17, Bancroft to Fish, no. 112, 16 July 1870. Hereafter cited as Despatches.
4. *Papers Relating to the Foreign Relations of the United States, 1870* (Washington, D.C.: Government Printing Office, 1870), p. 45.
5. Despatches, France, vol. 67, Washburne to Fish, telegram, 7 September 1870; no. 283, 9 September 1870; Instructions, France, vol. 18, Fish to Washburne, telegram, 9 September 1870; Instructions, Germany, vol. 15, Fish to Bancroft, 9 September 1870; Jeanette Keim, *Forty Years of German-American Political Relations* (Philadelphia: William Dornan, 1919), pp. 26-27, fn 35; Despatches, Germany, vol. 17, Bancroft to Fish, no. 132, 12 September 1870.
6. Instructions, Germany, vol. 15, Fish to Bancroft, no. 246, 30 September 1870.
7. Nevins, *Hamilton Fish,* I, 409; Despatches, Germany, vol. 18, Bancroft to Fish, no. 197, 27 February 1871; Despatches, Britain, vol. 109, Moran to Fish, telegram, 27 February 1871; Instructions, Germany, vol. 15, Fish to Bancroft, no. 305, 21 March 1871.
8. Despatches, Turkey, Morris to Fish, no. 374, 2 September 1870.
9. Despatches, Austria, vol. 10, Jay to Fish, telegram, 12 November 1870; Britain, vol, 106, Motley to Fish, no. 514, 15 November 1870; Russia, vol. 22, Curtin to Fish, no. 83, 12 November 1870.
10. Hamilton Fish, Diary, quoted in Nevins, *Hamilton Fish,* I, 430.
11. Joseph Fuller, "Hamilton Fish," in Samuel F. Bemis, ed., *The American Secretaries of State and Their Diplomacy* (New York, Pageant Books, 1958), VII, 156, 160; Charles F. Adams Jr., *Lee at Appomattox and other Papers* (2nd ed., Boston: Houghton Mifflin Company, 1903), p. 162; Despatches, Austria, vol. 11, Jay to Fish, no. 179. 19 November 1870; Instructions, Austria, vol. 1, Fish to Jay, no. 89, 8 December 1870.
12. Nevins, *Hamilton Fish,* I, 430, 434.
13. See Goldwin Smith, *The Treaty of Washington, 1871: A Study in Imperial History* (Ithaca, New York: Cornell University Press, 1941); Caleb Cushing, *The Treaty of Washington: Its Negotiation, Execution, and the Discussions Relating Thereto* (New York: Harper and Bros., 1873); and Charles Campbell, *The Transformation of American Foreign Relations, 1865-1890* (New York: Harper and Row, 1976).
14. John B. Brebner, *North Atlantic Triangle: The Interplay of Canada, The United States, and Great Britain* (New York: Russell and Russell, 1970), p. 196; Kenneth Bourne, *Britain and the Balance of Power in North America, 1815-1908* (Berkeley: University of California Press, 1967), pp. 300-03.

15. James W. Cortada, *Two Nations over Time: Spain and the United States, 1776-1977* (Westport, Connecticut: Greenwood Press, 1978), p. 92.
16. Cortada, *Two Nations over Time,* p. 90; Instructions, Spain, vol. 16, Fish to Sickles, nos. 2,3, 29 June 1869; see also Nevins, *Hamilton Fish,* I, 191-200, 231-33, for the story of Paul Forbes, a businessman who was commissioned as Special Agent to Spain to work for the same objectives for Cuba and to guarantee payment to Spain on behalf of the United States.
17. *Nevins, Hamilton Fish,* I, 181-82, 235-43; Instructions, Spain, vol. 16, Fish to Sickles, telegram, 1 September 1869, and telegram, 23 September 1869.
18. Instructions, Spain, vol. 16, Fish to Sickles, no. 26, 26 January 1870; no. 109, 25 November 1870.
19. Cortada, *Two Nations over Time,* p. 91; Instructions, Spain, vol. 16, Fish to Sicles, no. 127, 16 December 1870; no. 138, 10 January 1871.
20. Instructions, Spain, vol. 16, Fish to Sickles, no. 219, 19 April 1872.
21. *Ibid.,* Fish to Sickles, no. 270, 29 October 1872; see also nos. 247 and 253, 31 August and 25 September 1872 respectively.
22. Fish to Sickles, no. 272, 6 November 1872.
23. Nevins, *Hamilton Fish,* II, 627.
24. *Ibid.,* pp. 628-30.
25. Instructions, Spain, vol. 16, Fish to Sickles, no. 323, 23 April 1873.
26. *Ibid.*
27. Nevins, *Hamilton Fish,* II, *637.*
28. Instructions, Spain, vol. 16, Fish to Sickles, no. 366, 27 August 1873.
29. Fish to Sickles, no. 391, 15 October 1873.
30. Nevins, *Hamilton Fish,* II, 667; Instructions, Spain, vol. 16, Fish to Sickles, no. 404, 12 November 1873; telegram, 12 November 1873.
31. Fish to Sickles, telegram, 14 November 1873.
32. Fish to Sickles, telegram, 19 November 1873; telegram, 21 November 1873; telegram, 25 November 1873; Nevins, *Hamilton Fish,* II, 684-85.
33. Fish to Sickles, telegram, 1 December 1873.
34. Fish to Sickles, telegram, 20 December 1873.
35. Fish to Cushing, no. 2, 6 February 1873.
36. Instructions, Spain, vol. 17, Fish to Cushing, no. 31, 9 June 1874; no. 57, 15 August 1874; no. 59, 21 August 1874.
37. Fish to Cushing, no. 80, 27 October 1874; no. 84, 29 October 1874; telegram, 25 November 1874; telegram, 28 November 1874; telegram, 11 December 1874; no. 107, 29 December 1874; telegram, 17 and 24 February 1875; no. 152, 6 April 1875; no. 172, 8 May 1875.
38. Fish to Cushing, no. 185, 4 June 1875; no. 238, 22 September 1875; telegram, 28 September 1875; no. 265, 5 November 1875.
39. Fish to Cushing, no. 266, 5 November 1875.
40. Fish to Cushing, telegram, 6 December 1875.

41. Fish to Cushing, telegrams, 13 and 20 December 1875.
42. Nevins, *Hamilton Fish,* II, 883-84.
43. Instructions, Spain, vol. 17, Fish to Cushing, no. 323, 1 March 1876, in reply to Cushing to Fish, no. 777, 16 January 1876.
44. Fish to Cushing, no. 383, 16 June 1876; quote from Fish to Cushing, no. 405, 7 August 1876.
45. Cortada, *Two Nations over Time,* p. 99; Philip S. Foner, *A History of Cuba and its Relations with the United States, 1845-1895: From the Era of Annexation to the Outbreak of the Second War for Independence* (New York: International Publishers, 1963), II, 261-65.
46. *Ibid.,* p. 265.
47. Fish to Hall, 7 August 1877, cited in Foner, *A History of Cuba,* vol. 2, p. 262.
48. Joseph Fuller, "Hamilton Fish," in Bemis, *American Secretaries of State,* VII, 206-07.
49. Charles Campbell, *The Transformation of American Foreign Relations,* p. 60.
50. James Chapin, "Hamilton Fish and American Expansion," Unpublished Ph.D. Dissertation, Cornell University, 1971, pp. 510-39.
51. Despatches, Hawaii, vol. 13, Peirce to Fish, nos. 64 and 101, 30 July 1870 and 25 February 1871 respectively.
52. Hamilton Fish, Diary, Library of Congress, Washington, D.C., October 18, December 18, December 20, 1870; March 21, April 7, 1871.
53. Instructions, Hawaii, vol. 2, Fish to Peirce, no. 86, 25 March 1873.
54. Despatches, Hawaii, vol. 15, Peirce to Fish, no. 213, 7 July 1873.
55. Campbell, *The Transformation of American Foreign Relations,* p. 68.
56. Chapin, "Hamilton Fish and American Expansion," p. 538.
57. *Ibid.,* pp. 272, 274, 276, 566.
58. *New York Times,* September 8, 1893, Editorial, p. 4.
59. Robert Beisner, *From the Old Diplomacy to the New, 1865-1900* (New York: Thomas Y. Crowell Company, 1975), pp. 29, 39-43, 50-54.

2

WILLIAM MCKINLEY: RELUCTANT WARRIOR, CAUTIOUS IMPERIALIST

Richard E. Welch Jr.

Historians have had no difficulty in agreeing upon the physical portrait of William McKinley: the erect posture seeking to disguise the spreading waistline, the deep-set, dark-shadowed eyes, the stern Roman profile blurred by sagging muscles in cheeks and jawline. Where they have disagreed is over the character of McKinley as presidential leader and his direction of foreign policy in an administration that saw a war with Spain, the acquisition of a colonial empire, and important developments in United States relations with Great Britain and China.

The typical textbook account has pictured McKinley as a weak executive whose foreign policy reflected a timid dependence on public opinion. By this account, McKinley was subject to the manipulation of popular hysteria and the influence of such strong-minded expansionists as Theodore Roosevelt and Henry Cabot Lodge. Lacking any experience in diplomacy, he lacked as well any understanding of the purposes and stratagems of international relations. Initially created by partisan opponents, this derogatory picture of McKinley as a bumbling and timid president pushed by public opinion and stronger men into policies he neither wanted nor understood has achieved over the years the certitude that accompanies repetition.[1] It was popular with the Progressive Historians who saw the McKinley administration as the epitome of the selfish class politics of Big Business Republicanism and were not prepared to credit McKinley with any measure of mastery in the field of foreign relations. The Spanish American War was unnecessary and a stronger president would have pursued a diplomacy that withstood the jingoes and secured justice for the Cubans without war and without the accompanying aberration of overseas territorial expansion. In the years since World War II, this interpretation—though tempered in tone and altered in detail—has retained its majority status.[2] It has received an indirect measure of support from the "Revisionist school" of diplomatic historians and an ambivalent rebuttal from historians associated, somewhat haphazardly, with the Radical Left.

The "Realists" accept the idea that the Spanish-American War was inspired by humanitarian impulses and the jingoistic agitation of press and public, but their disapproval of the foreign policy of the McKinley administration is cast in broader terms. They see the McKinley years as the time when American foreign policy took a decisive turn for the worse. Forgetting the lessons of the American past, when diplomats supposedly had a keen sense of the core national interest, the United States in the McKinley years embarked on the slippery slope of crusader moralism. McKinley is less to be derided than deplored for allowing popular whims and fuzzy idealism rather than strategic considerations to determine policy. McKinley had no sense of America's true security interests or the realities of the balance of power in Europe and Asia; no understanding of the necessity to correlate policy goals and physical power. He introduced the "Utopian Period" in American diplomatic history, a period when moral abstractions and ideological simplifications would becloud an appreciation of the national interest. McKinley was the epitome of the short-sighted politician-amateur who would substitute good intentions for a hard-earned knowledge of Realpolitik.[3]

Revisionist historians associated with Marxist ideology or the New Left have sought to replace the weak-kneed McKinley of traditional accounts with a figure symbolic not of the dangers of moralism but the evils of economic imperialism. These authors range widely in the temper of their indictment, but they share a conviction that McKinley was the spokesman of Big Business in his foreign policies as well as his advocacy of the Gold Standard. For some McKinley was the unwitting tool of a policy that capitalized on a war with Spain to conquer overseas markets in the Caribbean and Pacific in behalf of an industrial economy embarrassed by surplus production. For others, McKinley was the wily and willing agent of a calculated policy of territorial conquest and commercial expansion. Their derogation of McKinley differs widely from that of the typical textbook account, but their strictures are no less severe.[4]

There is another group of revisionists, however, who would offer McKinley a fair measure of praise and sympathy. For them McKinley has been the victim of caricature and misunderstanding. Neither the timid politico of legend nor the tool of monopoly capitalism. McKinley was a keen-witted and strong Chief Executive who was the commander-in-chief of his administration's foreign policies. He pursued a consistent and logical diplomacy with Spain and chose war only when Spanish obduracy denied the prospect of meaningful negotiation. He carefully deliberated the question of Philippine annexation and then maneuvered to gain the approval of public opinion and the Senate in support of his conclusion that annexation offered strategic and economic advantages for the United States. He left the details of isthmian canal diplomacy and the Open Door Notes to John Hay but retained supervisory control of the State Department at all times. Skilled in the arts of cajolery and concealment, McKinley was a strong President determined to have his own way.[5]

By the Procrustean necessities of historiographical classification, this essay will fall in the last-named camp—that which sees McKinley as neither the timid politician reacting to the whipsaw of public opinion nor the agent of monopoly capitalism plotting a policy of economic imperialism. McKinley was not as courageous or intelligent as some of his recent defenders have suggested, but neither does he fit the stereotypes of his many detractors. The ideas and policies of the McKinley administration are of major importance in the history of American diplomacy. They encompass errors as well as achievements and they deserve neither uniform praise nor derogatory labels. Obviously there is some truth in the interpretations of McKinley's various critics. McKinley was a professional politician concerned with popular favor; he did prate frequently of duty and moral imperatives; he listened to business correspondents worried by industrial surplus and its association with social unrest. Neither his ideas nor his policies, however, have the consistency that his detractors and champions imply. Those ideas and policies deserve reassessment in an effort to understand an influential presidential diplomatist and an important transition period in the history of American foreign policy.

II

One reason for the continuing historiographical dispute over the character of McKinley and the nature of his diplomacy lies in the difficulty of gaining evidence for McKinley's thoughts on the goals and purposes of American foreign policy. McKinley was a secretive man who refused to take his contemporaries into his confidence or leave a written record of his private hopes and anxieties for posterity. Fearful of giving his political enemies an advantage and accustomed to test the political waters before divulging his intentions, McKinley saw oracular circumlocutions and a public pose of indecision as useful weapons and indirection and secretiveness as positive virtues. His determination to keep his own counsel led many of his contemporaries to suspect that McKinley lacked independent ideas in the area of foreign policy. They were mistaken.

McKinley was neither a Bismarck nor a Mahan but he did not lack for ideas and prejudices in the realm of foreign policy. If he had no developed philosophy of international relations, he had a set of nationalist ambitions and an auxiliary set of fears and antipathies. They were the product of several sources but the most important was a strong sense of nationalism and a conviction that the nationalist orientation of such earlier Republicans as James G. Blaine offered the surest guide for the expansion of American influence and power in a widening portion of the globe.

Prior to his inauguration on March 4, 1897, McKinley's political career had been primarily associated with such domestic issues as the protective tariff, monetary inflation, and the battle of the standards, and he came to the presidential office with no clearly defined record on foreign policy questions. But already there were indications that he would pursue a foreign policy of selective expansionism if conditions were favorable. He had given unqualified support to the foreign policy planks of the Republican platform: American control of the Hawaiian Islands, purchase of the Danish West Indies, construction of an isthmian canal through Nicaragua, and government encouragement of foreign trade and commerce.

McKinley's identification with the economic virtues of high protectionism did not imply a disbelief in the economic benefit of foreign trade expansion. Like many Americans, McKinley wished it both ways—a protected home market for U.S. manufactures and an expanding market for U.S. exports. Only with the year 1901 would McKinley begin to give serious attention to a policy of tariff reciprocity and a graduated reduction of the protective tariff system as a means of expanding U.S. foreign markets, but his growing interest in commercial expansion as an auxiliary means of assuring domestic economic growth was indicated in several public addresses in the years 1899-1900. The Republican platform of 1900, which received McKinley's advance approval, reflected this growing interest in its calls for a new cabinet department of Commerce and Industry, an overhaul of the consular system, advocacy of the rights of American traders in China, and the early construction of an isthmian canal.

McKinley never became a convert to the theory of certain contemporary publicists that the conquest of foreign markets was the overriding concern of American foreign policy, but one reason for his decision to acquire the Philippines was the belief that their possession would encourage the expansion of America's China trade. Foreign trade expansion would stimulate the nation's reviving economy in the immediate present and promote the long-term goal of American preeminence among the commercial powers of the world. Foreign trade was not merely a matter of economic profit, it was witness to the beneficial role of America as supplier for the world's needs. It should be a source of national pride.

The timing and the location of territorial expansion in the McKinley years was partly the product of accidental circumstance. But as a strong nationalist convinced of the beneficence of American influence and anxious for the increased recognition of America by other powers, McKinley was fully prepared to take advantage of the opportunities provided by American military success. If not a student of international politics, he was not unmindful of the suspected designs of other powers in the Caribbean and Pacific, and he advocated a strengthened national defense and a strong navy, even while a conservative fear of budgetary deficits inhibited him from urging major increases in military expenditures.

McKinley worked within the framework of the immediate future, and within that parameter he gave consideration to questions of national advantage. He judged the removal of Spain from Cuba to be aidful to the achievement of American strategic and economic goals in the Caribbean, and when Spain refused to acquiesce to McKinley's demands, he decided that there was no alternative to military intervention. Similarly, in his deliberations respecting the Philippines, strategic as well as economic ambitions were more important than those of moral duty and partisan advantage. McKinley was aware of the recommendations of certain naval officers for shore facilities that would enhance American naval power in the western Pacific, and he believed that possession of the Philippines would strengthen U.S. diplomatic authority in the Far East.

McKinley's public addresses tended to wrap considerations of national defense, influence, and gain in the gauze of morality and humanitarian obligation, but United States interests were always paramount. Aspirations to elevate "the little brown man" or advance the work of Christian missionaries were not hypocritical, but they were subsidiary. Subsidiary and complementary. McKinley was convinced that the expansion of American power and influence would be beneficial to the world as well as America, and certainly to those peoples who were the subjects of this country's benevolent indoctrination. He persuaded himself without conscious effort that in controlling a colonial empire, the United States was performing a good deed as well as pursuing the national advantage. Mission and self-interest found their resolution in the intention of the United States to give to its colonial dependencies efficient government and the prospect of home rule in some indeterminate future. United States control of such colonies as Puerto Rico and the Philippines would prove advantageous not only to America's own defense and commercial requirements but to backward peoples, presently vulnerable to foreign enemies and domestic anarchy, as well.

McKinley was a nationalist, a commercial expansionist, and a halting but not unwilling territorial imperialist. Was he—even by contemporary definition—an internationalist? H. Wayne Morgan has written: "He proclaimed the end of diplomatic isolation, called for international cooperation, and insisted that America accept the burdens of greatness in world affairs whether she wished them or not."[6] There is insufficient evidence to suggest that McKinley had the prevision to see the United States as leader among the world powers and champion of international cooperation. McKinley gradually became convinced that the foreign policy of the United States must adapt to the demands of a new century and the United States play a larger role in world affairs, but he continued to be uncertain of the dimensions of that role and its military defense requirements. McKinley shared with past presidents an antipathy to foreign alliances and entanglements. Though he wished to contribute to a more peaceful world as well as a more powerful United States, he had no coordinated plan for the implementation of those aims. McKinley was more the opportunistic tactician than the long-term strategist and more the ambitious expansionist than the internationalist.

McKinley lacked the personal traits to be a world leader but was ideally suited to pursue a foreign policy reflective of the confidence and ethnocentricity of middle-class America. Not a man of bold originality, McKinley was a hard worker and a quick learner, patient, cautious, and obstinate. Unlike most successful politician-presidents he was not much concerned with receiving personal credit so long as he got his way. He was habitually slow to make up his mind and, once he had done so, unalterably convinced of the righteousness of his decision. He was as confident of the wisdom of his policies as he was of the superiority of the American people and the brightness of the American future.

McKinley was a devout man living in an age of evangelical missionary labor and YMCA Christian Endeavor. His attribution of certain decisions to the compulsions of moral duty was a reflection of natural piety as well as honest self-deception. It was as well a recognition that many of his countrymen responded to the rhetoric of humanitarian duty and felt a need to be reassured that novel diplomatic adventures found justification in old certitudes and traditional moral values. During his presidency William McKinley was greatly admired by a majority of middle-class Americans in all sections. He successfully identified himself not only with Industrial America and the Republican party but with the nation's future and the aspirations and aggressive nationalism of his countrymen. McKinley mirrored the ambitious optimism as well as the cultural and intellectual limitations of turn-of-the-century America, and he achieved a measure of popular trust essential to the pursuit of his diplomatic policies. McKinley's foreign policy ideas are indeed best evidenced in those policies and in his relations with Spain and the Cuban revolutionaries, with the Filipinos and other "colonial peoples," and with Great Britain and China.

III

The most dramatic and surely the most analyzed feature of McKinley's foreign policy was his decision to go to war with Spain in April, 1898. It has been the subject of debate, misinterpretation, and retrospective guilt feelings. Any interpretation of McKinley's Spanish diplomacy must ultimately rest on one's judgment respecting the right of any country to determine the methods and time frame whereby another nation may subdue an insurrection. Did

McKinley have the right initially to set rules for the manner in which Spain should conduct its war in Cuba and then to set the terms under which Spain must conclude that conflict? Answer those questions in the affirmative and McKinley's Spanish diplomacy was consistent and his final decision for war, unavoidable. Hamilton Fish had seen it differently.

The Cuban Insurrection erupted in 1895 during the Cleveland administration, and McKinley was in some measure the inheritor of an American policy that sought to combine the posture of neutrality and the right to offer warnings to Spain respecting the nature of military tactics that would be judged "civilized." Shortly after his inauguration, however, McKinley purposely tilted American diplomacy in a pro-Cuban direction. In his instructions of July, 1897, to the new American minister to Madrid, Stewart Woodford, McKinley reiterated an earlier United States offer of its good offices to secure a settlement of the Cuban struggle and declared that such a settlement must be just and acceptable to the Cubans. Woodford was to inform the Spanish foreign minister that the United States could not stand aside indefinitely and see the war continue along existing lines.[7]

The failure of Spain to alter the harsh pacification tactics of General Valeriano Weyler in Cuba or admit any right of the United States to interfere in the domestic affairs of the Spanish people appeared to offer McKinley only the option of backing off or delivering a more explicit threat of American intervention. By the late summer of 1897, some members of Congress were already predicting war, but the assassination of the Spanish Prime Minister Casanovas in Madrid gave McKinley's diplomacy of graduated pressure a second chance. By October a new "Liberal" ministry had come to power under the leadership of Praxedes Sagasta. Sagasta informed the United States that his government was prepared to recall General Weyler, alter the *reconcentrado* policy, and consider offering some undefined measure of autonomy for the Cubans.

Tensions between Spain and the United States appeared to lessen in the months of November-December, 1897. The winter of 1898 would produce a sharp reversal and begin a momentum of mutual animosity and suspicion that culminated in war by the last week of April. The January 12 anti-autonomy riots in Havana, the publication of a private letter from Enrique Dupey de Lôme, the Spanish minister to Washington, with its derogatory references to McKinley, and then the sinking of the U.S. battleship *Maine* in

Havana harbor not only heightened the war hysteria in certain sections of the American press and public but persuaded McKinley that events had overtaken the possibility of putting an end to the struggle in Cuba by means of Spanish reforms and limited autonomy. Spanish promises had lost credibility and any variety of home rule status would be judged unsatisfactory by the Cubans as well as the American Congress. A military solution appeared beyond Spanish capabilities and McKinley now determined that U.S. requirements should include the immediate prospect of Spanish withdrawal and Cuban independence. The latter should be obtained under American tutelage so that Cuba would have a government stable and sensible as well as independent. The last week of March saw McKinley make his final effort to coerce the Spanish ministry into an acceptance of Cuban pacification on terms of the United States.

On March 27, Secretary of State William R. Day instructed Woodford to deliver a three-part proposal which represented, in effect, an American ultimatum. Spain must immediately abandon its reconcentration policy and accept relief for its victims from the United States. Spain must agree to an immediate armistice, suspending all hostilities until October 1, with the President of the United States to arrange and supervise negotiations between Spain and the Cuban insurgents in the interim. If no agreement had been reached by October 1, the President was to serve as "the final arbiter between Spain and insurgents."[8] Although these demands did not explicitly mention Cuban independence, the President, in a dispatch to Woodford on the previous day, had indicated that in his role as mediator he would demand for Cuba "full self-government with reasonable indemnity." When Woodford requested a more specific definition of the phrase "full self-government," Day replied on March 28 that "full self-government with indemnity would mean Cuban independence."[9]

The reply of the Sagasta ministry of March 31 was unsatisfactory. American mediation was rejected and the Spanish declared that a suspension of hostilities would be granted only if the insurgents requested it, which all parties knew the insurgents would never do. There was, of course, another Spanish reply, that of April 9. In that reply the Spanish declared their agreement to a proposal by the Vatican for an "armistice" in Cuba. This Spanish note of April 9 is frequently interpreted as a "total capitulation" to American demands. It is emphasized by those historians who label the Spanish American War unnecessary as well as unfortunate. The

Spanish note fell considerably short of a "capitulation." Not only did it make no mention of Cuban independence or United States mediation, but its promise of an armistice was hedged with qualifications. McKinley might well have given it more attention in his "war message" to Congress of April 11, but he had reason to suspect that what the Spanish proposed was not a true armistice but a time-delaying truce.

An assessment of McKinley's decision for military intervention must emphasize McKinley's alteration of the aims of his Spanish diplomacy to include a demand for ultimate Cuban independence under United States tutelage. McKinley's gamble that Spain would acquiesce to American demands had always reflected a measure of wishful thinking, but when those demands changed from pacification of Cuba by means of a grant of limited autonomy to pacification as a result of Spanish withdrawal, McKinley's hopes lost contact with reality. McKinley was then asking nothing less than a total reversal of Spain's Cuban policy. There were legitimate reasons why he should feel that the United States had a direct interest in ending the Cuban insurrection, but he had little reason to believe that he could obtain Cuban independence or Spanish acceptance of U.S. arbitration short of American military intervention.

Several authors have laid great stress on the role of business in guiding McKinley's diplomacy in the spring of 1898, while others have emphasized McKinley's fear of Republican division were he not to take the nation to war. Many spokesmen for the industrial and financial communities were prepared by March, 1898, to judge war a lesser evil than continued economic uncertainty; many Republican politicians were urging McKinley to assure party success with a war that would satisfy the expectations of an increasingly bellicose press and Congress. These, however, were but auxiliary influences in McKinley's decision to request authority to employ the armed services of the United States to end the war in Cuba. McKinley went to war because his Spanish diplomacy of escalating diplomatic pressure and threats had failed. The form of his ultimatum to Spain as well as the form of his "war message" of April 11 reflects the fact that his overriding aim was not a desire to assist the Cuban insurgents nor a desire to acquire Spanish territory for the United States. He wished an end to a civil war in Cuba that was proving increasingly damaging to the political harmony and strategic and economic interests of the United States. He sought a stable and peaceful Cuba that would cause no further problems for American diplomacy and had come to the conclusion that a peaceful Cuba could only be secured by U.S. intervention and tutelage.[10]

To say that McKinley was not pushed into war by popular hysteria and motives of political cowardice is not to argue the wisdom of his Spanish diplomacy. War came because diplomacy failed and there was a measure of ambivalence between the immediate and long-range inspirations for McKinley's decision for war.

McKinley's decision to forego further efforts at exerting pressure on Spain to make incremental concessions was the result of many factors. He was influenced by the exaggerated portrayal of Spanish conduct in Cuba, by humanitarian sympathies, by the prospect of continued political animosity in Washington, and by the economic losses suffered by U.S. traders and investors, but he went to war neither at the behest of the *Missionary Herald* nor the *Journal of Commerce,* nor to appease Republican jingoes in the Senate. He went to war because he could not obtain Spanish agreement to U.S. mediation and Cuban independence. He had threatened intervention if peaceful pressure and veiled threats failed, and he judged that they had failed. When Spain continued to delay and procrastinate, offering but vague and limited concessions, McKinley could see no alternative to war. War was not the outcome he had desired, but it would end the suffering in Cuba, give the United States a chance to supervise the establishment of a stable and sensible government in that island, and end the current uncertainty in United States political and economic affairs that had been created by the long and bloody Cuban Rebellion.

In the immediate view, McKinley judged U.S. armed intervention necessary to end an intolerable situation, free Cuba from Spanish misrule, and put the island on its feet as an independent nation. In the longer view, McKinley saw war and the dismissal of Spain from the Caribbean as aidful to increased United States authority in that region. Were the United States to build an isthmian canal, it would be strategically desirable that the decaying empire of Spain be eliminated from the Caribbean and the United States Navy placed in uncontested control of the windward passage. It was also desirable that our commercial interests in Cuba be restored and expanded.

IV

As it was McKinley who effectively made the final decision for war, so it was McKinley who served as the war's chief strategist. An operations room was established at the White House, ringed with large wall maps dotted with colored pins to show the disposition of American sea and land forces. Twenty-five telephone lines were installed to connect the President with branches of the War and Navy Departments, and McKinley broke ground by arranging a formal schedule of meetings with the Secretaries of War and Navy, the Commanding General of the Army, and the new Naval War Board. It was McKinley more than any of his advisers who decided on the strategy of "the indirect approach"—the strategy of attacking with maximum force the periphery of the Spanish empire with the goal of achieving victory as cheaply and quickly as possible.[11] McKinley only threatened naval operations against the Atlantic coast of Spain and, when he decided that a Cuban campaign was necessary, avoided an attack on the Spanish stronghold at Havana and confined United States military operation to the easier target of Santiago on the eastern end of the island. Similar considerations dictated his decision to send an army expedition against the weakly defended city of Manila in the Philippines.

The first engagement of the Spanish American War occurred in Manila Harbor where Commodore George Dewey destroyed the decrepit Spanish Pacific fleet under Admiral Patricio Montojo on May 1. That the first engagement in a war declaredly fought to free Cuba took place in the western Pacific has naturally inspired the accusation that the United States went to war to acquire the Philippine archipelago. The suspicion is understandable and the accusation erroneous. The destruction of Montojo's fleet was the result neither of a conspiracy by a Roosevelt-led cabal in Washington nor a covert imperialist plot of William McKinley. Several years earlier the Navy Department had sketched out a contingency plan in the event of a war with Spain and it included the destruction of Spain's Pacific fleet stationed at Manila. An enemy fleet is always a natural target in wartime and one of the most well-worn platitudes of military strategy is to hit the enemy where he is most vulnerable.

It was not the naval victory in Manila Harbor that suggests that McKinley was interested in a territorial indemnity at the war's conclusion but his decision within a week of Dewey's victory to send a sizeable contingent of American soldiers to take and occupy the city of Manila. Dewey requested the dispatch of U.S. armed forces and McKinley quickly acceded to that request.[12] It would appear that McKinley very early after the commencement of the war with Spain decided that he wanted as wide a variety of options as possible respecting U.S. claims of territorial indemnity. It is still more certain that McKinley believed that the occupation of Manila would exert further pressure on Spain to admit defeat and end the war. The occupation of Manila would force the Spanish government to order a surrender in Cuba.

McKinley's policy of attacking the periphery of the Spanish empire did not prevent heavy American casualties in the assault on Santiago, but by July 16, 1898, the United States received the capitulation of Santiago. On August 12, an armistice was signed in Washington. McKinley determined the language as well as the terms of the armistice agreement.[13] Spain must relinquish Cuba and evacuate that island immediately. Spain must cede to the United States Puerto Rico and an island in the Ladrones. The United States would hold the city, bay, and harbor of Manila pending "final disposition of the islands" at the peace conference. The stage was set for the most controversial foreign policy decision of the McKinley administration: the acquisition of the Philippines. McKinley would seek the advice of many persons while making that decision, but he alone would make it.[14]

V

The composition of the commission sent to the Paris peace conference indicated that McKinley was, by early September, leaning toward the acquisition of the entire Philippine archipelago. Three of the five commissioners were strong expansionists. When McKinley gave them a farewell dinner on September 16, on the eve of their departure, he professed continued uncertainty as to the extent of American territorial demands while observing that "the march of events rules and over-rules human action." This Delphic declaration was clarified by the instruction that the United States could accept nothing less than acquisition of the island of Luzon. On October 28 the commissioners would receive McKinley's instruction to demand Spanish cession of the Philippines. The islands were not divisible as either a commercial or a strategic unit. If the United States took Luzon alone, the other islands might become a source of temptation for England, Germany, and Japan. This would make possession of Luzon troublesome and costly. It was all or nothing and it should be all.

McKinley had made his decision by the first days of October, but he enunciated that decision only after a speaking tour of the Middle West had convinced him that it would not endanger the popularity of his administration. It was made, however, not in answer to popular demand but because McKinley judged the acquisition of a colonial empire in the Pacific to be in the national interest. McKinley was aware by the summer of 1898 that many trade journals were offering optimistic forecasts of the value of the Philippines as a source of customers and raw materials. It would not be until the autumn of 1899 that McKinley would publicly emphasize the economic importance of the Philippines and their utility for the expansion of our China trade, but from the beginning he realized that the Philippines might bring commercial advantage and furnish the equivalent of a leasehold on the continent of Asia. Economic arguments were only peripheral in McKinley's decision to go to war with Spain; they were more important in his decision to acquire the Philippines.

On strategic grounds, McKinley believed that the islands would not only furnish a coaling station and naval base but would assure a greater readiness by the other powers to acknowledge American interests in the political and economic affairs of China. Serving as the terminus of an island chain from Hawaii to Guam, the Philippines must enhance the position of the United States in East Asia as well as the Pacific.[15]

In communications with his commissioners and the United States Senate, McKinley made much of American obligations to the Filipinos and the lack of any satisfactory alternative to annexation. These were supportive rather than primary considerations in McKinley's evaluation. He did believe that the United States, having supposedly destroyed all Spanish authority in the Philippines, had an obligation to the Filipinos. Having decided that the United States should acquire the islands, he soon convinced himself that there was no argument to be made for any other option. His ethnocentrism and self-concealed racial bias assured that McKinley would doubt Filipino capacity and see Philippine nationalism as the rationalization of a few Tagalog bandits seeking their own aggrandizement. Philippine independence was quickly rejected as a possible option and such alternatives as an American protectorate or international neutralization agreement were also cavalierly dismissed. "Duty determines destiny," McKinley informed the peace commissioners, but it was McKinley alone who defined "duty." It was his interpretation of the national interest, not divine guidance, that shaped his decision.[16] McKinley was in fact fully prepared to take responsibility for a decision he judged both necessary and wise. He preferred, however, to mask considerations of national advantage in vague abstractions about duty, destiny, and Christian obligation.

McKinley was the author of the peace treaty signed in Paris on December 10, 1898, and the author as well of the Executive Order of December 21 that proclaimed that the sovereign authority of the United States extended over all the islands of the Philippine archipelago.[17] McKinley's Executive Order preceded Senate deliberations on the Treaty of Paris and the chronology was not accidental. By proclaiming the unrestricted sovereignty of the United States, McKinley presented the Senate with a *fait accompli.* If the Senate were now to refuse to confirm the treaty, it would be repudiating the word of the Commander-in-Chief as well as the achievement of his peace commissioners.

McKinley had laid claim to the Philippines in the name of the Republic, and thereby offered the Senate a carefully limited choice: to accept or repeal their annexation. McKinley so arranged matters that psychological inertia as well as the calls of duty and profit favored ratification. The debate in the Senate would be lengthy and hard fought, but McKinley was confident that neither Philippine annexation nor the President would be repudiated. Nor were they. The treaty was confirmed by a vote of 57 to 27. Possibly William Jennings Bryan's muddled advocacy of confirmation influenced two Western senators, but the three most important factors in determining the vote in the Senate were the arguments furnished the Republican majority by William McKinley, McKinley's promises of patronage favors to several wavering senators, and the Executive Order of December 21.[18]

McKinley's assessment that annexation of the Philippines would prove a source of commercial and strategic advantage for the United States is open to challenge. A strong case can be made that for the American nation as a whole the Philippines would prove of greater economic cost than benefit and would serve less as a naval drydock than as a hostage to Japanese imperial ambitions. In the more immediate term, one can argue that by disregarding the "Republic of the Philippines" proclaimed by Emilio Aguinaldo and the insurgent leaders, and by replacing Spain as their unwanted master, McKinley provoked the "Philippine Insurrection." Whatever one's evaluation of the immediate or long-term disadvantages of American annexation of the Philippines, it should be acknowledged that America acquired a colonial empire in the years 1898–99 not in a fit of absent-mindedness nor as the result of popular demand or some vague psychic crisis, but by the conscious act and decision of William McKinley.

VI

Having acquired a colonial empire, McKinley was determined to exert Executive control over its administration and thereby prove the identity of mission and self-interest. He was prepared to turn Guam, Wake, and American Samoa over to the Navy Department. The Republic of Hawaii, annexed by a joint resolution of Congress in June, 1898, was easily transformed into an incorporated territory with its current government. Cuba, Puerto Rico, and the Philippines were McKinley's main concerns, and there he would insist on presidential authority over the duration of military government and the transition to civilian government. He would insist on freedom of action for both the United States and himself. Neither the "natives" nor the Congress should interfere with a policy of enlightened colonization characterized by benevolent indoctrination.

A military government was established in Cuba, under the war powers of the President, and McKinley would not end military occupation until the Cuban insurgent army had been disbanded, prospects for a sensible Cuban government improved, and the terms of U.S. guardianship formally accepted. After a period of American tutelage, Cuban independence would be acknowledged, but independence must not endanger the special relationship of the island with its liberator. McKinley supervised and approved Elihu Root's draft of the misnamed "Platt Amendment." That amendment, approved by Congress on March 2, 1901, declared that the United States had the right to intervene in Cuba whenever there was a threat of domestic anarchy or "foreign" interference. The Cubans were instructed that its terms must be included in the new Cuban constitution. Appreciating that the alternative was continued American occupation, the Cubans reluctantly agreed on June 12, 1901.

Puerto Rico offered fewer problems and there McKinley exhibited more confusion of purpose. After initially calling for a policy of free trade for Puerto Rican exports to the United States, he backed off and accepted a preferential tariff bill for an indeterminate period. After advocating a single-chamber civilian legislature composed of appointed U.S. officials, he accepted a bicameral legislature with a lower house chosen by a restricted Puerto Rican electorate. McKinley's uncertainty was in part the result of his fear of creating precedents in Puerto Rico that might inhibit future U.S. policy in the Philippines, and it was the Philippines that was McKinley's major interest and the source of his greatest difficulty.

The "Philippine Insurrection" that began two days before Senate confirmation of the Treaty of Paris would continue throughout the McKinley presidency. McKinley's policy of paternalistic indoctrination in the Philippines was necessarily delayed by his determination to administer a decisive defeat to the insurrectos and gain Filipino acceptance of U.S. sovereignty. McKinley was convinced, however, that the United States must take steps toward civilian rule and Philippine participation in local government as a demonstration of America's generous intentions. McKinley wished simultaneously to extend the stick and the carrot: to crush opposition to the American army while sending to the Philippines commissioner-emissaries to assure the Filipinos of the benefits that would be theirs once they cooperated in defeating the bandit chief Aguinaldo and his deluded guerrillas.[19] McKinley's efforts to direct the military strategy of the war were sporadic and ill-informed; his faith in General Elwell Otis was misplaced and his understanding of the inspirations and strength of Philippine nationalism, negligible, but McKinley had no doubts about the wisdom of his Philippine policy. Military victory must precede any institutionalization of limited home rule, and although it was right to hold out political inducements to the Filipinos as a means of ending popular support for the insurrectos, there must be no promise of future Philippine independence. The United States alone would decide the criteria for determining the readiness of the Filipinos for graduated degrees of self-government. The Filipinos must not be distracted by visions of future independence; they must concentrate on obedience and moral improvement. When McKinley died, September 14, 1901, the "Insurrection" continued but it was in its final phase. Aguinaldo had been captured, the Taft Commission had assumed executive authority in Manila, and the broad outlines of a policy characterized by American instruction and Philippine dependence had been established.[20]

Enlightened colonization was McKinley's goal and it was he who determined its definition in the Philippines and the other new possessions. Presidential control of colonial policy was indeed the creation of William McKinley. In its exercise, McKinley was guilty of undue optimism that American political institutions were adaptive to other peoples and cultures.

VII

The most important and characteristic foreign policies of the McKinley presidency are those related to the Spanish war and the acquisition and administration of a colonial empire. There were but two other major policy concerns: British-American relations and the question of an isthmian canal; efforts to assure the protection and expansion of American commerce with China. In these areas, McKinley's measure of control was less direct.

McKinley's third secretary of state, John Hay, was the recipient of more presidential confidence than his predecessors, and Hay was anxious to promote diplomatic understanding between the United States and Great Britain. McKinley did not share Hay's anglophile bias and did not wish to give his political enemies the opportunity to charge the administration with an intention to form a British-American alliance, but McKinley approved Hay's efforts to settle various disputes with Britain, so long as the settlement was in accord with the President's desire to extend United States dominance in the Caribbean and the North American continent.

In 1899, a peaceful division of the Samoan Islands was arranged with Britain and Germany. British-American cooperation was also demonstrated at the Hague Conference on international arbitration and in the attitudes of the two governments toward their respective military difficulties in South Africa and the Philippines. The McKinley years, however, saw no true British-American rapprochement, largely because of two sources of continued friction: the Alaskan-Canadian boundary and McKinley's determination to assure unilateral American control over the future construction of an isthmian canal. The Alaskan-Canadian boundary dispute was of long standing and was exacerbated by the discovery of gold in the Klondike. It would receive no resolution in the McKinley years. The dispute over the Clayton-Bulwer treaty was resolved, though only after hard-bargaining and a residue of ill feeling.

The Clayton-Bulwer treaty of 1850 had provided for joint British-American control over any future isthmian canal in Central America. McKinley believed that such a canal would promote American naval strength and commercial expansion, but only if it were under exclusive U.S. control. Abrogation of the Clayton-Bulwer treaty must be accomplished, however, by way of treaty negotiation, not through the unilateral action of hotheads in Congress. Hay was instructed to fashion a treaty with the British minister, Sir Julian Pauncefote, while McKinley worked with Senate Republican leaders to delay action on a House bill supporting unilateral U.S. construction of a Nicaraguan canal. The first Hay-Pauncefote treaty would be rejected by the Senate because of its provisions prohibiting fortification of the canal and requiring that the canal be open to the ships of all countries on an equal basis in peace and war. Disgusted by the Senate action, Hay offered his resignation. McKinley refused to accept it and persuaded Hay to try again. The second Hay-Pauncefote treaty, drafted in late April, 1901, met the Senate's objections: the Clayton-Bulwer treaty was explicitly abrogated, the ban on fortifications was omitted, and the United States—at least by implication—would not be obliged to observe neutralization in wartime. Though this treaty would not be formally signed or ratified until after McKinley's death, its terms had been fixed in the April draft and it should be attributed to the McKinley administration. It represented a major step toward the eventual construction of an isthmian canal and so toward McKinley's larger goal of U.S. dominance of the Caribbean region.

The United States policy of the "Open Door" in China is often described as the invention of John Hay. The attribution is false on two counts. The Open Door policy was but a redefinition of principles that can be traced back to Caleb Cushing's Treaty of Wanghia of 1844. Additionally authorship of the Open Door Notes must be shared by Hay with William Rockhill and William McKinley. The notes of September, 1899, and the circular of July, 1900, were reviewed by the President before they were sent to the governments of the China Powers.

McKinley was slow to share the concerns of various business correspondents that the "spheres of influence" claimed in China by Britain, France, Germany, Russia, and Japan would serve as a prelude for partition and thereby squeeze American commercial interests out of the China Market. From the first, however, McKinley was a staunch advocate of the American tradition of demanding most-favored-nation treatment for American traders wherever possible. McKinley needed little encouragement to advocate the principle of equal opportunity for all foreign commercial interests in China. He only wished assurance that it could be done without the dangers of an international alliance or military commitment. Hay furnished the solution. The Open Door Notes of September, 1899, were cast in terms of general principles and avoided the appearance of power politics while carefully ignoring all questions of implementation. Advocacy of the territorial integrity of China in 1900 was a comparatively bolder step, but the international consequences of the Boxer Rebellion persuaded McKinley of its propriety. Having taken the unprecedented action of dispatching U.S. troops as members of an international expeditionary force to raise the siege of Peking, McKinley judged it necessary and proper to couple a concern for the rights of American enterprise in China with a declaration in behalf of Chinese independence in Hay's circular note of July 3, 1900.

Neither McKinley nor Hay invented the principle of the Open Door, but they helped formalize the principles of equal commercial opportunity and Chinese territorial integrity as major precepts of U.S. Asian policy over the next forty years of American diplomatic history. On this and several other counts, the McKinley years were of greater significance for the evolution of American foreign policy than has been generally recognized.

VIII

At McKinley's death, the United States was a world power, a nation ready to play an enlarged role in East Asia, the Pacific, and the Caribbean, and strong enough to determine for itself the extent and nature of its participation. This was obviously the result of historical developments over the previous century and more, but the McKinley administration does provide an important chapter. Many have seen McKinley as but an accidental figure. They admit that the McKinley years saw an important evolution in the history of American expansion, but McKinley is often pictured as the somewhat witless agent of forces beyond his knowledge or control. McKinley was hardly the inventor of the expansionist sentiment and ambition of the 1890s, but he was the major architect of important developments in U.S. foreign policy. The overseas territorial acquisitions and altered economic and strategic inspirations of the McKinley years represented a significant change for U.S. expansionism, and the ability and readiness of the United to dominate the rest of the western hemisphere may be dated with the McKinley presidency.

The McKinley legacy for American foreign policy was one of

success and danger. Perhaps no president since James K. Polk achieved a greater measure of foreign policy success. Every foreign policy plank of the Republican platform of 1896 had been fulfilled or placed on the road to fulfillment by McKinley's death. But McKinley's ability to gain the acquiescence of Congress and the public was not matched by an aptitude for prediction or an understanding of the complexities of international relations. McKinley was an intelligent man but one whose intellectual horizon was limited to the immediate present. The Spanish War undoubtedly hastened America's acceptance of international responsibilities, but in equal measure American military success encouraged a national tendency to confuse the promotion of United States interests with the progress and well-being of other peoples. McKinley was a prototypical American and his expectation of international gratitude for actions of national self-service was widely shared. The twentieth-century history of American foreign policy has frequently demonstrated the inaccuracy of this expectation.

The most serious policy error of the McKinley years was the acquisition of the Philippine Islands. Not only would this lead to a long and grisly guerrilla war in the Philippines, but in the longer term the Philippines would prove not an asset but a liability. By extending the United States defense perimeter seven thousand miles into the Pacific, McKinley not only transformed the requirements of U.S. naval strength but laid the groundwork for a generation of fluctuating Japanese-American animosity. McKinley was not a weak president pandering to popular hysteria. Rather he was a stubborn president whose self-righteous optimism and overconfident nationalism reflected the majority mood of his countrymen with dangerous accuracy. McKinley's policies augmented the international authority of the United States as they illustrated the tendency of American diplomacy to confuse power with security.

NOTES

1. See the excellent historiographical essay by Joseph A. Fry, "William McKinley and the Coming of the Spanish-American War: A Study of the Besmirching and Redemption of an Historical Image," *Diplomatic History,* III (Winter 1979), pp. 77-97.
2. The justifiably praised studies by Ernest R. May and David F. Trask see McKinley forced into war in the final analysis by popular hysteria and political pressure. Ernest R. May, *Imperial Democracy: The Emergence of America as a Great Power* (New York, 1961);

David F. Trask, *The War With Spain In 1898* (New York, 1981).

3. See Hans Morganthau, *In Defense of the National Interest: A Critical Examination of American Foreign Policy* (New York, 1952); Robert E. Osgood, *Ideals and Self-Interest in America's Foreign Relations: The Great Transformation of the Twentieth Century* (Chicago, 1953); George F. Kennan, *American Diplomacy, 1900-1950* (Chicago, 1951); Norman A. Graebner, "The Year of Transition," *An Uncertain Tradition: American Secretaries of State in the Twentieth Century,* Norman A. Graebner, ed., (New York, 1961).
4. There is a wide difference, however, between the sophisticated interpretation of William A. Williams and the unqualified judgments of Philip Foner. Foner believes that McKinley's Cuban diplomacy in the winter/spring of 1898 was specifically directed toward the acquisition of a colonial empire. The Spanish-American War was "caused by United States imperialism in need of markets, sources of cheap raw materials, and new fields of investment." William McKinley was personally well aware "of the relationship between military action against Spain over Cuba and the establishment of an American base of operation in the Philippines from which to venture into the lucrative Far Eastern markets." William A. Williams, *The Tragedy of American Diplomacy* (New York, 1962), pp. 29-30, 37-38, 41-45; Philip Foner, *The Spanish-Cuban-American War and the Birth of American Imperialism, 1895-1902* (New York, 1972), I, 287-88, 295-97, 309-10.
5. The portrait of McKinley as a strong executive whose foreign policy was the result more of presidential initiative than public opinion began with a doctoral dissertation of John Offner and gained additional evidence and persuasiveness as the result of the scholarly labors of H. Wayne Morgan, Paul Holbo, and Lewis Gould. John L. Offner, "President McKinley and the Origins of the Spanish-American War," Ph.D. dissertation, Pennsylvania State University, 1957; H. Wayne Morgan, *William McKinley and His America* (Syracuse, 1963); H. Wayne Morgan, *America's Road to Empire: The War With Spain and Overseas Expansion* (New York, 1965); Paul Holbo, "Presidential Leadership in Foreign Affairs; William McKinley and the Turpie-Foraker Amendment," *American Historical Review,* LXXII (July 1967), pp. 1322-34; Lewis L. Gould, *The Presidency of William McKinley* (Lawrence, Kansas, 1980). Gould's book is the latest and offers the most detailed argument and the fullest documentation.
6. Morgan, *William McKinley and His America,* p. 529.
7. *Papers Relating to the Foreign Relations of the United States, 1898* (Washington, 1901), pp. 558-61. Earlier, in a dispatch from Secretary of State John Sherman to the Spanish Foreign Minister, McKinley had demanded revocation of the *reconcentrado* policy and pacification of the islands by means of a program of permanent reform. In

that dispatch, McKinley made clear his conviction that the United States had the right to monitor Spanish conduct: "[The President] is bound by the higher obligations of his representative office to protest against the uncivilized and inhumane conduct of the campaign in the island of Cuba. He conceives that he has a right to demand that a war, conducted almost within sight of our shores and grievously affecting American citizens and their interests throughout the length and breadth of the land, shall at least be conducted according to the military codes of civilization." *Foreign Relations, 1897,* pp. 507-08.

8. *Foreign Relations, 1898,* pp. 721-22.
9. *Ibid.,* pp. 704, 712-13. Woodford had earlier suggested—with little warrant—that there was the possibility of U.S. purchase of the island. Though McKinley had once briefly considered such a purchase, he now instructed Secretary Day to inform Woodford: "We do not want the island." *Foreign Relations, 1898,* pp. 685-93, 704; Ernest R. May, *Imperial Democracy,* pp. 149-50.
10. When certain Republican senators sought to add to the "war declaration" an amendment calling for U.S. recognition of the provisional government of the Republic of Cuba, McKinley successfully threatened the use of the presidential veto. Not only did McKinley wish no restrictions on the authority of the Executive to determine the nation's foreign policy but he was determined not to be inhibited in his war strategy by the necessity to consult with the dependent beneficiaries of American intervention. After the war, a period of American tutelage would be necessary to establish order and stability, and it should be the United States alone that would determine the nature and duration of American guidance. Paul Holbo, "Presidential Leadership in Foreign Affairs," pp. 1323-30.
11. David F. Trask, *The War With Spain In 1898,* pp. 423, 477-78.
12. According to an Army General Order of May 16, these troops were to occupy and secure Manila "and any and all of the Philippine Islands that may come under the control of the United States." *Correspondence Relating to the War with Spain, April 15, 1898–July 30, 1902,* II, 635, 676-78. Se also McKinley to John D. Long, May 19, 1898, Papers of William McKinley, Library of Congress.
13. Diary of George M. Cortelyou, July 31, 1898, cited in Charles S. Olcott, *Life of William McKinley* (Boston, 1916), II, 67.
14. Throughout the summer and autumn of 1898, American Philippine policy was the preserve of William McKinley and the executive branch of the government. Congress did nothing before the debate over the Treaty of Paris, and although Lodge and other Republican senators volunteered advice, there is no evidence that they influenced McKinley's decision.
15. The United States already possessed Midway Island; the Hawaiian Islands were annexed at McKinley's instigation by a joint congres-

sional resolution in July, 1898 and the United States Navy would take possession of Wake Island in January, 1899. Wake provided an anchor for a trans-Pacific cable between Honolulu and Manila.

16. Robert Ferrell has suggested that McKinley's famous explanation to a delegation of Methodists of how his decision to acquire the Philippines was assisted by divine guidance may have been an invention of one of the members of the Methodist delegation, General James F. Rusling. Robert H. Ferrell, *American Diplomacy: A History* (3d ed., New York, 1975), pp. 367-69.
17. A key passage ran as follows: "All persons who . . . cooperate with the Government of the United States . . . will receive the reward of its support and protection. All others will be brought within the lawful rule we have assumed, with firmness if need be, but without severity so far as may be possible. . . . It should be the earnest and paramount aim of the military to . . . [prove] that the mission of the United States is one of benevolent assimilation, substituting the mild sway of justice and right for arbitrary rule." *Correspondence Relating to the War with Spain,* II, 719. See also Adjutant General to Otis, December 28, 1898, telegram, Dewey Papers, Library of Congress.
18. Some of McKinley's contemporaries recognized McKinley's central role in the passage of the treaty. Andrew Carnegie and Carl Schurz, two anti-imperialist opponents of the treaty, agreed that it was McKinley and his determination to use the full powers of the presidential office who assured passage. See Carnegie to Schurz, February 10, 1899, Carnegie Papers, Library of Congress.
19. McKinley's dual policy of military subjugation and promises of subsequent kindness was continuously denounced by such Anti-Imperialists as E. L. Godkin of *The Nation.* For Godkin, McKinley was trying to combine the roles of the vandal chieftain and the Christian missionary, expressing "a tender concern for the souls of the men he is about to kill." He was conducting "a philanthropic war"; "killing people tenderly," with tears in his eyes. See *The Nation,* LXVIII (May 18, 1899), pp. 368-69; LXIX (August 24, 1899), p. 140, (September 7, 1899), p. 182, (September 21, 1899), p. 218; LXX (March 22, 1900), pp. 217-18, (April 5, 1900), p. 252.
20. In the Philippines as in Cuba, Congress was largely restricted to responding to McKinley's policies and legislative requests. In March, 1901, McKinley skillfully secured passage of the "Spooner Amendment" which gave him broad authority to proceed with the establishment of civil government in the Philippines.

3

THEODORE ROOSEVELT AND THE CONSERVATIVE REVIVAL

Frederick W. Marks III

Anyone living in Washington at the dawn of the century could not have failed to notice that a curious group of men regularly traversed Rock Creek Park at a frenetic clip. Oblivious to weather and scorning well-trodden paths, they beat their way through thick and thin, up sheerest rocks and down wooded ravines, until they reached the Potomac. The regular leader of this pack, with large white teeth, mustache, steel-rimmed spectacles, and close-cropped hair, was unmistakably the president of the United States, while by his side or bringing up the rear could be seen various members of the diplomatic corps, including the handsome and charming French ambassador, Jules Jusserand. It is said that on one occasion, after the members of his party had reached the river, shed their clothing, and were about to plunge in, Roosevelt asked the Frenchman why he persisted in keeping his gloves on. But Monsieur le Président, exclaimed Jusserand, "we might meet [the] ladies!"[1]

Such a story serves to illustrate Theodore Roosevelt's uniquely personal approach to diplomacy, his penchant for conducting affairs of state astride a horse or on the tennis court. By the same token, however, the colorful side of a large personality can easily obscure Roosevelt's extraordinary gift for statesmanship. It has long been fashionable, particularly among Americans, to take T.R. less than seriously, despite the fact that he has one of the most impressive peace records in U.S. history. He became the first president, and one of only two, to win the Nobel Peace Prize. This was based in part upon his role in ending the Russo-Japanese War. By bringing both sides together at Portsmouth and employing a judicious mixture of firmness and tact, he succeeded in eliminating a serious threat to world peace, one which he did not fail to recognize as a menace to the peace of his own country. Basing his strategy upon the concept of a balance of power, in this case between Japan and Russia, he brought a fair degree of stability to the Far East, at least temporarily.

Nor is this to neglect the part he played in averting World War I. Events leading to the Algeciras Conference of 1906 featured an American president who refused to favor France or Germany and thus facilitated a compromise settlement on the German position in Morocco. Closer to home, his standing allowed him to mediate between Guatemala and El Salvador, as well as between Nicaragua and Honduras. He was instrumental in setting up a Central American Court of Justice which for more than a generation kept the lid on revolution and political intrigue over a region stretching from Mexico to Colombia. Above all, the first Roosevelt demonstrated his mastery of foreign policy by keeping the United States continually at peace. During his term of office, a period lasting almost eight years, not one soldier or sailor was ever ordered to fire on a foreign foe. Instead, he wound down a police action in the Philippines and while he engaged in two interventions, one in Cuba, the other in the Dominican Republic, both were carried out by invitation of the host country. In each case, the U.S. contingent behaved in such a way as to earn the respect of the native populace.

T.R.'s Big Stick is often portrayed as a policy of unvarnished power when in fact it was a series of cautionary principles involving flexibility and a wide array of tactics. The same Roosevelt who fought for naval appropriations also argued that a reduction in the tariff could lead to greater economic interdependence and therefore to a more secure peace. He not only approved of international adjudication but furthered its cause significantly. By way of resolving a dispute with Mexico (the Pious Fund Case), he became the first leader ever to refer a case to the Hague Court of Arbitration. Not content to sit behind a wall of battleships, he looked forward in the future to some form of world government. In the meantime he pressed steadily for arms limitation agreements. As the sponsor of some twenty-four bilateral arbitration treaties, he backed Britain's demand for arbitration on the question of Panama tolls and worked hard for American compliance with an unfavorable Hague ruling on the fisheries.[2] When war hysteria reared its head, as it did periodically, he could be counted upon to react calmly. By the same token, when his system of "balanced antagonisms" seemed about to break down, he stood ready to shore it up. Thus it was that he fostered two informal alliances, one between the United States and Britain, the other between Britain and France.

Where he parted company with the "world gush creatures" was in his fear that organized peace movements might lull America to sleep and cause her to regard a set of genuinely helpful tactics as an alternative to "the fighting edge."[3] If history taught anything, it taught that conflicts would arise which were irreconcilable, alike from the point of view of national interest and moral conviction. The United States must therefore prepare to meet whatever challenges lay in store. In accepting the Nobel Prize, he endorsed arbitration, a world court, and a league of nations while warning that righteousness must come before peace and that there was no substitute for a demonstrable readiness to employ force. His most bitter sarcasm was reserved for "maudlin sentimentalists," "flubdubs and flapdoodle mollycoddles"—the "peace at any price boys" who were always ready to belittle the importance of the military. In his opinion, weakness and timidity could do more harm than violence and injustice. Little trust, he warned, was to be placed in world opinion or disarmament as peace panaceas; as for sentimentality, it was "the most broken reed" upon which righteousness could lean.[4]

II

Theodore Roosevelt came to power at a time when the nation's history was well-laced with strife. Already, there had been six wars and within the next sixty years there would be four more. The fact is that he could look on either side of himself and find presidents who left behind a legacy of bloodshed. It is of more than passing interest, then, to inquire whether or not there may be a discernible pattern, or set of patterns, which could help to explain how he managed to pilot the ship of state through disputes involving three of the world's foremost powers.

Roosevelt did indeed operate according to a pattern, nor was he at a loss when it came to articulating it. Few chief executives have taken it upon themselves to advise their countrymen as he did on how to manage the conduct of foreign relations. None, certainly, have been any more effective at translating words into action. It was in this dual role as preacher and doer of the word that he liked to refer to the White House as his "bully pulpit," and it was from this very pulpit that he handed down a credo which can be reduced to ten constituent parts. Perhaps as much as the record itself, it is this diplomatic decalogue which distinguishes T.R. from all his peers in the presidency. His celebrated eleventh commandment, "Thou Shalt Not Slop Over" (or, to put it another way, "rely not upon atmospherics") was just what its name implied, an eleventh commandment accompanied by ten others.[5] He even defined one cardinal sin—but more on that later. There is hardly space in a short essay to explore every facet of the man's thought, but it may be helpful to single out a few of T.R.'s basic precepts in order to observe their operation in practice.

First came the notion of preparedness, the idea that if one would have peace, one must prepare for war. In the years 1901-1909, the standing of the U.S. fleet rose from 5th in the world to 2nd. Its prestige was never higher than under this one-time assistant secretary of the navy whose birthday, October 27, is still celebrated as Navy Day and whose presidency gave birth to the slogan, "Join the Navy and See the World." T.R. was never prepared to admit that power, when cautiously excercised, was likely to be provocative. It was weakness, he maintained, which would invite attack. The American navy had been "an infinitely more potent factor for peace than all the peace societies of every kind and sort."[6] When the minister from Istanbul complained that the presence of American warships in Turkish waters implied sympathy for a group of insurgents, Roosevelt reminded him that the fleet was merely supporting legitimate demands and that any false impression regarding American sympathy would be dispelled the moment the Turkish government complied with its obligations.

"Never draw," he counseled, "unless you intend to shoot," and never strike unless you are "prepared to strike hard."[7] Bluff was "the one unpardonable sin" because it undermined that most precious of all commodities, credibility. A great nation, he felt, must be prepared on occasion to act decisively as no feeling on the part of an adversary could be more dangerous than that of contempt.[8] The British, he said, had better throw fifty thousand more troops into South Africa than they felt they needed. Likewise, President McKinley should send more than one warship to Turkey to demonstrate American displeasure over local events (he eventually sent three). When China threatened reprisals against American life in 1906, Roosevelt notified the army that it must triple the size of an expeditionary force it was planning to send rather than "take any chances" of underestimating Chinese prowess.[9]

In one of the more vivid scenes for which his presidency is remembered, sixteen American battleships steamed into the Pacific on a round-the-world cruise. Beneath the official rhetoric about sixteen "messengers of peace," Roosevelt was plainly offering an earnest of American determination to hold its own. At the time Tokyo was justifiably angry over the shabbiness with which her nationals were being treated in California. At the same time, Japanese diplomats appeared to be casting a propriatory eye on the Philippines and Roosevelt detected a slightly threatening tone in their correspondence—what he termed "a very very slight undertone of veiled truculence." The initial upshot was a gentlemen's agreement whereby Tokyo undertook to call a voluntary halt to its emigration and Washington agreed to obtain redress for those Japanese who had already settled on the west coast. Although T.R. moved at once to carry out his side of the agreement, he soon discovered that reciprocal action was not forthcoming. It was at this point that he decided to dispatch all of his battle cruisers to within striking distance of Nippon. Needless to say, all of this was done without fanfare, almost as if by improvisation, and from start to finish with elaborate courtesy. In the end, Japan, with her pride still intact, came full circle and subscribed to a series of arrangements which put Pacific relations on a more than satisfactory footing. Roosevelt's fleet commanders were received in port and given a royal welcome.[10]

There was, of course, another side to the principle of tailoring power to policy. From time to time, policy itself had to be whittled down to the level of national resolution. No sooner had T.R. taken office in 1901 than he singled out the Philippines as America's achilles heel. At the root of the problem was the fact that he did not have the means to defend Manila against a determined enemy, and any fleet large enough to do so would pose a threat to the Japanese home islands. Thus, while he persuaded Congress to furnish funds for temporary defense, he did not think his countrymen would prove willing in the long run to sustain such a force.[11] Even as it was, he insisted on substituting Pearl Harbor for Manila as the bulwark of western defense. Along similar lines, he could not reconcile the Open Door policy in its broadest form with political realism. Any effort to underwrite Chinese sovereignty, anything in fact beyond the traditional concern for commercial access, seemed to him more than Congress could possibly be expected to furnish since it would require an army the size of Germany's and a fleet of the caliber of the Royal Navy. This, then, was the rule that governed his Korean policy. It was "hands off" not because he was unsympathetic, but because Korean nationalists had not proven themselves capable of lifting a finger in their own defense.[12] So highly did he come to regard Japan that he accorded her a Monroe Doctrine of her own and warned his successors against clashing with the imperial navy. Under no circumstances should the main U.S. battlefleet be divided (advice which was disregarded by FDR in 1941).[13] In 1900, he came out against an invasion of the Turkish port of Smyrna since he doubted the commitment could be sustained in strength. Turkey, he recalled had fielded 200,000 men against the Greeks and gone through them "like a hot knife through butter." There were no better ground forces in Europe and the reception which would lie in store for American invaders would make the Boer War seem pleasant by comparison.[14]

Roosevelt is often represented as being an ardent imperialist even though the area of the United States actually shrank under his stewardship. He yielded a strip of Alaskan panhandle larger than the size of the Canal Zone. On the one hand, he realized that an isthmian canal was imminent and felt strongly that it should be under the protection of the United States rather than in the hands of France, Britain, or Germany. Logically, therefore, it followed that the United States should lay claim to whatever naval bases might be needed to control the canal's approaches. Beyond this, however, he would not go. He was quite honest when he protested: "I am no more anxious to annex Santo Domingo than a gorged boa constrictor would be to swallow a porcupine wrong-end-to." The Navy lobbied for outposts in the Caribbean as well as bases along the coast of China; Colombia offered offshore real estate; there was an option to acquire Cuba's Isle of Pines. In every instance, however, the attitude of the White House was plainly negative.[15]

Similar caution acted as a brake upon all of Roosevelt's operations. The Great White Fleet was not permitted to sail without an advance screen of torpedo boats, and shore patrol was invented to insure against unfortunate incidents between American and Japanese tars. It might also be pointed out that T.R. did not send his armada into the teeth of the Anglo-Japanese alliance without first enlisting the aid of a powerful potential ally. American and German warships rendez-voused in Samoa and sixteen of the kaiser's warships sallied forth from the Baltic on their maiden voyage outside home waters just as Roosevelt was facing off against

Tokyo. Even the famous telegram which brought delegates to their feet at the 1904 Republican nominating convention, "We Want Perdicaris Alive or Raisuli Dead!", was fired off against a backdrop of patient and meticulous planning. By this time, he had exhausted every expedient other than force in dealing with Morocco and he was proceeding with the tacit support of France and Britain should a landing party prove necessary. This was the Roosevelt who warned his son Kermit in 1908, just before embarking on a big game hunt:

> We must be very cautious . . . always ready to back one another up, and probably we ought each to have a spare rifle when we move in to the attack.

Kermit later remembered how careful his father had been in preparing every detail of the expedition.[16]

III

Ordinarily, one might suppose that Roosevelt's brand of realism would leave little room for considerations of a moral or ideal nature. Such is not the case, though. Hard-headed and practical as he was, T.R. was also one of the more sensitive of presidents when it came to the realm of right and wrong. He built an entire career on the concept of a "square deal," whether in his struggle for civil service reform, the stands he took as police commissioner, or his fight against graft in the New York Assembly. The presidency itself affords still another example. His writings positively hum with the word "righteousness," intended always in the biblical sense of "thou shalt not steal," "thou shalt not bear false witness." It was a brand of morality which refused to admit distinction between nations and individuals. Applications might vary depending upon the situation, but the principle remained the same. When Russia's minister, Count Cassini, lied to Roosevelt, knowing perfectly well the latter knew he was lying, the president exploded at what he considered brazen and contemptuous effrontery. Upright behavior, along with preparedness, was to Roosevelt the indispensable shield of the republic, and it is with this in mind that he likened his country to "the just man armed."[17]

Issues such as democracy and self-determination, regarded in some quarters as the absolute benchmark of morality, were to Roosevelt matters of expediency dependent for their effect upon time and place. He did not believe, for example, that democracy would take hold in the Orient as it had in the West. It was not suitable for Turkey. It had positively ruined Haiti. France could not take it in the same dosage as England. Even in the United States, said Roosevelt, "it may be that 'the voice of the people is the voice of God' in fifty-one cases out of a hundred, but in the remaining forty-nine it is quite as likely to be the voice of the devil, or, what is worse still, the voice of a fool." As for imperialism, this again was a matter of ethical rather than moral import. Some parts of Eastern Europe were ripe for self-government. Others were not. Turkestan should remain under Russian jurisdiction just as Bosnia and Herzegovina were better off for the time being under Austria-Hungary. He could never forget that when British forces had left the Sudan, it had led to the slaughter of two thirds of the native population.[18]

Among other things, the moral law meant *noblesse oblige.* It meant the faithful support of one's allies. An imperial power must act as trustee for the world at large and no form of imperialism could be legitimate which did not benefit the subject people.[19] Roosevelt's code, whether domestic or foreign, stipulated fairness over and above ethnic, national, or economic considerations. Just so, he believed the concept of social justice should be applied equally to rich and poor, and he refused to accept poverty or weakness among nations as a license for wrong-doing. At home, he proved himself again and again an arbiter rather than a partisan in the struggle between big labor and big business. Characteristic is the following extract from a speech given in Canton, Ohio: "There is only one thing as important as the discouragement of a feeling of envy and hostility toward honest businessmen, toward honest men of means; that is, the discouragement of dishonest businessmen." Although the latter part of the phrase was enthusiastically applauded, the first was not. So he continued: "Wait a minute my friends, I don't want you to applaud this part unless you are willing to applaud also the part I read first to which you listened in silence. . . . I will read a little of it over again." This he did, with the crowd cheering and applauding lustily. Both at home and abroad, Roosevelt came to be regarded as an honest broker, and herein lies one of the main keys to his success. Had this not been the case, he would never have been able to render useful service when a resurgent Germany began to butt horns with France and when Japan felt that it had a wounded bear on the run.[20]

The strong, in Roosevelt's view, should always be slow to assert their rights against the weak, but such patience could not be compared with abdication in the face of blackmail or chronic wrongdoing.[21] His role in the separation of Panama from its mother state, Colombia, has frequently been cited as a black mark on the record of the United States. But such a perception sets aside those very elements that T.R. felt to be at the heart of the moral equation. In the first place, Panama had a supportable cause for revolt. The relationship between Colón and Bogotá had long been one of exploitation. Inevitably, this had given rise to armed insurrection which in turn necessitated the intervention of the United States—on the side of Bogotá—in order to maintain peace. Equally important in Roosevelt's estimate was the fact that José Marroquín, Colombia's chief executive, had given the equivalent of a pledge that he would support the Hay-Herrán Treaty. This was a treaty which would open the way to an American-built canal. It had been signed in good faith after months of labor and great pains on both sides and few impartial observers doubted its fairness to Colombia. Once Roosevelt had committed his prestige, along with that of his administration, Marroquín executed a sudden about-face, letting it be known that he wanted sums over and above what had been agreed. Such tactics drew down the full fury of which Roosevelt's passionate soul was capable. This is not to imply that other considerations were absent. At no time did T.R. ever lose sight of the national interest. It is simply to observe that in this particular case morality was a spur, rather than a stumbling block, to bold and forceful action.[22]

One other facet of the Roosevelt *modus operandi,* and one which can be seen as integral to his pursuit of peace, was face-saving.[23] The *amour propre* of other nations was fully as important to T.R. as that of his own. Not once did he engage in serious confrontation that he did not afford his opponent a graceful means of escape. His famous slogan, "Speak softly and carry a big stick," did not imply any mincing of words.[24] On the contrary, Roosevelt was candid and straightforward in spelling out the limits of American tolerance. But such information was invariably dispensed *sub rosa* and behind closed doors. In other words, wherever possible in the delicate process of negotiation, he availed himself of secrecy. For weeks prior to the announcement of the Portsmouth talks, he refused to take even the secretary of state into his confidence, and he threw a similar shroud over his role leading up to Algeciras. Not surprisingly, it took historians twenty years to uncover the Taft-Katsura memorandum with Japan. Roosevelt also knew how to be self-effacing. He could praise the kaiser for defending Chinese territorial integrity in 1904 just as he could applaud the czar for sparking the second Hague Conference. Needless to say, the initiative in both instances had come from him. By the same token, he saw the Algeciras Conference as a convenient means of preserving German honor while awarding Paris "the kernel of the nut." After adjourment, he congratulated the kaiser on a "great triumph" while warning French officials to "abstain from a noisy celebration of victory."[25]

Foreigners were impressed by Roosevelt's insistence upon confidentiality because it compensated for what they regarded as one of America's worst weaknesses, its unbridled press. One British cabinet report to the Crown referred to Washington, D.C. "with its omnipresent unscrupulous press, its senators who have to be separately conciliated, and its diplomatic methods unchecked by any long diplomatic tradition," as "probably the most difficult theatre in the world for carrying on delicate negotiations." In talks leading to the Portsmouth Peace Conference, the Japanese hesitated to confide in Roosevelt because they considered the democratic process unreliable in handling sensitive matters. Ambassador Takahira, who had given his opinion on Manchuria assuming that it would be held in strict confidence, was appalled to find it three days later in the columns of the *New York Sun*. Where Roosevelt was concerned, such embarrassments were not likely to occur. The president would call envoys to his office in the late evening or early morning with the express purpose of avoiding reporters. During the Portsmouth negotiations, Baron Rosen of the Russian delegation was awakened at 2 A.M. to be told that the president was hailing him for a 7 A.M. train departure to Oyster Bay. The next day, his host received him on the tennis court, racquet in hand, and they conversed during "intervals of the game."[26]

In a serious crisis, T.R. was likely to rely upon unofficial envoys such as Oliver Wendell Holmes or Henry Cabot Lodge. Occasionally, he would cross Lafayette Square *incognito* to dine in the company of Secretary Hay or the British ambassador, and he thought nothing of sending important messages through trusted representatives of foreign countries. In the spring of 1902, Whitehall was informed that Roosevelt was relying more upon British envoys Cecil Spring Rice and Colonel Kitson than he was upon his own state department which might at any time be forced by Congress to turn over its most confidential files. From time to time, he went out of his way to summon foreign friends whose judgment and discretion were beyond doubt. Coming from places as far away as St. Petersburg, they would cross the Atlantic for a tête à tête and report back to their governments in person. On December 27, 1904, Roosevelt wrote to Spring Rice, then secretary of the British embassy in Russia: "I wish to Heaven you could come over if only for a week or two, and I think it would be very important for your government." The Englishman did come, as it developed, and he stayed with Henry Adams. But no one knew exactly why he had come and there was no mention of any foreign visitor by the press. Adams noted Hay's tendency to settle as many questions as possible by word of mouth and to write few papers. But if this was true of Hay, it was all the more applicable to Hay's chief who prided himself on the kind of diplomacy "which consists of not uttering one word that can be avoided."[27]

IV

Nowhere is Roosevelt's style better illustrated than in two serious brushes with Downing Street. The first of these, involving an Anglo-German blockade of Venezuela, can be briefly sketched. Venezuelan strong man Cipriano Castro had for years proven himself impervious to European demands for the payment of outstanding debts. Roosevelt, who held no brief for Castro, would like nothing better than to have seen him soundly thrashed by his European creditors.[28] Real danger, however, lurked in the possibility that police action on the part of either the British or the Germans might take the form of sending 20,000 troops to Caracas. Occupation of Venezuela could well open the door to a foreign naval base on the rim of the Caribbean. This, in turn, would undermine American prestige, threaten control of a future canal, and knock the Monroe Doctrine into a cocked hat. A year of tension, punctuated by threats, led to the blockade of the Venezuelan coast. British and German warships bombarded coastal forts, sank Venezuelan craft, and landed troop detachments. While England had more guns in action than did Germany, the Wilhelmstrasse could not be discounted.

The first thing Roosevelt did was to issue a crystal-clear warning against any form of permanent occupation. For added emphasis, he held naval excercises off the coast of Puerto Rico (at Culebra) and commissioned military studies of the Venezuelan coast. In November of 1902, as the pressure on Caracas mounted, he ordered every one of his battleships and torpedo boats to within close range of the German-British blockade. Finally, he summoned

Germany's chargé d'affaires, Theodor von Holleben, in complete secrecy and told him that Germany (hence Britain, too) had exactly ten days to resolve the dispute peacefully. In London, Roosevelt's highly trusted chargé conveyed urgent warnings to the highest officials of the British government. When day followed day, however, without any sure sign of improvement, Roosevelt ordered his firepower into the actual operating area of the blockade. He was thus openly prepared to go to extremes when he heard of London's decision two days later to yield, carrying Berlin close behind.

Just as important as the quiet mobilization of naval power and equally quiet ultimatum was the way Roosevelt managed to prevent Congress from forcing his hand. His annual address of December 2 reported "not a cloud on the horizon" and Senator Lodge maneuvered successfully in the upper house to limit debate. On December 16, at the moment of greatest suspense, the president assured reporters that he did not regard the Caribbean situation as especially grave. Not one presidential threat ever found its way into the press. British Foreign Secretary Lord Lansdowne requested that Washington strike out a number of heated words from the published version of the diplomatic correspondence and his request was duly granted. The trail was actually very well covered. Just how far the White House went to maintain its diplomatic silence may be gathered from an inexplicable void still visible in the daily record of the American embassy in Berlin. It begins in mid-sentence on October 17 and runs all the way through to December 12. Important envoys from Berlin and London conferred with Roosevelt during the final stage of the crisis, but the transcripts of the conversation, if they ever existed, have disappeared without trace.[29]

Shifting for a moment to the Alaskan Boundary Dispute between the United States and Canada, the basic facts may again be quickly stated. When gold was discovered in the Canadian Yukon in 1896, it became a matter of some import as to whether Canada could lay claim to ports of call along the nearby Pacific coast. Traditionally, it was assumed that Alaska's 400-mile panhandle precluded Canadian access to the sea. Soon after the discovery of gold, however, Canadian leaders began to assert that enough of the panhandle belonged to Ottawa to put the Yukon on navigable water. In time, they promised their constituents they would persuade the United States to submit to arbitration. Roosevelt's reaction was an angry one: this was a preposterous fraud. Every map for at least sixty years, including the one hanging in Parliament House, Ottawa, supported the U.S. claim. Thus Canada had no more right to additional territory than the United States did to Cornwall or Devon.[30] He was willing to show flexibility by agreeing to abide by a *modus vivendi* arranged under President McKinley, but he sent 800 cavalrymen to the disputed area lest there be any misunderstanding as to where he himself stood on the matter. By January of 1903, Washington and Ottawa had agreed to a quasi-arbitral judicial commission whereby the case would be judged by three Americans, two Canadians, and one Briton, all of whom were to be "impartial jurists." Without question, the purpose was to permit Canada to save face. Roosevelt made this abundantly clear when he vowed he would not tolerate any substantial infringement on the American claim and ruled out any form of regular arbitration which implied splitting the difference. He felt that he had arrived at a gentlemen's agreement with leaders who admitted the weakness of their case and assured him they did not anticipate substantial gain. At the same time, he was under heavy pressure from senators not to give way on American rights or even to use the word "arbitral."

Given the above facts, it may well be imagined how T.R. reacted when both of Canada's judges held out against important sections of the American brief and a third judge, Chief Justice Lord Alverstone of Great Britain, appeared to side with them. Although Roosevelt had not appointed truly "impartial" jurists (due in part to the exigencies of domestic politics), he nonetheless felt that he was allowing enough in the way of concession to honor his side of the bargain.[31] Even though Ottawa's primary goal, direct access to the sea, remained unacceptable, he was willing to yield a sizable strip of land, not to mention two substantial islands in the Portland Channel. All along, he let it be known that he would insist absolutely on the implied basis for agreement. To London *Times* correspondent George Smalley, he confided that he was prepared to be "ugly." To Britain's chargé he hinted at "drastic" measures. Oliver Wendell Holmes was given a strong letter intended for the eye of Joseph Chamberlain at the Colonial Office.[32] As contradictory rumors began to filter across the Atlantic, Andrew Carnegie became the courier for yet another Roosevelt missive. Finally, at the eleventh hour, Lord Alverstone sided with the American brief on all essential points.[33]

Naturally, the Canadians expressed pique, but T.R., true to form, congratulated them for having emerged as winners and insisted that the award "offered signal proof of the fairness and good will with which two friendly nations can approach and determine issues." By the time he left the White House, his neighbors to the north were sufficiently well disposed to name one of their mountain peaks after Lord Alverstone and the chief surveyor of Canada was not afraid to admit that Ottawa never had a leg to stand on. Thus were the early years of the century a culminating phase of what Bradford Perkins has called the great rapprochement. Virtually every source of discord between Britain and America was eliminated by 1909, including the Newfoundland fisheries dispute which had festered for over a hundred years.

The Alaskan boundary dispute remains one of the better examples of what T.R. meant by the phrase, "speak softly and carry a big stick." Inclined to be breezy and candid in conversational banter, he was virtually always discrete in affairs of state. His 1911 boast to a college audience that "I took the Canal Zone" has been rehearsed by successive generations of historians to evince proof of an impulsive nature. One can cite dozens of counterexamples, however, which go to prove the opposite. When Admiral Dewey made public reference to Venezuela as "an object lesson to the kaiser," he was instantly called on the White House carpet to be reminded by the commander-in-chief that "we are too big a people to be able to be careless as to what we say."[34]

As this was a statecraft which demanded trustworthy channels of communication, it is interesting to observe how sedulously Roosevelt strove to cultivate foreign members of the diplomatic corps. Ultimately, his personal relationship with figures such as Cecil Spring Rice and Arthur Lee, both of Britain, as well as Jules Jusserand and Speck von Sternburg of France and Germany respectively, insured that he would be able to deal directly with difficult questions without tipping his hand in public. "Springy" did not receive an official appointment to Washington until after 1909, but he did correspond with the president (addressing his letters to Mrs. Roosevelt) and he did come to the White House during moments of exceptional strain.

V

All of this leads to one final observation about T.R.'s diplomatic style and outlook. It is not the normal thing for an American to write a naval history of the War of 1812, particularly one so fair to the British side that its author should be invited to contribute to an English history of the Royal Navy. Roosevelt was such a person. Superbly cosmopolitan, he read Japanese poetry and studied the Samurai code of chivalry. After traveling to Latin America in 1913, he published accounts of the various ways in which Latin American civilization struck him as superior to his own. He had long been aware that his own country ranked relatively low when it came to artistic achievement. Moreover, there was a courtesy and refinement about his southern neighbors which he found greatly attractive. The women whom he met in Brazil, Argentina, Chile, and elsewhere impressed him with their high standard of education, professional astuteness, and linguistic facility even as they retained a full complement of feminine charm and managed to rear a large family. He marveled at the way his brethren had adapted themselves to racial diversity—more effectively, he thought, than the people of North America. The beauty of the parks, plazas, and public buildings was not lost on him. And all of this, along with a number of sharper comments, found expression in the series of articles which appeared under his name in *Outlook* magazine.[35]

He lectured his fellow countrymen as they were never lectured before or since for their rudeness to Oriental immigrants. In one of his addresses to Congress, he thundered, "No nation is fit to teach unless it is willing to learn." When China struck back at the United States for its treatment of Chinese immigrants by boycotting American goods, T.R. readied the marines, but he also warned the people of the United States that "we cannot receive equity unless we are willing to do equity." He returned a lion's share of the Boxer indemnity to China, and when a new ambassador arrived from Peking, one who made a host of enemies, T.R. admitted: "He is a bad old Chink and if he had his way he would put us all to heavy death . . . [but] I do not object to any Chinaman showing a feeling that he would like to retaliate now and then for our insolence." In sum, he is one of the few presidents who has suggested to Americans that their outlook on the rest of the world might leave something to be desired.[36]

Ironically, Roosevelt is frequently perceived as a chauvinist. This may be due in part to his insistence on what he liked to call 100% Americanism; it may stem from the scorn that he heaped upon such expatriates as Henry James. There can be no doubt that his personality was home-grown. Celebrated for informality, he was the first president to be known by his initials, the first to prefer the title "Mr. President" to "Your Excellency." Germany's Wilhelm he called "Bill the Kaiser" while Russia's Czar Nicholas was simply "Nicky." At the same time, there was a definite line beyond which he would not go and beyond which he did not wish to see others go: "A good deal of the fuss and feathers of traditional diplomacy," he once wrote, "does not come easily to Americans. But on the whole, I think I prefer the European idea to that which is cherished by a large section of my fellow countrymen—that shirt-sleeves and bad manners are inseparable from true democracy."[37]

One of the outstanding paradoxes in the Roosevelt personality is precisely this juxtaposition between the native and the foreign. Only one other American comes to mind who, like T.R., managed to be at once thoroughly American and altogether cosmopolitan. Benjamin Franklin is remembered for his fur hat, homespun suit, and gnarled cane, yet he was nothing if not adept at representing his countrymen in the courts of Europe, something he did for twenty-six years. The other similarity is that T.R., like Franklin, was a renaissance man. He spoke French and German, published over thirty books, served as president of the American Historical Association, and contributed to scholarly journals of science while in the White House. Because he could converse on nearly any topic, current or ancient, he had automatic rapport with virtually any person he met. Wherever he went, he extended the same genuinely friendly hand, to ranchers and cowboys, to artists and architects. Alert to any sign of bias in his own makeup, he once wrote his sister that a certain group of foreigners "simply can't be as dirty as they would like to be." He then hastened to add, "I have a nice, charitable feeling towards foreigners, you see; in fact one of my most charming and amiable characteristics is my gentle tolerance of modes of thought and habits of life that differ from my own."[38] Vintage Roosevelt.

It is this self-deprecatory tone, coupled with an ardent desire to appreciate things foreign that, along with other qualities, constituted him the most internationally popular and respected of all the presidents. To the Sultan of Morocco, whose people had not seen an American warship since the days of Andrew Jackson, the United States appeared to be the holder of the international balance of power. Italian leaders admired him for his straightforward ways and looked to him for a lead on their China policy. His post-presidential tour of Europe in 1910 turned out to be one continuous love fest. In Hungary he regaled his hosts with his knowledge of the Arpad dynasty. The French distributed 57,000 copies of a speech which he delivered at the Sorbonne, while the British showered him with invitations and bestowed honorary degrees on him at Oxford and Cambridge. He must have been especially pleased when they laughed at his jokes and put teddy bears in his path. During his brief visit to Berlin, he became the first civilian ever to review the German imperial troops. In Japan, his portrait was hung beside that of the emperor. And in Brazil, a river was named after him, the Rio Teodoro which he himself had discovered during one of his wilderness expeditions.

T.R. is not generally viewed as the originator of the Good Neighbor Policy, yet it was he who shifted the Rio-London axis to run more nearly between Rio and Washington. No other president has been voted a special commendation at a Pan-American congress nor has any other chief executive been given a warmer welcome south of the border. This applies equally to his secretary of state, Elihu Root, another winner of the Nobel Peace Prize, who traveled to Latin America in 1906. An assembly hall specially erected for the Third Conference of American Republics was named the Palacio de Monroe, and enthusiastic students had to be dissuaded from pulling Root's carriage through the streets of Rio. T.R. was not only admired as a *caudillo* in the eyes of Latin America. He was a man who once having promised to pull American troops out of Cuba did so (in contrast with the British and Japanese who had failed to honor similar commitments in Egypt and Korea). It was Roosevelt who succeeded in winning a berth for Latin American delegates at the Second Hague Peace Conference, something unprecedented. He it was who helped to secure international acceptance of the Drago Doctrine, which holds that economic grounds are insufficient to justify military intervention across a national boundary. One should not find it strange, therefore, to learn that the Monroe Doctrine was more toasted than roasted in Latin America just as T.R.'s intervention in the Panamian revolution on the side of the insurgents was widely approved. Anti-Americanism of the type prevalent later in the century had yet to gain a significant hold.

Perhaps it may be said by way of conclusion that Roosevelt's prime significance as a statesman is three-fold. He brought a relatively inexperienced nation into the club of great powers; he did so by following time-tested patterns of diplomatic strategy; and he articulated these patterns for posterity. As an American, he belongs in the tradition of leaders like George Washington and John Quincy Adams. Washington, who came to office during a time of war against Indian nations backed by Britain and Spain, made peace. Adams, who began with peace, maintained it while enhancing the position of the nation overseas. Both Washington and Adams were highly experienced in dealing at first-hand with foreigners.[39] Each maneuvered to face their adversaries from a position of strength, and while they succeeded in maximizing the nation's military potential, they wielded it with notable restraint. Like T.R., they dealt with other nations on an impartial and non-ideological basis, Washington warning against passionate attachments and Adams stating in no uncertain language that while America would hope for the victory of Republican causes around the world, she was the champion and vindicator only of her own. This was the diplomatic tradition known to Europeans as *Realpolitik.* And just as it found successful practitioners overseas, so too did it find periodic favor in America before 1900 as well as in the years thereafter.

NOTES

1. Jean Jules Jusserand, *What Me Befell* (New York: Houghton Mifflin, 1933), pp. 335-36.
2. Theodore Roosevelt, *An Autobiography* (New York: Macmillan, 1919), p. 582 (hereafter cited simply as *Autobiography*). For T.R.'s positive attitude toward arbitration, see Roosevelt to de Constant, 1 September 1903; to Abbot, 8 June 1905; to Carnegie, 5 April 1907; to William II, 6 May 1908; Elting E. Morison and John M. Blum, eds., *The Letters of Theodore Roosevelt,* 8 vols. (Cambridge, Harvard University Press, 1951-1954), III, 584; IV, 1208; V, 641; VI, 1023 (hereafter cited simply as *Letters*).
3. *Autobiography,* p. 275.
4. Frederick W. Marks III, *Velvet on Iron: The Diplomacy of Theodore Roosevelt* (Lincoln, Nebraska: University of Nebraska Press, 1979), p. 138 (hereafter cited as *Velvet on Iron*); Roosevelt to Grey, 28 February 1907; to Oliver 22 July 1915, *Letters,* V, 601; VIII, 955.
5. *Velvet on Iron,* p. 138. On one occasion, Roosevelt felt that the cables he was receiving from Wilhelm and Edward were "too gushing." He therefore made his own replies "entirely dignified"; Roosevelt to Ireland, 31 July 1903, *Letters,* III, 537.
6. Roosevelt to Hall, 29 November 1899; to Eliot, 22 September 1906, *Letters,* II, 1100; V, 421.
7. Roosevelt to Lodge, 27 March 1901; to Key, 6 July 1901; to Taft, 22 December 1910, *Letters,* III, 32, 111; VII, 190.
8. Roosevelt to Root, 30 April 1900; to Trevelyan, 1 October 1911, *Letters,* II, 1275; VII, 352.
9. *Velvet on Iron,* pp. 152-53; Roosevelt to McKinley, 26 April 1897; to Strachey, 27 January 1900; to Taft, 11 January 1906; to Oliver,

6 December 1907, *Letters,* I, 602; II, 1145; V, 133, 863.
10. *Velvet on Iron,* pp. 57-58; Roosevelt to Trevelyan, 1 October 1911, *Letters,* VII, 393.
11. Roosevelt to Eliot, 14 December 1900; to Coudert, 3 July 1901; to Taft, 21 August 1907, *Letters,* II, 1415; III, 105; V, 762.
12. *Autobiography,* p. 545; *Velvet on Iron,* p. 139; Roosevelt to Hay, 22 April 1903; to Taft 22 December 1910, *Letters,* III, 478; VII, 190.
13. Roosevelt to Taft, 3 April 1909, *Letters,* VI, 1543.
14. Roosevelt to Root, 20 April 1900, *Letters,* II, 1268-69.
15. *Velvet on Iron,* p. 140. See also, Roosevelt to Coudert, 3 July 1901, *Letters,* III, 105: "We do not want to expand over another people capable of self-government unless that people desires to go in with us—and not necessarily even then . . . Barring the possible necessity of fortifying the Isthmian Canal, or getting a naval station, I hope it will not become our duty to take a foot of soil south of us."
16. Roosevelt to Kermit Roosevelt, 6 June 1908, *Letters,* VI, 1060; *Velvet on Iron,* pp. 145-46, 156.
17. Roosevelt to Shaw, 22 June 1903; to Burton, 23 February 1904; to Mott, 12 October 1908; to Oliver 22 July 1915, *Letters,* III, 497; IV, 737; VI, 1282; VIII, 956. Righteousness for Roosevelt came before peace; *Autobiography,* p. 275; Roosevelt to Schurz, 8 September 1905, *Letters,* V, 16. See also, *Autobiography,* p. 500, where he employs the word "honest" three times in one sentence.
18. Roosevelt to Coudert, 3 July 1901; to Francis Joseph, 15 August 1904, *Letters,* III, 106-107; IV, 897; *Autobiography,* p. 576; *Velvet on Iron,* p. 192.
19. Roosevelt to Moot, 13 February 1900, *Letters,* II, 1183.
20. Jusserand, *What Me Befell,* p. 345. The railroads should pay proper wages and render proper service, but they could not do so "unless they make money"; *Autobiography,* p. 539.
21. *Autobiography,* pp. 419, 543, 552.
22. See *Velvet on Iron,* chapter 3. In Roosevelt's words, to yield to Marroquín would have earned him "a place in Dante's inferno beside the faint-hearted cleric who was guilty of '*il gran rifiuto*' "; *Autobiography,* p. 566.
23. See, for example, Roosevelt to Lodge, 2 July 1899, *Letters,* II, 1038; *Autobiography,* p. 305.
24. Roosevelt to Sprague, 26 January 1900, *Letters,* II, 1141.
25. Of the kaiser he wrote: "I have been sedulously anxious to build a bridge of gold for him"; Roosevelt to White, 14 August 1906, *Letters,* V, 358-59. See also, Roosevelt to Sternburg, 25 June 1905; to Reid, 28 April 1906, *ibid.,* IV, 1257; V, 242.
26. *Velvet on Iron,* p. 51.
27. *Autobiography,* p. 110; *Velvet on Iron,* p. 49.
28. Roosevelt to Sternburg, 12 July 1901, *Letters,* III, 116.

29. *Velvet on Iron,* pp. 38-54.
30. Roosevelt to Lee, 18 March and 24 April 1901; to Hay, 10 July 1902, *Letters,* III, 20, 66, 287-88.
31. Roosevelt to Holmes, 25 July 1903, *Letters,* III, 530.
32. Roosevelt to Holmes, 20 October 1903, *Letters,* III, 634.
33. See *Velvet on Iron,* pp. 61-64, 105-11.
34. *Ibid.,* p. 61.
35. *Ibid.,* pp. 184-85; Roosevelt to Hitchcock, 22 July 1903, *Letters,* III, 523.
36. *Autobiography,* pp. 412, 415; *Velvet on Iron,* p. 93; Roosevelt to von Mach, 7 November 1914, *Letters,* VIII, 834.
37. Roosevelt to Adee, 2 September 1904; to Department of State, 2 December 1908, *Letters,* IV, 915; VI, 1406; *Velvet on Iron,* p. 14.
38. Roosevelt to Corinne Roosevelt Robinson, 8 February 1887, *Letters,* I, 121.
39. John Quincy Adams is widely recognized as one of the most cosmopolitan of all the founding fathers; but Washington deserves recognition as belonging to this class also. As a young man, he carried messages and ultimatums from Governor Dinwiddie to the French along the frontier. He also bore the burden of negotiating with various Indian chieftains. Later, as a general, he had to lead a multinational coalition against Great Britain. During these critical years, the success of the revolution depended in large measure upon his personal relationship with such men as Lafayette, von Steuben, Kosciusko, and Pulaski. No general in charge of an undertaking as widely based as the American Revolution could have been a stranger to the world of diplomacy.

4

WOODROW WILSON AND THE QUEST FOR ORDERLY PROGRESS

Lloyd Ambrosius

One central theme characterized President Woodrow Wilson's leadership in world affairs. He consistently endeavored to establish his control over American foreign relations. Seeking to dominate the policy-making process in the United States and to project American influence into other countries, he intended to use the full powers of the presidency. This search for control at home and abroad occurred within the context of a changing nation and a revolutionary world. Science and technology had enabled Americans to develop industry and build cities. Transforming the personal relationships of traditional rural communities into a bureaucratic pattern, industrialization and urbanization created a modern corporate or organizational society in the United States. These profound social and economic changes necessitated a new role for the American government in both domestic and foreign affairs. What American democracy required, according to Wilson, was "progressive order."[1] Like other progressives, he hoped to avert uncontrollable chaos or anarchy by managing orderly change. The maintenance of the *status quo* no longer appeared feasible to him either in the United States or abroad. As a typical American progressive, he preferred reform to revolution. This preference shaped his attitude toward revolutions in other countries. He welcomed moderate changes, especially when these resulted in greater American influence, but opposed radical revolution. In short, under Wilson's leadership the United States searched for a dynamic form of control, not merely for order.[2]

Wilson experienced the fundamental dilemma facing American policy-makers in the twentieth century. On one side, the world's growing interdependence prevented the United States from ignoring events in other places. Apparently remote developments, such as those leading to the outbreak of the European war in 1914, eventually involved the United States. On the other side, the continuing pluralism of the modern world prevented this nation from winning universal acceptance for its own ideals and practices. Foreign leaders simply refused to behave in the way the American president desired. Under these circumstances the United States needed to define a foreign policy that would protect its own legitimate interests in an international environment it could neither avoid nor control. Wilson ultimately failed in this task. He overestimated his ability to shape the world according to his particular vision of interdependence. Even military intervention did not give him this power. The League of Nations, which epitomized his vision, never transformed the structure of international relations as he expected. On the contrary, it generated conflict both at the Paris Peace Conference of 1919 and in the United States. The Allies as well as Germany declined to play the role Wilson assigned to them during the peacemaking after World War I, and so did the Republican senators in the United States. The persistence of pluralism prevented the Democratic president from reforming the world in accordance with his ideals. Seeking in vain for control over foreign affairs, he failed to reconcile the realities of interdependence and pluralism in his definition of American foreign policy. The fundamental dilemma created by these two contemporary features consequently continued to plague future American diplomatists. Wilson's legacy provided only inadequate guidance for them.[3]

II

When Wilson entered the White House in 1913, changes already occurring in the United States and around the world pointed toward a significantly different role for the president in foreign affairs. By the beginning of the twentieth century the United States had emerged as an industrial giant. New technologies enabled its factories to produce an expanding volume of commodities for both domestic and foreign markets. Industrial development also promoted commercial agriculture. With new machinery American farmers began to produce foodstuffs for sale in cities, not only at home but also abroad. Because of abundant raw materials, both industry and agriculture were relatively self-sufficient. Although foreign trade was increasingly important, it was not absolutely essential for the prosperity of the American economy. Other countries depended more on the United States for industrial and agricultural products than this nation did on them. As a consequence, the economic basis for the emergence of the United States as a world power already existed. This reality the Spanish American War of 1898 had clearly demonstrated. Americans had then translated their economic supremacy over Spain into military victory in Cuba as well as the acquisition of Puerto Rico, Guam and the Philippines.

As they expanded their empire into the Caribbean and across the Pacific, Americans encountered other emerging world powers. Japan and Germany also began to challenge the traditional empires of Europe and Asia. The maritime nations of western Europe no longer dominated global politics. The British and French empires, although still extensive, could not prevent the new rivals from staking out their claims. The Chinese and Russian empires experienced even greater difficulty as they both lost control over some of their possessions. Before it finally collapsed in 1912, the Manchu dynasty in China had made numerous territorial and economic concessions to all of the great powers, both old and new. After suffering a humiliating defeat in the Russo-Japanese War of 1904–05, the Russians acknowledged Japan's hegemony over Korea and other nearby territory. For the first time in modern history, an Asian nation militarily defeated a European empire, giving rise to fears of a "yellow peril" in Europe and the United States. Racial prejudice compounded the problems of economic and political conflict among nations.

Europe, and especially western Europe, increasingly lost its traditional dominance in world affairs. The peace conference that ended the Russo-Japanese War was not held in London, Paris, or Berlin, but in Portsmouth, New Hampshire. Hosted by President Theodore Roosevelt, it symbolically represented the new status of the United States as a great power. Roosevelt's contribution as well to the peaceful resolution of the Moroccan crisis of 1905–06 between Germany, on one side, and France and Great Britain on the other, further indicated the shift of influence in international relations away from western Europe. The maintenance of the

European balance of power no longer depended merely on the decisions and actions of the Europeans themselves. While the Japanese expanded into eastern Asia and the Pacific, the Americans now exerted their influence not only there but also in Europe and Africa. Not confined to their own continent or even to Latin America, their involvement now extended beyond the Western Hemisphere.[4]

The potential collapse of the European balance of power and the simultaneous emergence of the United States created the conditions for Wilson's self-assigned role in world affairs. Under his leadership, for both external and internal reasons, this nation could not avoid entangling itself in the wars and politics of the Old World as it had during most of the nineteenth century. The "free security" that Americans had previously enjoyed was no longer possible.[5] World War I engulfed the United States in 1917 despite Wilson's genuine attempt to preserve American neutrality. Global interdependence prevented this nation from escaping the war's impact. Although both the Allies and the Central Powers jeopardized America's maritime interests, Germany's submarine warfare posed the most direct threat and eventually provoked the United States to intervene. Once Wilson decided to enter the war, he began to articulate a new American foreign policy for the future peace. Summarized in the Fourteen Points, his vision of a new system of international relations provided his justification for the war's costs. At the peace conference in Paris where he sought to implement his program, the president devoted himself primarily to creating the League of Nations. This international organization, he hoped, would overcome the traditional rivalries among nations and inaugurate a new era of peace.

Ill-prepared for his new role of global leadership, Wilson drew upon his own personal experience and ideas for guidance. Unable to understand the diversity of values and interests among the various peoples of the world, he typically assumed that they shared his own perspective. If foreign leaders disagreed, as they frequently did, he attributed this disagreement to their failure to represent the true interests of their own nations. He projected his conception of American nationalism onto the rest of the world, presupposing its universal validity. Viewing the United States as the vanguard, he expected other nations to follow its example and develop in the same way. His vision of the future consequently combined both universalism and unilateralism. While proclaiming a new era of internationalism, the president actually expected others to conform to his particular understanding of American ideals and practices. This paradoxical approach to foreign affairs sometimes made Wilson appear hypocritical, but the real problem was his inability to distinguish between the interests of the United States and those of other nations. Despite his growing appreciation of the modern world's interdependence, he still failed to comprehend its pluralism. This failure appeared in his response not only to the European war but also to various revolutions during his presidency. Those in Mexico and China began before his inauguration. Others in the Russian, German and Austro-Hungarian empires came under the impact of war and military defeat. Reacting to these revolutions without fully comprehending the forces they unleashed, Wilson lacked intellectual categories to understand them on their own terms. When he sought to influence their direction, the consequences were invariably different from his expectations. Peoples in other countries refused to behave in accordance with his own national perspective.

Wilson's search for control at home and abroad exemplified a typical impulse of progressive Americans. With the human scientific and technological conquest over nature of the nineteenth century, they now optimistically expected a similar achievement in the social, economic, and political relationships within human society itself. Social scientists at the beginning of the twentieth century began to articulate the concept of social control. Sociologist Edward A. Ross, who had studied under Wilson at Princeton, examined the various methods by which society influenced individuals in *Social Control* (1901).[6] An economist, John Bates Clark, anticipated Wilson's New Freedom with his argument for preventing the monopolistic tendencies of American corporations by preserving free competition in *The Control of Trusts* (1901).[7] Franklin H. Giddings, a leading sociologist and, like Clark, a personal friend of Wilson, offered his defense of the United States as a "democratic empire." Appealing to both Social Darwinism and the Social Gospel, he justified the American war against Spain in 1898 and the new imperialism in its wake. "My studies of theoretical sociology," he proclaimed in *Democracy and Empire* (1900), "long ago led me to believe that the combination of small states into larger political aggregates must continue until all the semi-civilized, barbarian, and savage communities of the world are brought under the protection of the larger civilized nations."[8] Convinced that the United States and Great Britain could best assume this burden, he urged his fellow Americans to undertake this new role in world affairs.

Significantly, both Clark and Giddings became early and steadfast advocates of American participation in the League of Nations.

Wilson likewise welcomed the consequences of the Spanish-American War for American leadership, and especially for presidential primacy in foreign affairs. In 1900 he affirmed that the president of the United States "must utter every initial judgment, take every first step of action, supply the information upon which it is to act, suggest and in large measure control its conduct."[9] This conception of presidential control over American foreign relations continued to characterize Wilson's thought. Elaborating on it in *Constitutional Government in the United States* (1908), he asserted that the chief executive's powers in this field were "very absolute." "The initiative in foreign affairs, which the President possesses without any restriction whatever," Wilson contended, "is virtually the power to control them absolutely. The President cannot conclude a treaty with a foreign power without the consent of the Senate, but he may guide every step of diplomacy, and to guide diplomacy is to determine what treaties must be made, if the faith and prestige of the government are to be maintained. He need disclose no step of negotiation until it is virtually committed. Whatever its disinclination, the Senate may feel itself committed also."[10] Unfortunately for Wilson, this interpretation of the Constitution failed to persuade the Republican senators under Henry Cabot Lodge's leadership after World War I. They declined to approve the Versailles Treaty with the League of Nations Covenant exactly as he had presented it to them. The outcome of the treaty fight in 1919–20 demonstrated that the president's control over American foreign relations was considerably less absolute than he desired. Wilson's arguments persuaded other prominent political scientists such as Edward S. Corwin and Quincy Wright, but not the Senate.[11]

Like the social scientists, progressive journalists contributed to the concept of control. In *The Promise of American Life* (1909), Herbert Croly advocated "a certain measure of discipline" and "a large measure of individual subordination and self-denial" to improve the social and economic conditions of the United States, while preserving its democratic political institutions. In the name of the national interest, he urged greater executive leadership both at home and abroad. "As much in foreign as in domestic affairs must the American people seek to unite national efficiency with democratic idealism," he argued. Anticipating the end of American isolation from the Old World, he wanted the United States to prepare for its inescapable involvement in the international political economy. Reform at home would equip the nation for its new role overseas. Noting the world's growing interdependence, Croly foresaw the prospect of American intervention in a future European war to foster democracy and promote international peace. He outlined the rationale that Wilson would later use to justify the American declaration of war against Germany in 1917. In his view American belligerency might be justified for the sake of extending this nation's control over the Old World to establish democracy and peace.[12]

Walter Lippmann agreed with Croly that progressive American leadership was essential to avoid chaos in the changing world. Because the traditional *status quo* was already disintegrating, the only choice for Americans was between "drift" and "mastery." He advocated rational or pragmatic control over human affairs to combine both progress and order. In *Drift and Mastery* (1914) he viewed the United States as the nation best prepared to adopt this method for dealing with the world's chaotic conditions. "Civilization, it seems to me," Lippmann concluded, "is just this constant effort to introduce plan where there has been clash, and purpose into the jungles of disordered growth."[13]

Given these attitudes, both Croly and Lippmann readily supported Wilson's foreign policy during World War I. These editors of the *New Republic* welcomed his endorsement of the idea of collective security and employed it to justify American intervention in 1917. Along with philosopher John Dewey, they heralded American belligerency as a crusade for democracy. Reconciling their liberal idealism with pragmatism, which required them to justify the war's costs by its results, they anticipated a postwar world of democracy and peace. Lippmann even contributed directly to the preparation of Wilson's Fourteen Points as secretary of the Inquiry.[14] Croly, Lippmann, and Dewey, like the President, wanted the United States to redeem the Old World and transform international relations through the League of Nations. But they were inevitably disappointed by the peace treaty with Germany, for their idealistic hopes could never be achieved. Their unrealistic expectation that the United States could easily impose its will on other countries resulted in their disillusionment with the Versailles Treaty. Denouncing it, these liberals now opposed American membership in the League. The bitter disappointment of Croly, Lippmann, and Dewey after the war reflected the high hopes they had earlier placed—or really misplaced—in Wilson's leadership. The problem of liberal disillusionment was theirs more than his, for no American President could accomplish the kind of universal control over foreign affairs that they all desired.[15]

III

Challenging the prevailing liberal attitudes of American progressives, journalist Randolph S. Bourne offered a radical critique of Wilson's foreign policy. In 1917 he asserted that "the 'liberals' who claim a realistic and pragmatic attitude in politics have disappointed us in setting up and then clinging wistfully to the belief that our war could get itself justified for an idealistic flavor, or at least for a world-renovating social purpose, that they had more or less denied to the other belligerents." He understood, as they did not, that no statesman could impose rational control over the war. Warning that Wilson could never accomplish "any liberal control of events," Bourne denounced the illusion that the United States could utilize the war to regenerate the world and establish peace through a postwar League.[16] Convinced that American progressives, including the social scientists, could never discover scientific laws of human behavior that would enable them to predict and control the future, the radical Bourne shared a fundamental premise with the conservative Henry Adams. Adams had searched for some unifying principle in history, but failed to discover it. Neither religion nor science provided him an adequate explanation of cause and effect. "Historians," he warned in *The Education of Henry Adams* (1918), "have got into far too much trouble by following schools of theology in their efforts to enlarge their synthesis, that they should willingly repeat the process in science."[17] Senator Lodge, who edited this autobiography for publication, shared Adams' skepticism. Doubting that intellectuals or statesmen could comprehend and consequently control the world's destiny as the progressives believed, the conservative senator never shared the president's attitude toward world affairs. He refused to believe the exaggerated promises of a redemptive foreign policy. For this reason, rather than merely because of partisan politics, Lodge criticized Wilson's plan for the League of Nations.[18]

Although Christianity furnished no unifying principle for Adams, it did for Wilson. His faith in God undergirded his belief in the world's universality. Combining the Social Gospel with Social Darwinism, he expected a better world to emerge from conflict.

Progress would result from competition. Identifying the United States with Christianity, and patriotism with religion, he proclaimed that "America was born a Christian nation. America was born to exemplify that devotion to the elements of righteousness which are derived from the revelations of Holy Scriptures."[19] This view of the United States enabled Wilson to define the war as a crusade. "He cunningly hopes," observed the Social Gospel theologian George D. Herron, "he divinely schemes, to bring it about that America, awake at last to her national selfhood and calling, shall become as a colossal Christian apostle, shepherding the world into the kingdom of God." This motif lay behind the president's yearning for the redemption of the Old World, as Herron explained in *Woodrow Wilson and the World's Peace* (1917).[20] Praising this book, Wilson himself applauded "Herron's singular insight into all the elements of a complicated situation and into my own motives and purposes."[21] From this theological perspective, the Presbyterian President decided to call the League's constitution a Covenant and to locate its headquarters in Calvinist Geneva. Religion as well as science furnish the intellectual content of his foreign policy.[22]

Wilson's conception of the global mission of the United States emerged from his Latin American policy. In it he combined the elements of unilateralism and universalism that would later characterize his vision of the League. In conformity with the Roosevelt Corollary to the Monroe Doctrine, he intervened unilaterally to exclude European influence from the Caribbean nations. But he hoped to achieve multilateral approval from the other nations in the Western Hemisphere for his own actions to replace European with American predominance. "The United States has nothing to seek in Central and South America," the president announced soon after his inauguration, "except the lasting interests of the people of the two continents, the security of governments, intended for the people, and for no special group or interest, and the development of personal and trade relationships between the two continents, which shall redound to the profit and advantage of both and interfere with the rights and liberties of neither."[23] The fulfillment of this goal depended upon Wilson's ability to win universal acceptance of his own ideals and practices by the nations of Latin America. He anticipated resistance from some of their leaders, but deluded himself into believing that the peoples shared his aspirations. He ignored the pluralism of the region.

Announcing his new Latin American policy in 1913, the president emphasized "the development of constitutional liberty in the world." He thought the new Panama Canal, linking the Atlantic and Pacific oceans, would foster closer ties between North and South America. When it opened in 1914, it would unite the two continents with common political and military as well as commercial interests. From this perspective he stressed the idea of Pan-Americanism. At the suggestion of his friend, Edward M. House, Wilson attempted to negotiate a Pan-American treaty of nonaggression and political cooperation with the ABC countries, Argentina, Brazil, and Chile. While he saw this multilateral treaty as an extension of the Monroe Doctrine to guarantee the territorial integrity and republican political institutions of these countries, they saw the danger of American hegemony. Despite their resistance throughout 1915, the president continued to hope for the Pan-American treaty's successful conclusion. "Our concern for the independence and prosperity of the states of Central and South America is not altered," he affirmed in his annual message to Congress. "We retain unabated the spirit that has inspired us throughout the whole life of our government and which was so frankly put into words by President [James] Monroe. We still mean always to make a common cause of national independence and of political liberty in America. But that purpose is now better understood so far as it concerns ourselves. It is known not to be a selfish purpose. It is known to have in it no thought of taking advantage of any government in this hemisphere or playing its political fortunes for our own benefit. All the governments of America stand, so far as we are concerned, upon a footing of genuine equality and unquestioned independence."

Wilson believed that the United States, unlike other great powers, played an exceptional role in world politics. It served the common welfare of mankind rather than its own imperial ends. "This is Pan-Americanism," he explained. "It has none of the spirit of empire in it. It is the embodiment, the effectual embodiment, of the spirit of law and independence and liberty and mutual service." Denying the similarity between the hegemony of the United States over its weaker neighbors and that of other empires, the president presupposed that his view of progressive American politics coincided with the interests of Latin American nations. Addressing the Pan-American Scientific Congress in Washington early in 1916, he reiterated his vision of Pan-Americanism: "For politics I conceive to be nothing more than the science of the ordered progress of society along the lines of greatest usefulness and convenience to itself." As he had earlier for the United States, Wilson now prescribed "progressive order" for Latin America to avoid uncontrollable chaos. The Latin Americans, however, were no more eager to submit to American than to European control. After more than two years of fruitless effort, by early 1917 the president quietly dropped his proposal for a Pan-American treaty.[24]

At the same time that he promoted his multilateral conception of Pan-Americanism, Wilson intervened unilaterally in Latin America. He dispatched American troops to more countries there than any of his predecessors in the White House. Despite his denunciation of "dollar diplomacy," he fully intended to protect American economic and commercial interests in the region. He also appreciated the strategic importance of the Caribbean as a vital seaway to the Panama Canal. Fearful that the European powers, and especially Germany, might establish a naval base that could threaten this seaway, he sought to counter this prospect by preventive action. By fostering governments in the Latin American countries around the Caribbean that were friendly to the United States, and if necessary by imposing them through military intervention, the president sought to guard against any threatening European influence. In practice, however, the distinction between defensive and offensive acts disappeared as he asserted American control over weak Latin American nations. The occupation of Haiti in 1915 and the Dominican Republic in 1916 exemplified this pattern. Wilson sent the American navy to these island nations to force them to establish governments acceptable to him and to control their finances. Although he spoke about constitutional liberty, the military intervention that he practiced in these countries overrode their own constitutions. His real objective was American control rather than democracy or merely order. Facing internal resistance, the American marines in Haiti and the Dominican Republic trained local police forces to crush it. The United States ensured the election of its own clients to the top political offices or simply established its own military government. While preventing Germany or any other European power from interfering, the president consolidated American hegemony in the Caribbean.[25]

Mexico gave Wilson more difficulty than any other country in the Western Hemisphere. Here the American-European rivalry in Latin America became most intense. Great Britain and Germany enjoyed considerable political as well as economic influence in that country. Like the United States, these European powers endeavored to protect their interests during Mexico's revolution by playing off one faction against another. Early in 1913, through a successful coup against the revolutionary government of Francisco Madero, General Victoriano Huerta established himself in Mexico City. Although the American ambassador had participated in planning this counter-revolutionary coup, which resulted in Madero's murder, the new American president refused to recognize the Huerta government. For over a year Wilson attempted various methods, ranging from diplomatic mediation to military intervention, to replace it with an acceptable alternative. As he once remarked, "I am going to teach the South American Republics to elect good men!"[26] The president desired neither to annex any of Mexico's territory nor to establish a formal protectorate over the country, but he nevertheless intended to impose his will. To counter the United States, Huerta turned to Europe and especially to Great Britain. He resisted Wilson's plan to replace him through a democratic election. The failure of the United States to shape Mexico's political institutions by peaceful methods led the president to resort to military intervention. The occupation of Veracruz in April 1914, although timed to prevent the landing of a German ship with munitions and justified by the brief detainment of American sailors at the port of Tampico, resulted from his determination to remove Huerta. Unexpected Mexican resistance and consequent American casualties induced Wilson to accept mediation by the ABC countries as a face-saving way to extricate the United States from a dangerous situation. He could not control Mexico as easily as he had originally anticipated.[27]

Venustiano Carranza, leader of the Constitutionalists, eventually succeeded Huerta as president of Mexico. Wilson recognized his government. Yet Carranza, too, endeavored to protect his country's independence from American paternalism. On occasion he collaborated with the United States to strengthen his position against his internal foes, notably Francisco "Pancho" Villa. But when Wilson sent General John J. Pershing's punative expedition into Mexico in March 1916, the Mexican president saw it as a threat. Villa had raided Columbus, New Mexico, to provoke American military intervention, and succeeded in accomplishing his objective. While Pershing vainly attempted to capture him, Villa recruited more troops and waged guerilla warfare against both the Americans and Carranza's government. Pershing's troops clashed not only with Villa's but also with Carranza's. Under these circumstances the Mexican government turned to Berlin for military assistance. In January, 1917, Germany's foreign secretary, Arthur

Zimmerman, responded by proposing an alliance against the United States. Although the German government never intended to give Mexico much support to reconquer Texas, New Mexico and Arizona, it hoped to divert the United States from Europe by embroiling it in a war with Mexico. This plan failed disastrously as British intelligence intercepted the Zimmermann telegram and gave it to Washington. Releasing it to the press, the president used the Zimmermann telegram as dramatic evidence of Germany's threat to the United States. As the United States moved toward war against Germany, he ordered Pershing to withdraw from Mexico despite the punative expedition's failure to achieve its objective. This withdrawal improved Mexican-American relations, but left a legacy of distrust. Carranza continued to oppose Wilson's vision of regional interdependence as he denounced the Monroe Doctrine. He did not welcome the endorsement of this doctrine in the League of Nations Covenant.[28]

IV

Disclosure of the Zimmermann telegram contributed to the already deteriorating German-American relationship. Germany's submarine warfare had moved the United States to the brink of war by the spring of 1917. At the beginning of the European war in 1914, Wilson had proclaimed a policy of impartial neutrality. The sinking of the British passenger liner *Lusitania* in May, 1915, by a German submarine prompted him to condemn this new form of warfare. "The rights of neutrals in time of war," he protested with reference to the American passengers who lost their lives, "are based upon principles, not upon expediency, and the principles are immutable." Because the president refused to make a comparable protest against British maritime practices, Secretary of State William Jennings Bryan resigned during this crisis. He wanted to continue impartial neutrality. Yet Wilson himself, despite his moral condemnation of Germany, intended to keep the United States out of the war. "The example of America," he explained, "must be the example not merely of peace because it will not fight, but of peace because peace is the healing and elevating influence of the world and strife is not. There is such a thing as a man being too proud to fight. There is such a thing as a nation being so right that it does not need to convince others by force that it is right."[29] The *Lusitania* incident convinced Robert Lansing, Bryan's successor at the State Department, that "the German ambition for world dominion" threatened all democracies, including the United States. He thought that "the military oligarchy which rules Germany is a bitter enemy of democracy in every form; that, if that oligarchy triumphs over the liberal governments of Great Britain and France, it will then turn upon us as its next obstacle to imperial rule over the world; and that it is safer and surer and wiser for us to be one of many enemies than to be in the future alone against a victorious Germany."[30] Yet even Lansing still wanted to maintain American neutrality. In October, 1915, the president approved his recommendation to protest against Great Britain's off-shore blockade and definition of contraband. Continuing to criticize British maritime practices, the secretary of state proposed, in January, 1916, a *modus vivendi* between the Allies and the Central Powers. With Wilson's endorsement, he attempted to convince the Allies to disarm their merchant ships in exchange for a pledge from the Central Powers that their submarines would follow the rules of cruiser warfare under international law. The purpose of this *modus vivendi* was to keep the United States out of the war.

Wilson endeavored both to protect American rights on the high seas and to avoid war. "No matter what military or naval force the United States might develop," he proclaimed in 1915 as he launched his plans for enlarging the American armed forces, "statesmen throughout the whole world might rest assured that we were gathering that force, not for attack in any quarter, not for aggression of any kind, not for the satisfaction of any political or international ambition, but merely to make sure of our own security. . . . The mission of America in the world is essentially a mission of peace and good will among men."[31] During his campaign for preparedness early in 1916, he reiterated this theme. Wilson contended that "there is a moral obligation laid upon us to keep out of this war if possible. But by the same token there is a moral obligation laid upon us to keep free the courses of our commerce and of our finance, and I believe that America stands ready to vindicate those rights." Moreover, he thought the defense of North and South America might require the United States to enter the war. Pan-Americanism might justify American belligerency. "We have," he announced, "made ourselves the guarantors of the rights of national sovereignty and of popular sovereignty on this side of the water in both the continents of the Western Hemisphere."[32]

To prevent Germany's submarines from drawing the United States into the war, Wilson offered American mediation. He sent Colonel House to Europe during the spring of 1915 and again in

1916. Neither Germany nor the Allies welcomed House's vague proposals for ending the war without victory. To divert him from the divisive issues of the current war, British Foreign Secretary Edward Grey encouraged him to think about the methods for guaranteeing future peace. In response House and later Wilson began to formulate the idea of a postwar League of Nations. They hoped somehow to transcend the bitter rivalries of the war by promising American participation in the future preservation of peace. The President first publicly endorsed this idea of collective security in a speech to the League to Enforce Peace in May, 1916. He announced "that henceforth alliance must not be set up against alliance, understanding against understanding, but that there must be a common agreement for a common object, and that at the heart of the common object must lie the inviolable rights of peoples and of mankind."[33] This proclamation of universal human rights offered no guidelines for resolving the territorial and economic issues separating the Central Powers from the Allies. Wilson turned his attention to these issues for the first time in December, 1916, when he sent peace notes to the belligerents. Having abandoned House's earlier plan for American mediation through the convening of an international peace conference, he now requested both sides in the war to state their aims. The German government, which had recently proposed direct negotiations with the Allies, refused to fulfill Wilson's request for a statement of war aims, while the Allied governments rejected Germany's proposal. In the context of this stalemate, the president delivered his famous "peace without victory" address to a joint session of Congress in January, 1917. Blaming the European balance of power and alliances for the Old World's problems, he called for a new system of collective security. "There must be," he said, "not a balance of power, but a community of power; not organized rivalries, but an organized common peace." His vision of a future League of Nations represented the world-wide expansion of the Monroe Doctrine. "I am proposing, as it were," Wilson explained, "that the nations should with one accord adopt the doctrine of President Monroe as the doctrine of the world: that no nation should seek to extend its polity over any other nation or people, but that every people should be left free to determine its own polity, its own way of development, unhindered, unthreatened, unafraid, the little along with the great and powerful."[34]

Wilson's policy of American neutrality collapsed with the beginning of Germany's unrestricted submarine warfare in February,

1917. Prior to this time the Germans had hesitated to use their submarines for fear of provoking the United States. After sinking the British freighter *Arabic* in August, 1915, and torpedoing the French channel steamer *Sussex* in March, 1916, they had promised not to attack merchant or passenger ships without giving a warning and rescuing the victims. This pledge to abide by the rules of cruiser warfare had effectively prevented Germany from using its submarines. As long as this condition prevailed, the United States experienced greater difficulty with British maritime practices. In July, 1916, after Great Britain published a blacklist of American firms which traded with the Central Powers, Wilson had vigorously protested against the continuing British violations of American rights. But these grievances now appeared relatively unimportant as the Germans broke their pledge and resumed submarine warfare. After the sinking of American ships in mid-March, 1917, Wilson called the Congress into session and recommended a declaration of war. Referring to his "peace without victory" address, he told the Congress: "Our object now, as then, is to vindicate the principles of peace and justice in the life of the world as against selfish and autocratic power and to set up amongst the really free and self-governed peoples of the world such a concert of purpose and of action as will henceforth insure the observance of those principles." Denouncing the autocratic government of Imperial Germany, he called for the liberation of the German people. "The world," he concluded, "must be made safe for democracy. Its peace must be planted upon the tested foundations of political liberty."[35] The Congress apparently agreed as it voted four days later, on April 6, 1917, to declare war against Germany.[36]

Revolution in Russia seemed to justify Wilson's wartime crusade for democracy. The new provisional government, which replaced the Romanov monarchy after the abdication of Czar Nicholas II in mid-March, promised to establish constitutional liberty and to keep Russia in the war. It immediately received diplomatic recognition from the United States. In his war message the president affirmed that "Russia was known by those who knew it best to have been always in fact democratic at heart, in all the vital habits of her thought, in all the intimate relationships of her people that spoke their natural instinct, their habitual attitude towards life. The autocracy that crowned the summit of her political structure, long as it had stood and terrible as was the reality of its power, was not in fact Russian in origin, character, or purpose; and now it has been shaken off and the great, generous Russian people have been added in all their naive majesty and might to the forces that are fighting for freedom in the world, for justice, and for peace."[37] Wilson promptly extended credits to the provisional government and sent a special mission led by the Republican elder statesman Elihu Root to encourage it. Naively assuming that the Russian people shared his own ideals and his current enthusiasm for the war, the president was totally unprepared for the Bolshevik revolution in November, 1917. He refused to recognize the radical Soviet regime of Vladimir I. Lenin. Nor did he welcome its appeal for the opening of peace negotiations. His hopes for democracy in Russia and victory in the war against Germany were now directly threatened by the Bolsheviks.

Wilson thought these adverse developments in Russia resulted from a misunderstanding of American and Allied war aims by the Russian people. Responding to the Bolsheviks, he decided to clarify these aims in a major address to Congress on January 8, 1918. "Whether their present leaders believe it or not," he proclaimed, "it is our heartfelt desire and hope that some way may be opened whereby we may be privileged to assist the people of Russia to attain their utmost hope of liberty and ordered peace." The president went on to outline the Fourteen Points of his peace program. Calling for open diplomacy and freedom of navigation and commerce, for disarmament and national self-determination, he concluded by advocating a postwar organization of collective security. Although quite general, this statement offered the most explicit definition of a European policy that any president had ever made. For the first time the American government was outlining its view of peace conditions for the continent of Europe. One central theme characterized this program, Wilson stressed: "It is the principle of justice to all peoples and nationalities, and their right to live on equal terms of liberty and safety with one another, whether they be strong or weak."[38]

Despite American efforts to foster democratic institutions in Russia and keep it in the war, the Bolsheviks remained in power and negotiated a separate peace with Germany in March, 1918. The Treaty of Brest-Litovsk, by ending the war on the Eastern Front, created a crisis in western Europe. During the summer of 1918 the Central Powers threatened to defeat the Allies before the United States could provide decisive relief. The American Expeditionary Forces under General Pershing were only beginning to appear on the Western Front. Because the United States had previously prepared for only a defensive war against Germany, it required a year after the American declaration of war before Pershing's troops were ready to make a sizable contribution. Meanwhile, the British and French forces encountered the German spring offensive.[39]

Under these circumstances Wilson finally agreed in July, 1918, to American military intervention in Russia. Although neither he nor his military advisers shared the British and French hopes for restoring the Eastern Front, he now relented to repeated Allied requests to send American troops into both Siberia and northern Russia. Their mission, as he defined it, was strictly limited. In Siberia he allowed the American army to assist a Czecho-Slovak corps, which had earlier fought on the Eastern Front, to leave Russia by proceeding along the Trans-Siberian Railway to the port at Vladivostok. From there they could depart for the Western Front. Both at Vladivostok and in the northern Russian ports of Murmansk and Archangel were supplies which he did not want to fall into hostile hands. He also hoped that the presence of American troops in Siberia would contain Japanese ambitions there and in northern Manchuria. Although Wilson wanted to avoid American military interference in the internal affairs of Russia, that was impossible. Despite his intentions, the American forces unavoidably participated in the Russian civil war against the Bolsheviks. The president limited this involvement as he had during the Mexican revolution. "My policy regarding Russia," he explained, "is very similar to my Mexican policy. I believe in letting them work out their own salvation, even though they wallow in anarchy for a while."[40] He attempted to influence both revolutions by encouraging constitutional governments favorable to the United States and even by intervening with American troops, but refrained from an all-out effort to use military power to replace undesirable regimes with American-made alternatives. That degree of control he restricted to the weak Caribbean nations.

Throughout the war Wilson maintained an aloofness from the Old World. The United States became an Associated rather than an Allied Power. Instead of merging with the Allied armies, the American Expeditionary Forces preserved their separate identity under Pershing's command. The President never endorsed the secret treaties of the Allies or their desire to crush the new Soviet government by intervening on the side of anti-Bolshevik factions in Russia. When he failed to secure Allied approval of his own peace program, Wilson proclaimed it unilaterally in his Fourteen Points. He wanted other nations to embrace American ideals and practices, but did not intend to sacrifice American independence. Expressing this paradoxical attitude in a major address in late September 1918, he affirmed: "We still read [George] Washington's immortal warning against 'entangling alliances' with full comprehension and an answering purpose. But only special and limited alliances entangle; and we recognize and accept the duty of a new day in which we are permitted to hope for a general alliance which will avoid entanglements and clear the air of the world for common understandings and the maintenance of common rights."[41]

Wilson identified with the American diplomatic tradition of isolation from the Old World as he heralded American participation in the future League of Nations. Both unilateralism and universalism characterized his diplomatic style. When Germany, after the failure of its summer offensive, turned to him for an armistice in October, 1918, he did not hesitate to handle the negotiations largely by himself. Experiencing military defeat, the Germans now appealed for peace on the basis of the Fourteen Points. Sending House to Paris to deal with the Allies, the President succeeded in gaining their approval as well for most of his peace program. The armistice on November 11, 1918, ended the war with commitments by the Allies and Germany to base the peace treaty on his Fourteen Points. Wilson's detachment from the Allies worried Republican leaders, including Roosevelt. "Above all," the ex-president stated, "we feel that at the Peace Conference, America should act, not as an umpire between our allies and our enemies, but as one of the allies bound to come to an agreement with them, and then to impose this common agreement upon our vanquished enemies."[42]

V

Wilson decided to participate personally in the negotiations at the Paris Peace Conference of 1919. This summit conference reflected the global character of world politics as delegates from every continent attended it. Of the five great powers, only three—Great Britain, France and Italy—were European. The United States and Japan were the other two. Russia was conspiciously absent as the victorious powers invited neither the Soviet government nor any of its rivals to Paris. The problems of the Russian civil war and of Bolshevism nevertheless intruded onto the proceedings. Other empires had followed Russia into revolution, creating the specter of the westward expansion of Bolshevism. On the eve of the armistice the Hohenzollern and Hapsburg monarchies in Germany and Austria-Hungary collapsed under the impact of military defeat. So did the Ottoman Empire of Turkey. Throughout Central and Eastern Europe and also the Middle East, new states emerged to supplant the previous empires. Some of them, such as Poland and Czechoslovakia, found immediate acceptance in Paris, but others waited on the outside. A delegation from the new Weimar Republic, which had replaced Kaiser Wilhelm II in Germany, arrived there only after Wilson and the Allied leaders had prepared the peace treaty for it to sign. Others were totally excluded. Representatives from the recently proclaimed Irish republic failed to receive a hearing of their case for independence from Great Britain. So did the revolutionary Ho Chi Minh, who wanted to emancipate Vietnam from French colonial rule. The Allies, with Wilson's concurrence, intended to exclude the internal affairs of their empires from the agenda.[43]

At the beginning of the peace conference, the President reiterated the redemptive theme of his foreign policy. He called upon the Allies to join the United States in a new international order to achieve universal justice and liberty. "In coming into this war," he proclaimed, "the United States never thought for a moment that she was intervening in the politics of Europe, or the politics of Asia, or the politics of any part of the world. Her thought was that all the world had now become conscious that there was a single cause which turned upon issues of this war. That was the cause of justice and liberty for men of every kind and place. Therefore, the United States would feel that her part in this war had been played in vain if there ensued upon it merely a body of European settlements."[44] The heart of Wilson's peace program was the League of Nations. He made the drafting of the Covenant for this postwar international organization his first priority in Paris. But before he could succeed in this task, he needed to accommodate the various interests of the principal Allies, for they did not share his particular conception of global interdependence.

Although the British delegates generally cooperated with Wilson in drafting the Covenant, Prime Minister David Lloyd George forced him to approve a colonial settlement and a naval agreement favorable to the British Empire. The President approved the British idea for a system of mandates under the League because he, too, believed that backward peoples needed the supervision of civilized nations. The mandates for the former German colonies in Africa and the Pacific barely disguised their acquisition by the British,

French and Japanese empires. He also agreed not to expand the American navy without consulting the British. French Premier Georges Clemenceau, who wanted to restore the European balance of power, hoped to transform the League into an anti-German alliance. Although the French delegates failed in that endeavor, Lloyd George and Wilson offered France separate treaties guaranteeing its security against German aggression. Clemenceau also gained their consent for continuing the temporary occupation of the Rhineland under the peace treaty with Germany. Not willing to depend upon Wilson's League or German disarmament for French security, Clemenceau preferred these more traditional methods. Rather than relying on the vague promises of Article 10 of the Covenant, which would obligate all nations in the League to respect and preserve the territorial integrity and political independence of each other, the French wanted to establish alliances and strategic frontiers for themselves and also for Poland and Czechoslovakia so as to prevent a resurgent Germany from again threatening its neighbors. Wilson also made concessions to Italy, although he rejected Premier Vittorio Orlando's claim to the Adriatic city of Fiume. "The whole question," he asserted, "resolved itself into this: we were trying to make peace on an entirely new basis and to establish a new order of international relations. . . . To put Fiume inside Italy would be absolutely inconsistent with the new order of international relations."[45] Failing to persuade Orlando, Wilson appealed over his head to the Italian people. The Italian delegation then left the peace conference. The unity that Wilson sought on the basis of universal ideals obviously did not exist. The Italians eventually returned to Paris, but only after Orlando had received a vote of confidence from the Italian parliament to demonstrate that he, not Wilson, accurately represented public opinion in his own country. Their temporary absence threatened the president's hopes for the League and consequently prompted him to compromise with the Japanese over the Shantung province of China. He did not want to risk the prospect that Japan as well as Italy might refuse to sign the peace treaty and remain outside the League, for that would shatter even the illusion of its universal character. Wilson finally succeeded in creating the postwar League, but only by accommodating the national interests of the Allies. Although in theory he emphasized the world's interdependence, in practice he acknowledged its pluralism as well. He could not escape from the dilemma which these two features created.[46]

The Shantung controversy at Paris reflected the ambiguity in

Wilson's attitude toward China and Japan. He wanted to protect the political independence and territorial integrity of the Chinese republic and to maintain the Open Door policy of the United States. Although critical of President William Howard Taft's earlier "dollar diplomacy," he, too, endeavored to preserve equal economic opportunities for American merchants and investors in China. Yet Wilson also sought to avoid conflict with Japan over China. He did not want to pay too high a price to protect American interests there. At the beginning of the European war in 1914, Japan declared war against Germany and sent its troops into China to seize the German concessions in Shantung. The United States could not prevent the Japanese from taking advantage of the war to expand their empire at Germany's—and also China's—expense. After consolidating their control over Shantung, the Japanese in January, 1915, asked the Chinese government to concede Twenty-one Demands. They wanted its approval not only for the transfer of German rights in Shantung to Japan, but also for the previously established Japanese dominance in Manchuria and Inner Mongolia, the concession of new mining and industrial rights in central China, the prohibition of future leaseholds for other powers along the Chinese coast, and the establishment of a virtual Japanese protectorate throughout China. In March Secretary Bryan expressed American opposition to the Twenty-one Demands, but he also acknowledged a special Japanese interest in northeastern China. After Japan delivered an ultimatum to the Chinese in May, Bryan reminded it of American interests. The United States, he affirmed, would not recognize any Sino-Japanese agreement that violated the rights of American citizens in China, the political and territorial integrity of the Chinese republic, or the Open Door policy. Nevertheless, the Japanese forced the Chinese to concede all of the Twenty-one Demands except for the protectorate. Whether the Wilson administration would acquiesce in these gains, regarding them as Japan's special interests, or oppose them as infringements on American rights in China, remained undetermined. The Lansing-Ishii agreement in November 1917, which encompassed both possible positions, perpetuated this ambiguity. Wilson began to take a harder line toward Japan as he reacted to its extensive intervention in Siberia. At the peace conference he attempted to deny its claim to succeed Germany in Shantung. In Paris the Japanese also demanded the affirmation of racial equality in the League of Nations Covenant. On this issue the Chinese agreed. But racial prejudice in the British Empire and the United States surfaced as Wilson supported the British in rejecting this principle. After defeating this Japanese proposal, he finally conceded on Shantung. He feared that otherwise Japan might not join the League. This compromise deeply disappointed the Chinese and resulted in their refusal to sign the Versailles Treaty. Clearly, Wilson's vision of a new international order failed to produce harmony in eastern Asia.[47]

By adjusting to the realities of global politics at the peace conference, the President succeeded in creating the League of Nations. But it did not inaugurate the new era of peace he had promised. Foreign nations still served their own interests rather than accept his particular vision of interdependence. The world's pluralism continued to produce conflict. Germany's strenuous objections to the peace treaty as a breach of the Fourteen Points provided only one example of the perpetual rivalry among nations, which the League did not overcome. The Germans naturally understood the Fourteen Points differently from the Allies or Wilson himself. The Versailles Treaty failed to fulfill their hopes for a "Wilson peace." They signed it on June 28, 1919, only under duress.[48] Like all statesmen, the President lacked the capacity to redeem the world. He could not control it. There was no universal consensus among nations. Not even all Americans shared his perspective. The peace treaty inevitably resulted in disappointment at home as well as abroad. By his exalted rhetoric, he had fostered false expectations and thereby contributed to postwar disillusionment. In the United States the Senate, especially critical of the League, rejected the treaty with Germany. Wilson's search for control at home and abroad ended in partial failure. He had extended American influence throughout the world, but never adequately defined a foreign policy for dealing with pluralism as well as interdependence. In a diverse international environment, the United States could not win universal acceptance for its own ideals and practices. It lacked the power to impose them on all nations. Yet it could not ignore foreign threats to its own legitimate interests. In the final analysis, Wilson failed to resolve this fundamental dilemma of American foreign relations in the interdependent and plural world. His legacy included no realistic definition of foreign policy for the United States in the twentieth century.

NOTES

1. "Nature of Democracy in the United States," in Arthur S. Link, ed., *The Papers of Woodrow Wilson* (Princeton: Princeton University Press, 1969), VI, 238.
2. For a different interpretation that emphasizes order instead of control, see Robert H. Wiebe, *The Search for Order: 1877-1920* (New York: Hill and Wang, 1967).
3. On the inadequacy of Wilson's legacy of collective security, for example, see Roland N. Stromberg, *Collective Security and American Foreign Policy: From the League of Nations to NATO* (New York: Frederick A. Praeger, Publishers, 1963).
4. For an excellent summary of the global transformation of the modern world, see Geoffrey Barraclough, *An Introduction to Contemporary History* (New York: Penguin Books, 1964).
5. C. Vann Woodward, "The Age of Reinterpretation," *American Historical Review,* LXVI (October 1960), pp. 1-19.
6. Edward Alsworth Ross, *Social Control: A Survey of the Foundations of Order* (New York: The Macmillan Company, 1901).
7. John Bates Clark, *The Control of Trusts: An Argument in Favor of Curbing the Power of Monopoly by a Natural Method* (New York: The Macmillan Company, 1901).
8. Franklin Henry Giddings, *Democracy and Empire: Their Psychological, Economic and Moral Foundations* (New York: The Macmillan Company, 1900), p. v.
9. Woodrow Wilson, *Congressional Government: A Study of American Politics* (Boston: Houghton Mifflin Company, 1885; 15th ed., 1900), pp. xi-xii.
10. Woodrow Wilson, *Constitutional Government in the United States* (New York: Columbia University Press, 1908), pp. 77-78.
11. Edward S. Corwin, *The President's Control of Foreign Relations* (Princeton: Princeton University Press, 1917); Quincy Wright, "The Control of Foreign Relations," *American Political Science Review,* XV (February 1921), pp. 1-26; Quincy Wright, *The Control of American Foreign Relations* (New York: The Macmillan Company, 1922).
12. Herbert Croly, *The Promise of American Life* (New York: Capricorn Books, 1964), pp. 22, 289-314.
13. Walter Lippmann, *Drift and Mastery: An Attempt to Diagnose the Current Unrest* (Englewood Cliffs: Prentice-Hall, Inc., 1961), p. 148.
14. Lawrence E. Gelfand, *The Inquiry: American Preparations for Peace, 1917-1919* (New Haven: Yale University Press, 1963).
15. Charles Forcey, *The Crossroads of Liberalism: Croly, Weyl, Lippmann, and the Progressive Era, 1900-1925* (New York: Oxford University Press, 1961), pp. 221-315; David W. Noble, *The Progressive Mind, 1890-1917* (Chicago: Rand McNally & Company, 1970), pp. 53-64,

165-79; John C. Farrell, "John Dewey and World War I: Armageddon Tests a Liberal's Faith," *Perspectives in American History,* IX (1975), pp. 299-340.

16. Randolph S. Bourne, "A War Diary," *The Seven Arts,* II (September 1917), pp. 535-47, in Carl Resek, ed., *War and the Intellectuals: Essays by Randolph S. Bourne, 1915-1919* (New York: Harper & Row, Publishers, 1964), pp. 36-47.
17. Henry Adams, *The Education of Henry Adams: An Autobiography* (Boston: Houghton Mifflin Company, 1918), p. 401.
18. For other aspects of his views, see William C. Widenor, *Henry Cabot Lodge and the Search for an American Foreign Policy* (Berkely: University of California Press, 1979).
19. "The Bible and Progress," in Ray Stannard Baker and William E. Dodd, eds., *The Public Papers of Woodrow Wilson: College and State* (New York: Harper & Brothers Publishers, 1925), II, 291-302; "Religion and Patriotism," in Arthur S. Link, ed., *The Papers of Woodrow Wilson* (Princeton: Princeton University Press, 1972), XII, 474-78.
20. George D. Herron, *Woodrow Wilson and the World's Peace* (New York: Mitchell Kennerley, 1917), pp. 68-69, 76-77.
21. Mitchell Pirie Briggs, *George D. Herron and the European Settlement* (Stanford: Stanford University Press, 1932), p. 249.
22. John M. Mulder, *Woodrow Wilson: The Years of Preparation* (Princeton: Princeton University Press, 1978), pp. 229-77.
23. Arthur S. Link, *Wilson,* Vol. II: *The New Freedom* (Princeton: Princeton University Press, 1956), p. 320.
24. Ray Stannard Baker and William E. Dodd, eds., *The Public Papers of Woodrow Wilson: The New Democracy* (New York: Harper & Brothers Publishers, 1926), III, 64-69, 406-28, 439-45; Mark T. Gilderhus, "Pan-American Initiatives: The Wilson Presidency and 'Regional Integration,' 1914-1917," *Diplomatic History,* IV (Fall 1980), pp. 409-23.
25. David Healy, *Gunboat Diplomacy in the Wilson Era: The U.S. Navy in Haiti, 1915-1916* (Madison: The University of Wisconsin Press, 1976); Hans Schmidt, *The United States Occupation of Haiti, 1915-1934* (New Brunswick: Rutgers University Press, 1971), pp. 3-107; Sumner Welles, *Naboth's Vinyard: The Dominican Republic, 1844-1924* (New York: Payson & Clarke Ltd., 1928), II, 700-835; Dana G. Munro, *Intervention and Dollar Diplomacy in the Caribbean, 1900-1921* (Princeton: Princeton University Press, 1964), pp. 269-529.
26. Link, *Wilson,* II, 375.
27. Robert E. Quirk, *An Affair of Honor: Woodrow Wilson and the Occupation of Veracruz* (Lexington: University of Kentucky Press, 1962); Friedrich Katz, *The Secret War in Mexico: Europe, the United States, and the Mexican Revolution* (Chicago: The University of

Chicago Press, 1981), pp. 3-249; Lloyd C. Gardner, "Woodrow Wilson and the Mexican Revolution," in Arthur S. Link, ed., *Woodrow Wilson and a Revolutionary World, 1913-1921* (Chapel Hill: The University of North Carolina Press, 1982), pp. 3-48.

28. Katz, *Secret War,* pp. 253-383; Barbara W. Tuchman, *The Zimmermann Telegram* (New York: Ballantine Books, 1958); Mark T. Gilderhus, "Wilson, Carranza, and the Monroe Doctrine: A Question in Regional Organization," *Diplomatic History,* VII (Spring 1983), pp. 103-15.
29. Lansing to Gerard, Washington, July 21, 1915, Department of State, *Papers Relating to the Foreign Relations of the United States, 1915, Supplement: The World War* (Washington: Government Printing Office, 1928), p. 481; Baker and Dodd, *Public Papers,* III, 321.
30. Robert Lansing Diary, July 11, 1915, Jan. 9, 1916, Library of Congress.
31. Baker and Dodd, *Public Papers,* III, 386.
32. *Ibid.,* IV, 91.
33. *Ibid.,* IV, 184-88.
34. *Ibid.,* IV, 407-14.
35. Ray Stannard Baker and William E. Dodd, eds., *The Public Papers of Woodrow Wilson: War and Peace* (New York: Harper & Brothers Publishers, 1927), V, 6-16.
36. For Wilson's transition from neutrality to intervention, see Edward H. Buehrig, *Woodrow Wilson and the Balance of Power* (Bloomington: Indiana University Press, 1955); Ernest R. May, *The World War and American Isolation, 1914-1917* (Cambridge: Harvard University Press, 1959); Daniel M. Smith, *The Great Departure: The United States and World War I, 1914-1920* (New York: John Wiley and Sons, Inc., 1965); Daniel M. Smith, "National Interest and American Intervention, 1917: An Historiographical Appraisal," *Journal of American History,* LII (June 1965), pp. 5-24; Arthur S. Link, *Wilson,* Vol. III: *The Struggle for Neutrality, 1914-1915* (Princeton: Princeton University Press, 1960), Vol. IV: *Confusions and Crisis, 1915-1916* (Princeton: Princeton University Press, 1964), and Vol. V: *Campaigns for Progressivism and Peace, 1916-1917* (Princeton: Princeton University Press, 1965).
37. Baker and Dodd, *Public Papers,* V, 12-13.
38. *Ibid.,* V, 155-62; Arno J. Mayer, *Political Origins of the New Diplomacy, 1917-1918* (New Haven: Yale University Press, 1959).
39. George F. Kennan, *Soviet-American Relations, 1917-1920,* Vol. I: *Russia Leaves the War* (Princeton: Princeton University Press, 1956); Edward M. Coffman, *The War To End All Wars: The American Military Experience in World War I* (New York: Oxford University Press, 1968); Edward M. Coffman, *The Hilt of the Sword: The Career of Peyton C. March* (Madison: The University of Wisconsin Press, 1966); Daniel R. Beaver, *Newton D. Baker and the American*

War Effort, 1917-1919 (Lincoln: University of Nebraska Press, 1966).

40. Betty Miller Unterberger, "Woodrow Wilson and the Russian Revolution," in Link, *Wilson and Revolutionary World,* pp. 49-104; George F. Kennan, *Soviet-American Relations, 1917-1920,* Vol. II: *The Decision to Intervene* (Princeton: Princeton University Press, 1958).
41. Baker and Dodd, *Public Papers,* V, 253-61.
42. Roosevelt to Balfour, New York, Dec. 10, 1918, Elting E. Morison, ed., *The Letters of Theodore Roosevelt* (Cambridge: Harvard University Press, 1954), VIII, 1414-15.
43. Gerhard Schulz, *Revolutions and Peace Treaties, 1917-1920* (London: Methuen & Co. Ltd., 1967); John M. Thompson, *Russia, Bolshevism, and the Versailles Peace* (Princeton: Princeton University Press, 1967); Arno J. Mayer, *Politics and Diplomacy of Peacemaking: Containment and Counterrevolution at Versailles, 1918-1919* (New York: Alfred A. Knopf, 1967); N. Gordon Levin, Jr., *Woodrow Wilson and World Politics: America's Response to War and Revolution* (New York: Oxford University Press, 1968); Alan J. Ward, *Ireland and Anglo-American Relations, 1899-1921* (London: Wiedenfeld and Nicholson, 1969), pp. 70-268.
44. Department of State, *Papers Relating to the Foreign Relations of the United States, 1919: The Paris Peace Conference* (Washington: Government Printing Office, 1943), III, 177-201; Baker and Dodd, *Public Papers,* V, 395-400.
45. Department of State, *Papers Relating to the Foreign Relations of the United States, 1919: The Paris Peace Conference* (Washington: Government Printing Office, 1944), V, 85-86.
46. David Hunter Miller, *The Drafting of the Covenant* (New York: G. P. Putnam's Sons, 1928), I, 3-555; Lloyd E. Ambrosius, "Wilson, Clemenceau and the German Problem at the Paris Peace Conference of 1919," *Rocky Mountain Social Science Journal,* XII (April 1975), pp. 69-79; Lloyd E. Ambrosius, "Wilson, the Republicans, and French Security after World War I," *Journal of American History,* LIX (September 1972), pp. 341-52; Inga Floto, "Woodrow Wilson: War Aims, Peace Strategy, and the European Left," in Link, *Wilson and Revolutionary World,* pp. 127-45.
47. Russell H. Fifield, *Woodrow Wilson and the Far East: The Diplomacy of the Shantung Question* (Hamden: Archon Books, 1965); Raymond A. Esthus, "The Open Door and Integrity of China, 1899-1922: Hazy Principles for Changing Policy," and David F. Trask, "Sino-Japanese-American Relations During the Paris Peace Conference of 1919," in Thomas H. Etzold, ed., *Aspects of Sino-American Relations since 1784* (New York: New Viewpoints, 1978), pp. 48-101; Paul Gordon Lauren, "Human Rights in History: Diplomacy and Racial Equality at the Paris Peace Conference," *Diplomatic History,* II (Summer 1978), pp. 257-78.

48. Klaus Schwabe, *Deutsche Revolution und Wilson Frieden: Die amerikanische und deutsche Friedensstrategie zwischen Ideologie und Machtpolitik 1918/19* (Düsseldorf: Droste Verlag, 1971); Peter Berg, *Deutschland und Amerika, 1918-1929: Über das deutsche Amerikabild der zwanziger Jahre* (Lübeck: Matthiesen Verlag, 1963), pp. 9-47; Lloyd E. Ambrosius, "The United States and the Weimar Republic: America's Response to the German Problem," in Jules Davids, ed., *Perspectives in American Diplomacy: Essays on Europe, Latin America, China, and the Cold War* (New York: Arno Press, 1976), pp. 78-104; J. Joseph Huthmacher and Warren I. Susman, eds., *Wilson's Diplomacy: An International Symposium* (Cambridge: Schenkman Publishing Company, 1973).

5

CHARLES EVANS HUGHES, RATIONALISM, AND FOREIGN AFFAIRS

Betty Glad

Before 1914 the United States had achieved its remarkable security, not through its own arms, but from three oceans surrounding the North American continent and the proclivities of Great Britain to adapt its power and policies to America's long-term interests.[1] During the Great War the conditions of this free security system were undercut by changes in technology and the world's political structure. The airplane made the oceans less significant as natural barriers. The rise of Germany, Japan, and ultimately the Soviet Union to the ranks of the great powers would soon undermine Britain's political position to the point where that country would be unable to manage the European balance of power as it had in previous generations. The commercial and imperial interests of the American people continued to push them more deeply into international affairs. The United States emerged from the war as a creditor nation in world markets. Clearly the war years had revolutionized America's relationship to its external environment.

As secretary of state for four years after March 5, 1921, Hughes would play the leading role in the effort to adapt the foreign policies of the United States to the new international milieu. Experience had prepared him for the task. As a former governor of New York, Associate Justice of the U.S. Supreme Court, and the Republican presidential nominee in 1916, he had shown himself to be moderate and progressive, capable of effective leadership. Aside from Elihu Root, then too old for public office, Hughes was the intellectual leader of the Republican Party, recognized as such by both presidents under whom he served.

When Warren Harding first introduced Hughes to reporters as his choice for secretary of state, Harding suggested that he would handle things differently from Woodrow Wilson. The secretary, he said, would speak for the State Department.[2] Hughes later would describe his relationship to Harding: "I did not go to him with a statement of difficulties and ask him what should be done, but supplemented my statements of the facts in particular cases by concrete proposals upon which he could act at once, and to which he almost invariably gave his approval." Harding, he added, was "always accessible, anxious fully to understand each problem as it arose."[3] Indeed, as other commentators noted, Harding appeared to be almost in awe of Hughes. Herbert Hoover, secretary of commerce, believed that the President was actually afraid of his secretary of state.[4] Calvin Coolidge, too, left the major responsibility for foreign affairs in Hughes's hands. The location of the secretary of state's office in the State, War, and Navy Building next door to the White House provided the physical foundation for a close working relationship. This permitted Hughes to stroll across the White House yard each afternoon to confer quietly with Coolidge.[5]

II

In defining the U.S. position vis-a-vis the rest of the world, Hughes would be guided by a world view shared by many others educated in Ivy League schools in the late nineteenth century. His only formal training in world politics consisted of a course in international law he had taught at Cornell University in 1892–1893 while the regular instructor was on leave. Hughes immersed himself in the prevailing rationalistic international law of his day.[6] That experience at Cornell, however, merely capped the broader social philosophy that Hughes had developed while a student at Brown University and the Columbia University Law School. From the then popular Scottish Realist philosophy he absorbed the idea that there was a rational universe which rewarded those who adhered to the puritanical virtues. Fusing this idea with the German idealistic philosophy of J. Lewis Diman, the instructor in political economy at Brown, he came to the view that reason was not static but a historically evolving force. Thus the line between the public and the private was never frozen, but changed as attitudes changed. The American polity, although still in the process of change, represented for Hughes the highest development of reason in the world of the day. From his study with Theodore Dwight at Columbia he came to see law as the highest embodiment of reason in human affairs.[7] In short, Hughes's entire education suggested that the United States had special qualities and that one should look to its traditions for guidance.

As secretary of state Hughes would forego Wilson's utopian plans for a moral and political transformation of the world and give Americans in search of "normalcy" a less elevated standard to follow. "Foreign policies are not built upon abstraction," he said. "They are the result of practical conceptions of national interest arising from some immediate exigency or standing out vividly in historical perspective."[8] Turning toward Europe, he noted that Americans still adhered to the principle of "not meddling" in Europe's political strife. This isolationist tradition, he agreed, was rooted in history and reason. As George Washington pointed out in his Farewell Address, Europe would be engaged in frequent controversies foreign to American concerns. Misreading historical notions, he saw the United States as even less subject to injuries from Europe than it had been during its formative years. Viewing power politics as a peculiarly European way of life, he assumed that American motives were purer: "The great advantage we have had is that, coming to independence in a world afflicted with the long rivalries of military powers, the traditions of conquest, and the dreams of empire, we sought simply the assurance of freedom, and our national instinct has been opposed to aggression and intervention. . . . "[9] Moreover, Europeans did not want American advice. Each one," he said, "would welcome our help against the other but not against itself."[10] No less than other isolationists Hughes believed that American influence benefited from detachment and would disappear the moment that the United States became a partisan in Europe's quarrels. Beyond these concerns, American domestic politics made isolationism a wise policy. Because of their varied origins Americans had ties, sentiments, and interests too narrowly focused to meet the requirements of national policy.[11]

Despite his highly provincial view of the nation's past, Hughes did not join the ultra-isolationists of his day. Tradition, he noted, never implied a complete separation from Europe. Our founding statesmen, he said, had "no thought of escaping constant dealing with these Powers, whose rivalries menaced our peace." Nor did the American people ever shirk cooperation with other nations when there was a consciousness of common interests and aims. These common purposes included the development of instruments for the peaceful settlement of disputes, the promotion of humanitarian efforts which required a community of action, the re-establishment of sound economic conditions, and participation in international conferences for the adjustment of differences and the formulation of useful conventions.[12]

For Latin America also Hughes looked to tradition—as he understood it—for guidance. The Monroe Doctrine had been an integral part of America's national purpose. It remained an essential policy to be applied as necessity required.[13] In resisting various Latin American attempts to multilateralize the Doctrine in the early twenties, Hughes insisted that the United States alone could interpret it. "It is a policy," he said, "declared by the Executive of the United States and repeated in one form and another by Presidents and Secretaries of State in the conduct of our foreign relations." While gratified at expressions of accord by other American states toward the declarations of the United States with respect to their independence, this government, he reminded Latin Americans, had "commonly avoided concerted action to maintain the doctrine, even with the American Republics." Tradition did not compel the United States to take any particular course of action should the Doctrine be challenged.[14]

Hughes stripped the Monroe Doctrine of some of its most extravagant pretensions. He rejected the claims of Theodore Roosevelt that the Doctrine might require U.S. intervention in the affairs of other American nations to correct chronic wrongdoing and administrative incompetence. For Hughes the assumption that intervention by non-American powers in American affairs would automatically endanger the safety of the United States was simply untrue.[15] In such statements Hughes anticipated the Clark Memorandum on the Monroe Doctrine which appeared in 1930. Like Clark, Hughes did not foreswear U.S. intervention in the other American republics, but he shifted the grounds for intervention from the Monroe Doctrine to the more general grounds of national security. On matters of national security the United States would act as if the Monroe Doctrine did not exist.[16] International law, he pointed out, allowed any nation to exercise its authority beyond its territorial limits should there be a direct threat to its peace and safety, or a denial of justice to its citizens.[17] Because of the Panama Canal, Hughes admitted, disturbances in the Caribbean region were of special concern to the United States.[18]

Outside the Caribbean area Hughes based his Latin American policies on the ideals of Pan Americanism. Occasionally he acknowledged the economic and cultural barriers within the Americas, but generally he emphasized the common interests and feelings of friendship which bound the republics of the New World into a peaceful political system. For Hughes Pan Americanism rested on the conviction "that there are primary and mutual interests which are peculiar to the republics of this hemisphere and that these can best be conserved by taking counsel together and by devising appropriate means of collaboration."[19] This commonality of purpose was based on contiguity, but economic and technological trends promised to bring an even greater intimacy, an even keener sense of neighborhood.[20] Beyond these factors the American system was based on a common history and shared values. "We have all revolted against tyranny," he recalled. "We have erected throughout the American continents the standards of national freedom and independence. We have thus been drawn together by a common sentiment which makes us neighbors in spirit."[21]

Although Hughes never made claims of America's moral superiority to Europe directly, there were intimations of this attitude in some of his statements. "If anyone," he argued, "is disposed . . . to emphasize differences and regrettable expressions of unneighborly points of view, let him consider conditions elsewhere throughout the world,—the jealousies, distrust, historic animosities, found in every region and, unless he is a hopeless cynic, I think that he will conclude that the relations of the American States do not suffer in comparison."[22] Hughes assumed that the American exemption from the historic antagonisms and ambitions which had vexed the peace of the rest of the world resulted from the alleged rejection of power politics in the Western Hemisphere where agreements rested on the "processes of reason, discussion and mutual accommodations."[23]

In defining American commercial interests abroad, Hughes again identified U.S. policy with the common good. He would smooth the paths of trade and investment through the pursuit of the open door abroad and the development of non-discriminatory tariffs, navigation, and other commercial rules at home. The unconditional most-favored-nation clause in trade agreements he saw as a lever for eliminating foreign rules and processes that discriminated against American commerce. "We are constantly insisting upon equality of opportunity," he observed, "and we cannot expect to be successful in removing discriminations against us when we think them injurious and at the same time insist on discriminations in our favor whenever we see fit." Hughes believed that the United States could hold its own throughout the world if it enjoyed equality of commercial opportunity.[24]

Although Hughes would do his best to buttress a nondiscriminatory world economic order, he had little faith in radical proposals for transforming the world's legal order. International cooperation, he believed, was possible only "within the narrow field not closed by divergent national ambitions or as interest yields to apprehension or obtains compensation through give and take."[25] The clash of fundamental national interests could produce war. Indeed, the most fundamental interest of a state—its national existence—ultimately depended on its ability and willingness to defend that existence.[26] Thus law at the international level had only a limited role in curtailing basic conflicts. Both lawmaking and law enforcement were decentralized. There was no legislature to impose its will by majority vote, no executive to give effect even to accepted rules. Lacking in effective sanction, international law was in "constant danger of being supplanted by considerations of expediency whenever the exigency is so severe, or the immediate advantages so great, or opinion so divided, as to warrant the risk." Indeed, when a state was wronged under international law, the only sanction at its disposal was the use of its own power.[27]

Hughes saw little chance for a radical change in the behavior of states through the introduction of abstract formulas to outlaw or limit war. Such proposals, he pointed out, sought to rule out wars of aggression, not wars for defense. But there was rarely a case of admitted aggression, said Hughes, "where on each side the cause is not believed to be just by the peoples who support the war." Proposals for collective security Hughes found equally problematical: "Great powers agreeing among themselves may indeed hold small powers in check. But who will hold great powers in check when powers disagree? The trust in force must in truth be trust in common agreement behind the force." Indeed, all mechanisms for the maintaining of peace by economic or military sanctions, he predicted, were "likely to fail when they are most needed, because national interests are diverse and unanimity of action under stress of crises involving conflicts of opinion is well-nigh impossible."[28] Not even the spread of democracy throughout the world would diminish the possibility of conflict. Great wars, involving vast populations, could not be fought without public support, but the most serious causes of war were precisely those which carried popular appeal.[29]

Despite this pessimistic portrait of the international system, Hughes did not give up hope for a more stable world order. Rational human effort, he thought, could reduce the likelihood of war. "Peace is a state of mind," he said. "If the state of mind exists, it will find expression in agreements and institutions, in the willingness to assume obligations of mutual self-restraint." Even the recent World War had some positive effect. People had begun to see that modern weapons provided no real security, that victory was hollow when measured by the cost of contemporary warfare.[30]

Diplomacy was the traditional means whereby nations reconciled their differences peacefully. When that broke down, nations could employ various forms of third party participation to achieve peaceful settlements of disputes. Arbitration, adjudication, and conciliation agreements, as well as the codification of international law, Hughes believed, were the most promising enterprizes of the era.[31] Arbitration arrangements were useful because they disposed nations to submit for decision issues which they were not otherwise inclined to submit. Yet the legally binding nature of the award encouraged them to find escape clauses from the need to arbitrate. Conciliation, because its results were not legally binding, was a more useful form of third-party assistance in controversies where political interests were at stake. It promoted agreements because it bought time for passions to cool and provided new recommendations which might open the way for compromise without humiliating concessions. The success of such efforts, however, rested always on the discovery of mutually acceptable compromises.[32]

No less than other proponents of international law, Hughes had difficulty in distinguishing controversies that were political, and thus outside the realm of law, from those that were justiciable, or subject to international law. Hughes assumed that a political controversy involved vital interests, and that conflicts under treaties would not touch vital interests and thus could be settled under international law. But it was apparent that this was not always the case. Following a war or political intervention a state could be forced to make serious political concessions. If at a later date the defeated state openly challenged the legal restraints placed upon it, the controversy would be covered by law but still involve vital interests. As J. L. Brierly has stated: "The dissatisfaction of a state with the status quo raises a question which is not a judicial one, and cannot be turned into a judicial question by adopting judicial methods of procedure; it raises a question which is essentially political, susceptible of amicable settlement, no doubt, but only by appropriate political methods. . . . "[33] It would have been less confusing had Hughes distinguished between justiciable and legal disputes on the basis of whether a state was making claims under the law or stating its basic national interests, regardless of the law, perhaps even contrary to it. By not seeing this distinction clearly, Hughes ran the constant danger of attempting legal settlements for political conflicts. It was not clear that the codification of international law, which Hughes favored, would resolve the questions of jurisdiction and applicability.[34]

In addition to the promotion of third-party settlements and the codification of international law, Hughes saw arms limitation as a way to secure peace. "Competitive armament," he said, "is an outward sign of an inward distrust and will go on until confidence replaces fear and suspicions."[35] Thus he recognized the "great cogency" of the argument that "the organization of security must precede a general limitation of armaments."[36] The arms race itself begat suspicion and distrust and invoked counter responses, making war almost inevitable. Arms control agreements, by enhancing feelings of security, would break the vicious cycle initiated by arms competitions. The objective in arms limitation, Hughes argued, was not to cripple reasonable means of defense. Rather the goal was to put an end to offensive armaments, the kind that "threatens aggression, breeds distrust, stimulates competition in arms and leads to war." The distinction, of course, was often a difficult one. But Hughes rejected the idea of certain masters of strategy that the best defense lay in the attack. This notion of defense, he said, invited the apprehension of others and similar preparations for offensive war by them. Hughes did not insist that all provocative arms be controlled at once. He favored a gradualistic and optimistic approach, backed by agreements "to any extent or in any area found practicable. . . . A measure of prevention is better than none."[37]

Hughes was in many respects a sensitive and intelligent political realist. In his analysis of the role of national interest and the limits of collective security and the outlawry of war he revealed a sophistication beyond that of many of his contemporaries. His faith in progress toward peace through the development of the institutions for peaceful adjustment, however, seems strangely incongruous, given the hard-headed realism that characterized much of his writing. To comprehend fully the faith he placed in these reforms, one must recall the prisms through which he viewed the world. Placing his reliance on a nineteenth-century rationalist philosophy, he saw reason as playing a significant role in the international order. At a lower evolutionary level than the nation-state, the world order was still in the stream of history. The progress toward the rule of reason which dominated the universe would direct events in that area as elsewhere. Yet progress, because it was based on the transformation of attitudes, had to be slow. Institutional development did not initiate changes in attitudes, but reflected them. Given the international system, then, the most one could hope for was the discovery of mutually satisfactory grounds for the accommodation of diverse national interests. Those institutions and instruments which promoted the discovery of these common interests were the distinctive developments of the age.

Two other facets of his thought would create difficulties for Hughes as secretary of state. The assumption that the triumph of reason guaranteed the discovery of mutual interests and the end of force blinded him to the role that power played in the development of legal and political institutions. Law, he did not see, often codified the special interests and power of dominant groups within a community. Nor did he seem fully aware of the extent to which agreements reflected assessments not only of what was fair, but also of the relative power of the contending parties. Associating accommodation with reason and consent as he did, he could scarcely appreciate the role that power played in the process. Finally, he failed to observe that tradition might not be the best source for defining the national interest when technology and the external political developments were creating a radically new international environment for the United States.

III

Despite his personal prestige and his well developed world view, Hughes would be limited in his efforts to define American foreign policy. Within the administration he would need to share power with Hoover, who would sometimes push trade with states that did not meet Hughes's standards.[38] President Harding would take more flexible stances than Hughes toward the revolutionary regimes in Mexico and Russia. But Hughes's major difficulties would be with the irreconcilables in the U.S. Senate.

Shortly after Harding announced that Hughes would be the new secretary of state, Boies Penrose, the powerful Pennsylvania Republican, commented: "I do not think it matters much who is Secretary of State. Congress—especially the Senate—will blaze the way in connection with foreign policy."[39] Certainly there was reason to expect special problems from the Senate Foreign Relations Committee. Henry Cabot Lodge, who chaired the committee until his death on November 9, 1924, was determined to exercise the kind of influence he had enjoyed when the Senate prevented League membership in 1919 and 1920. William E. Borah, who succeeded Lodge as chairman of the Committee, was even more troublesome. An ultra-isolationist, he was almost a compulsive nay-sayer. Several other irreconcilables—Frank Brandegee, Hiram Johnson, Joseph Medill McCormick, George Mose—retained their seats on the Committee. None of these men would be inclined to shift ideological gears merely to accommodate an administration of their own party. The tactics which had enabled them to frustrate Wilson's crusade for the League of Nations could be employed to defeat any internationalistic proclivities of the new Republican administration as well.

Harding added to Hughes's problems by refusing to confront his former congressional colleagues. Yet Hughes, who had made many political mistakes in dealing with the New York legislature as governor, would show considerable skill in handling the United States Senate. He wooed Senators who might come over to his side and avoided others. Learning from Wilson's painful experience, he determined to skirt a fight with the Senate unless public opinion was strongly behind him.[40]

Hughes had signed Elihu Root's "Manifesto of Thirty One" during the 1920 general election campaign. With other leading Republicans, he suggested in that document that U.S. entry into the League of Nations would be best assured by certain revisions in the Covenant and the election of Harding as President. However, when Harding, in his first speech to Congress as President, firmly announced that the United States would have nothing to do with the League, Hughes did not protest. Never inclined to political martyrdom, he wrote to George Wickersham, one of the co-signers, that none of the Thirty One "intended to assert a control they did not possess or to promise the impossible." Indeed, Harding's landslide had strengthened the League's opponents to the point where the President realized that had he proposed entry into the League, the administration would have been wrecked by "a most bitter fight and he would not have succeeded."[41] The hopes of Wickersham, A. Lawrence Lowell, and other co-signers of the Manifesto for some international association disintegrated completely when Hughes informed Lowell on July 20, 1922: "The President does not think, and I entirely agree with him, that he should refer again, at this time, to his desire for an association of nations."[42] Several months later he wrote Wickersham how his own earlier suggestions for a new association, not directly connected with the Versailles Treaty, had met with no approving response. "I do not believe," he concluded, "that there has been a time when the Administration could have proposed hopefully a project for a new association of nations."[43]

Although Hughes faced criticism among pro-League Americans for his desertion of the cause, they should not have been surprised. Philosophically, Hughes had reservations about such a dramatic reorganization of the world as envisaged in the League of Nations. Politically, he had hedged on proposals for the League since the war years. As the Republican candidate for the presidency in 1916 he gave his approval to the project of the League to Enforce Peace. But he favored only an international court and perhaps periodic international conferences. In a speech at Long Branch in the spring of 1917 he opposed any U.S. pledge to use force in unknown contingencies. During the remaining months of the war he kept his distance from the League to Enforce Peace. On March 30, 1918, he declined an invitation to become a member of that group's Executive Committee, and on May 16 refused to speak at the League conference in Philadelphia.[44]

When the draft proposal for the League of Nations first appeared in the United States, Hughes argued that Article X—that dealing with collective security—be dropped altogether. The guarantee made no allowance for changes in international boundaries and, he noted, "it ascribes a prescience and soundness of judgment to the present Peace Conference in erecting States and defining boundaries which nobody in the history of the world has ever possessed."[45] Even Hughes's subsequent recommendation that the United States join the League included a reservation to preserve U.S. freedom of action under Article X. Three other Hughes reservations would provide for the possible withdrawal of states from the League, the exemption of the Monroe Doctrine from League jurisdiction, and the removal of immigration and tariff matters (except as otherwise provided in international agreements) from League concern.[46]

Despite the American rejection, the League of Nations was a functioning organization by the spring of 1921, and Hughes faced the task of defining the U.S. relationship to it. There was no reason why Hughes should not have recognized the League as a corporate entity with which the United States could have limited dealings. Yet the existence of the League was an embarrassment to those Republicans who had predicted that the organization could not exist without U.S. membership. Hughes responded to this sentiment. Letters from the League were left unanswered for months, and when the State Department finally sent out an unsigned form letter in response to all League queries, they were not sent directly to the League Secretariat but were forwarded through the U.S. delegation at Geneva. Hughes addressed his later demands that the United States be consulted on the administration of the new mandates to the individual states involved rather than to the Council of the League. And when the Assistant Surgeon General of the United States finally attended a conference on the standardization of anti-toxin in serum, the Department acted as if he were collaborating with the old Office Internationale de Hygienge Publique in Paris rather than its official sponsor, the new Health Section of the League.

Hughes also played a crucial role in the refusal of the members of the American Panel of the Court of International Arbitration to make nominations for judges on the new World Court. The request for nominations had been forwarded only after considerable delay in the State Department. Shortly thereafter Hughes warned Root that such nominations would appear as actions of the U.S. government and risk controversy that would endanger the success of important policies the government was then pursuing.

Gradually the State Department came to recognize the corporate existence of the League. By 1922 the U.S. consul at Geneva brought information to the League Secretariat, although anonymously and not under official letterhead. Beginning in March of that year United States observers appeared at technical conferences—those on the traffic in women, the suppression of obscene publication, the Opium Advisory Committee, and the Temporary Mixed Commission to Deal with the International Arms Traffic. The State Department sent observers to the Council in 1923 when it considered making a loan to Greek refugees who had been driven from their homes in the recent dispute with Turkey. Drawing on a device initiated by his predecessor Bainbridge Colby, Hughes skirted the Congress with "unofficial observers." As he explained it, the United States could not act as a member of the League; thus it sent unofficial observers to deal with matters affecting American or humanitarian interests.[47] Finally in 1924 Hughes wrote to the Secretary General of the League, Eric Drummond, over his own signature.

Although this form of representation was the best possible, given the political climate in the United States, it created more problems than Hughes cared to admit. American observers were reluctant even to speak at public sessions. They had no authority to commit the United States to anything, even provisionally. As Georges Clemenceau of France once remarked, this practice meant that the United States was represented by "an ear but not by a mouth."[48] Hughes delineated the American relationship to the League in an address before the New York State Republican Convention on April 15, 1924. "[B]ecause several nations have formed an organization of which we are not a part," he said, "is no reason why we cannot co-operate in all matters affecting our proper concern. We simply adjust our forms of contact and negotiation to the existing conditions." Of course, the United States would not take up any subject that might draw it into matters not supported by the American public.[49]

Later, embarrassed by the trepidation with which he first approached the League, Hughes denied his role in these early policies. A dilatory mail clerk carried the blame for the American failure to answer mail from the League in early 1921. The American Panel which refused to make World Court nominations, Hughes insisted, had acted in accord with their own views of propriety. "While it is true that, in response to Mr. Root's request, I stated frankly my own opinion," he acknowledged, "I was careful to say that the members of the American group should act on their own responsibility."[50] Actually Hughes must bear more responsibility for U.S. behavior toward the League. One cannot fault him for refusing to resign when Harding insisted that the United States not join the League. But he had demonstrated bad political judgment if he really believed that a vote for Harding would increase the likelihood of U.S. entry into the League. The Manifesto was clearly a campaign document and its main purpose was to serve party ends. The State Department, moreover, remained cool to the League long after it discovered the actions of the dilatory mail clerk. And Hughes's objection to World Court nominations was crucial in the decision of Root and the other American judges not to forward them, as Root testified later.

IV

Aside from the League issue Hughes sought prescriptions for peace that accorded with the nation's isolationist sentiments. On February 17, 1923, he drafted a letter to President Harding recommending U.S. adherence to the World Court protocol.[51] A few days later Harding sent the letter on to the Senate with his own endorsement. Thereafter, to placate Senators Lodge, Borah, and the irreconcilables on the Senate Foreign Relations Committee, Hughes proposed four reservations. These conditions, as he explained in his letter to Harding, were to make it clear that U.S. adherence to the Court protocol would not involve it in any legal obligations under the League. These provisos outlined alternative arrangements for the United States to participate in the choosing of judges, the sharing of Court expenses, and the revision of the World Court statute.

Hughes was especially solicitous of Lodge. The secretary had made his first address advocating American membership on the Court in Boston, Lodge's home town, on October 30, 1922. The Department forwarded a copy of the address, with its favorable references to Lodge, to the Senator. Later Hughes met with Lodge several times in Washington, outlining the administration's plans regarding Court membership. Still Lodge would not budge. William A. King, a Democrat, introduced the resolution in the Senate. Lodge, taking advantage of a tie vote in the committee, was able to pigeonhole the project until his death in November, 1924. Borah's accession to the chairmanship of the Senate Foreign Relations Committee did not help the issue. Long before the floor vote on January 26, 1926, several months after Hughes had left the State Department, Borah and his allies had convinced a majority of the Senate to attach three reservations to U.S. adherence, in addition to those proposed by Hughes. One would sink the project. It required that the Court not render any advisory opinion except publicly, and that it not consider any request for an advisory opinion touching on any dispute in which the United States claimed an interest.

At first Hughes opposed this reservation. The Court, he pointed out to President Coolidge, could not legally bind the United States without its consent. He wondered whether John Basset Moore, the

United States judge on the World Court, who had authorized this reservation, was not really trying to keep the United States out of the Court.[52] When it became clear that the reservation had become a condition for U.S. entry, he tried to put the best face on the matter. "The reservation of the Senate as to advisory opinions," he said, "is a precaution, whether necessary or not, . . . which is in aide of the Court's appropriate jurisdiction. . . . " When the Council of the League, on March 18, 1926, proposed that the United States and other members of the Court meet at Geneva to clarify the U.S. conditions, Hughes agreed with Coolidge's flat refusal. American conditions and reservations were final.[53]

Even after the apparent failure of his World Court project Hughes devoted himself to other institutions of peace. As head of the U.S. delegation to the Sixth Pan American Conference in 1928 and a follow-up conference in Washington, Hughes played a major role in the negotiation of new arrangements for the arbitration of disputes within the Americas. At the latter conference the parties agreed to submit to compulsory arbitration all differences not resolved by diplomacy "which are judicial in their nature by reason of being susceptible to decision by the principles of law." Departing from the formulas developed twenty years earlier in the Root arbitration treaties, these arrangements did not exempt the vital interests, independence, and national honor of the United States from the obligation to arbitrate. They exempted only disputes within the domestic jurisdiction of the parties and not covered by international law. Other procedures facilitated the establishment of arbitration boards and the rules they would follow. Beyond this the conference drafted a conciliation treaty for the handling of political disputes. Building on the Bryan treaties of 1913-1915, it provided for a cooling-off period during which a panel of commissioners, selected in advance, would attempt to define the issues and offer possible solutions. These arrangements were valuable, said Hughes, because states would "not arbitrarily deny their clear obligations."[54]

V

On July 2, 1921, the U.S. Senate passed a resolution declaring the wars with Germany and Austria-Hungary at an end. It reserved to the United States all rights, reparations, and other advantages to which the United States and its nationals were entitled under the armistice agreement and the Versailles Treaty. Unilateral declarations such as these, Hughes knew, could not effectively secure the rights of the United States as a military victor. Moreover, there were certain rights regarding mandates, access to claims tribunals, and occupation costs under the Versailles Treaty that Hughes did not want to relinquish. Yet he knew that any effort to negotiate a new treaty with Germany would create legal complications with the Allies. At a White House meeting, attended by about fifteen Senators, Hughes suggested that the Treaty of Versailles, shorn of all references to the League, might serve as a peace with Germany. The irreconcilables retorted that any settlement based on the Versailles Treaty would never pass the Senate.[55] Eventually Hughes reached a compromise. The Department prepared a treaty consisting of the original text of the congressional resolution of July 2, with a series of cross references to specific articles of the Versailles Treaty stipulating rights and privileges beneficial to the United States. This secured German recognition of American rights as well as consent of the Senate. The Treaty of Berlin was signed on August 25, 1921. Similar treaties with Austria and Hungary were signed that same month.

The Treaty of Berlin did not end Hughes's problems with the Senate on European matters. In the summer of 1922 Senator Oscar W. Underwood attempted to resolve another problem with Germany by unilateral fiat. He proposed to settle all claims of American citizens arising out of Germany's wartime activities through a commission composed solely of Americans. In this case Hughes overrode the Senate. Inviting Borah to his office, Hughes told him that the administration would proceed on its own in the formation of a German-American Claims Commission. He offered legal precedent for such an executive arrangement. The agreement was signed on August 10, 1922.[56] In his efforts to secure a peace with Germany and to provide for the settlement of claims against that country, Hughes simply tried to normalize U.S. relations with a defeated country in accordance with standard international practice.

Hughes's attempt to work out a practical program for the Allied repayment of war debts to the United States involved him in problems for which conventional answers would be inadequate. The question of debts arose from the U.S. loans of over $10 billion to the Allied governments in 1917 and 1918. As early as 1920 the Allies, awaiting a downward adjustment of U.S. interest rates, suspended interest payment on the loans. Congress, choosing to deal with the issue rather than permitting the administration to take the lead, passed a law in 1922 which called for the repayment of these loans in 25 years with a downward adjustment of the interest rates. A Foreign Debt Commission, which included Hughes and other administration officials, would work out the details in separate funding agreements with each country. Unfortunately the Allies faced practical difficulties in obtaining the dollars to meet even the new terms. The Fordney-McCumber Tariff of 1922, which Hughes and the administration supported, raised the U.S. tariff level to a new high. Against such barriers the European nations could not make sufficient exports to the United States to gain the dollars necessary to repay the loans. The alternative of massive gold shipments to the United States would have undermined the stability of the European currencies. Germany, moreover, was in the midst of a major currency inflation and thus unable to send war reparations to the Allies which would have helped their economic recoveries. In these circumstances the Allies insisted that the repayment of their loans rested on Germany's reparations payments to them. The British, in the Balfour notes of the summer of 1922, officially proposed the cancellation of all inter-Allied debts.

Some American financiers argued that Washington accept the proposal. As banker Otto Kahn pointed out, there was no way that the loans could be repaid "without consequences ruinous to most of our debtors and highly damaging to ourselves."[57] But most Americans, including Republican leaders in the Senate, preferred to ignore the technical balance-of-trade and payments questions. Falling back on an eternal verity—that debts must be repaid—they insisted that the Allies had a moral duty to meet their obligations. Hughes likewise never questioned the obligations of the Europeans to pay off their loans, but in his address to the American Historical Association in December, 1922, he moved close to the European position when he admitted that the debts were connected to German reparations. Throwing out some token bones to meet prevailing American opinion, he noted that Germany's ability to pay did not affect the inter-Allied debts to the United States. (No one had ever made that claim.) But Hughes then agreed with the Allied position that the ability to repay debts was based on German reparations payments. "Moreover, so far as the debtors to the United States are concerned," he said, "they have unsettled credit balances, and their condition and capacity to pay cannot be properly determined until the amount that can be realized on these credits for reparations has been determined."[58] Going beyond mere rhetoric, Hughes suggested that a commission of experts look into the matter of German reparations.[59] But even going public did not bring immediate acceptance of his proposals. Almost a year passed before the French, chastened by their failure in 1923 to secure the payments through their occupation of the Ruhr, were more willing to listen. On November 30, 1923, the Reparations Commission agreed to proceed on Hughes's plan to appoint experts to serve on two committees, one to deal with the balancing of the German budget and the stabilization of the German economy, the other to study the return of certain capital exports to Germany.

On April 9, 1924, the First Committee, headed by Charles G. Dawes of the United States, recommended a graduated scale for reparations payments, a reorganization of the *Reichsbank* under Allied supervision, and the floating of a large foreign loan to Germany to bolster its economy. Subsequent to the approval of this plan on August 30, 1924, American dollars began to pour into Germany. These payments freed German funds so that Berlin could make reparations payments to the former Allies who, in turn, could repay their loans to the United States. The Dawes Plan, in short, was a recognition that the implementation of the funding agreements signed with the various European countries was dependent on German reparations payments.

No clear explanation of this relationship ever reached the American public. Moreover, Hughes insisted that the negotiations leading to the Dawes loans had been the simple result of the efforts, choices, and decisions of private individuals. Contrary to these claims, however, Hughes's concern with the outcome of these talks was evident in his many activities to establish the commission and to secure support for its recommendations afterwards. He played a key role in the selection of the commission members and the reparations agents. American diplomats received instructions to work with government officials and bankers in Paris and London to make the terms of the loan acceptable to American investors. Traveling to London in July, 1924, to address a Bar Association meeting, Hughes privately took side trips to Paris and in London in an effort to obtain support for the projects worked out by the Dawes commission. Ultimately Hughes personally persuaded J. P. Morgan to bear most of the load of the U.S. portion of the loan.[60]

Actually the Dawes Plan only papered over the problem. Allies would service their war debts only as long as U.S. loans to Germany continued, and those loans would stop with the crash of 1929. Moreover, private experts and financiers made decisions purportedly on their own, but major foreign policy concerns were driving them. Senator Joseph T. Robinson of Arkansas, an influential Senate Democrat, criticized Hughes for attempting to conduct foreign policy through American investors: "The responsibility of conducting foreign affairs must not be left to bankers, merchants, and bond brokers in their private capacities. . . . The issue [*sic*] to be met are Government. Therefore, the power that should grapple with them is not a private responsibility, but public authority." Norman Davis found this sort of participation in world affairs "inadequate, undignified and cowardly."[61]

The reasons for Hughes's pretense are clear. To do almost anything constructive on the matter of debts he had to avoid the Senate. "If I had sought to obtain the consent of Congress to the appointment of a committee officially representing our Government," he confided in his Biographical Notes, "I should have been involved in a controversy which would have defeated the entire plan."[62] He admitted in a public forum, his address before the Pilgrims Society of Westminister Hall in London in 1924: "[H]ad we attempted to make America's contribution to the recent plan of adjustment a governmental matter, we should have been involved in a hopeless debate, and there would have been no adequate action. That is not the way to make an American contribution to economic revival."[63]

Overall Hughes accomplished much in Europe, given the strength of American isolationism and the institutional and political framework in which he worked. He defined his goals in accordance with preponderant public sentiment, but dealt with the facts in an attempt to provide the practical basis for the satisfaction of his goals. With considerable resourcefulness he developed the means for avoiding the irreconcilables who, while most insistent on the satisfaction of American claims against Europe, consistently threw roadblocks in the path of their actual accomplishment. The objectives on which most Americans agreed, he knew, could not be effectively secured through self-righteous proclamations, unilateral fiat, or threats to wash one's hands of European affairs should European governments refuse to follow the American lead. For all his concern with practical matters Hughes failed to resolve the war debt and balance of payment problem. He was aware that repayment of the war debts required Germany's economic recovery. What he did not admit was that even the revived economies of the Allies would not have generated sufficient income to repay the war loans unless the United States lowered its tariffs. Without increased European exports the debts could be serviced only as long as

American dollars went through Germany and back to the United States in the form of debt payments.

VI

Hughes's greatest achievement as secretary of state came in an area where he was least circumscribed by the Senate and national tradition: naval arms limitation. The burgeoning naval arms race among the United States, Britain, and Japan, he acknowledged, was in part the consequence of the U.S. naval building program initiated by Wilson in 1916. Any halt to this race would require a voluntary agreement. Hence any proposal, to be successful, would recognize the vital interests of other powers as well as those of the United States.

In planning for the Washington naval limitation conference of 1921-1922 Hughes needed first to destroy the prevailing pessimism regarding the possibility of an agreement. To that end he decided that the conference should open with a proposal so dramatic that demands for an agreement would come from around the world.[64] Only nine men knew his surprise. The final copy of his speech was mimeographed by an admiral in the Navy and then locked in a safe in his office until the morning of the delivery. Choosing the first session of the conference for the unveiling, Hughes would give the world press a full weekend to play up the American proposal and bring pressure on the various governments to accept the American formula. Even more important than the timing was the content of the proposals. By taking account of the interests of the other major naval powers, and by specifying the sacrifices his own country would make, Hughes would demonstrate that the United States took the question of arms limitation seriously.

Discovering the proposals which might succeed had not been easy. Early in his preparation Hughes had looked at the specific demands and needs of the major powers. He soon concluded that this approach would involve the nations in a morass of subjective claims and counterclaims. Then, early in October, he found an alternative: he would base his proposal on the principle of maintaining the status quo in naval strength then existing among the major powers. Sending State Department counselor J. Reuben Clark to the Navy Department with a request for charts based on this principle, he asked the Navy for its advice. On its recommendation Hughes settled on capital ships tonnage as the key element and decided to try to limit auxiliary craft by the same ratio. As he said in his opening address at the Naval Conference, the naval experts had advised the American delegation "that the tonnage of capital ships may fairly be taken to measure the relative strength of navies. . . . "[65]

Working from these principles and the detailed information provided by the Navy, Hughes came up with detailed proposals for the destruction of specific vessels then being built by the United States, Japan, and Great Britain. President Harding approved them; then Hughes distributed his statement to the other members of the American delegation. In thus shifting the ground of the discussion from naval needs to the maintenance of the status quo, Hughes had found the one formula that assured the success of the conference. As his secretary later observed, had we "left the solid ground of what each country had and entered upon the consideration of what in the opinion of technical advisors was necessary or advisable no agreement would be possible."[66]

Hughes declared in his opening speech that the time for action had come. He then proceeded to outline a program for the limitation of capital ships, giving tonnage figures, specifying the vessels to be kept by each power, those to be scrapped. In less than fifteen minutes, as one British observer noted, he sank more ships "than all the admirals of the world have sunk in the cycle of centuries."[67] When he had finished, the galleries stood up and cheered for a solid ten minutes and newsmen went around smiling, slapping each other on the back. That weekend newspapers in London, Tokyo, and Paris spoke of the miracle of Washington. The *New York Times* correspondent in Rome reported that Hughes's speech was generally perceived as a "spectacularly clever move." Any power that was reluctant to follow his lead "would be placed in a bad light before the whole world."[68]

Hughes's political sophistication was even more apparent in the management of the subsequent talks. The U.S. delegation included Lodge, chairman of the Senate Foreign Relations Committee, and Underwood, leader of the committee's Democratic minority. This guaranteed bipartisan support for the conference and it eliminated the more dogmatic Borah whose presence on the delegation would have complicated the negotiations. Military men who might have resisted the cutbacks of some of their favorite weapons Hughes silenced by assigning them to advisory groups working with the official U.S. delegation. Hughes limited the participation in each of the several discussions going on in Washington to those whose interests were directly involved; all meetings were conducted in secret. As Hughes knew, the process of horsetrading would have faltered under world press scrutiny. Moreover, Hughes made the necessary concessions to secure agreements. After much debate, he allowed the Japanese to keep the *Mutsu* in exchange for the American completion of two battleships of the West Virginia class. Britain would be permitted to build two super-dreadnoughts authorized the preceding summer. To maintain the original ratio, certain light ships retained under the original proposal would now be scrapped.

Hughes made his most important concession without much debate. Early in December, Baron Kato, the head of the Japanese delegation, declared that Japan might accept the short end of the 5-5-3 ratio if the United States and Britain would agree to maintain the status quo with respect to fortifications in their Pacific possessions. On December 12 Hughes accepted this condition, although he exempted Hawaii from the arrangement. In the resulting Article 19 of the Five Power Treaty, the United States, Britain, and Japan agreed to the status quo at the time of the signing of the treaty with regard to fortifications and naval bases.

Every attempt to extend the capital ship ratio to auxiliary craft failed. Hughes made a direct appeal to Britain over the head of the French delegation to obtain French approval of a capital ship ratio of 1.75 for France. Troubled by France's decline as a naval power and their exclusion from the Big Three naval discussions at the State Department, the French insisted on maintaining such a high submarine capability that agreement on auxiliary craft became impossible. Italy eventually agreed to the 1.75 ratio as well. The Five Power Treaty, signed on February 6, 1922, was substantially based on Hughes's initial proposals. It provided for a ten-year naval holiday from the construction of capital ships (with limited replacement of superannuated ships from then until 1936). It marked for scrapping certain other ships already built or in the process of being built. The signatories were to arrive ultimately at a capital ship ratio of 5-5-3-1.75-1.75. To make the limitation meaningful, tonnage and gun-caliber limitations were added. Hughes believed that the Five Power Treaty reduced tensions among the big powers. "The effect of the limitation," he said, " . . . was to give a practical assurance to each Power against invasion by the other. It was a demonstration of nonaggressive purposes and thus it furnished in an important sphere an illustration of the practicality of avoiding provocative armament."[69]

VII

Although he seldom spoke of the balance of power, Hughes's policies at the Washington Conference made it clear that one of his major goals was to check Japanese ambition in the Far East. In this regard the Four Power Treaty of Washington was his most important achievement. Since the spring of 1920 various American officials, including Hughes, had opposed the renewal of the Anglo-Japanese alliance of 1902. London's support of Japanese claims to Shantung at the Paris Peace Conference and its acquiescence in Japan's occupation of Siberia thereafter had fed the concern that the alliance was but a shield for Japanese expansion. Hughes warned the British ambassador, Sir Auckland Geddes, in June, 1921, that the alliance would continue to feed the more extremist ambitions of Japan in the Far East. Thus any U.S. protest against new Japanese adventures, continued Hughes, could lead to a conflict between the United States and Great Britain.[70]

With considerable ingenuity Hughes fashioned a way for the British to escape their alliance without unduly alarming Japan. The bipartite arrangement between those countries would be replaced by an agreement among Britain, Japan, and the United States. The three powers invited France, sensitive because of its exclusion from the naval talks, to join the new political arrangement. These four countries agreed to respect each others' rights to their insular possessions and dominions in the Pacific and, in the event of a threat to the Pacific possessions of any one of them, to consult on the matter of a proper response. Hughes, in effect, exchanged the recognition of Japan's acquisition of the German islands in the northern Pacific for the dissolution of the Anglo-Japanese alliance and a Japanese promise not to expand further.

To prop up a weak China against a strong Japan and protect American interests in China Hughes retreated to the traditional policies of the United States in support of the Open Door and the territorial integrity of China. In the Nine Power Treaty of February 6, 1922, Hughes secured the international recognition of these principles in a multilateral treaty. Article III went beyond any previous commitment in specifying the meaning of the Open Door. It forbade any move which would give a foreign country superiority of opportunity in Chinese territory.[71] In essence the Four Power Treaty and the Nine Power Pact were attempts to freeze, through international agreements, the new status quo in the Far East.

In other negotiations not formally part of the Washington Conference, Hughes secured Japanese promises to retreat from Chinese and Russian territories occupied during and immediately after the war.[72] Acting as a mediator between Japan and China, Hughes played an important role in securing the Sino-Japanese treaty on Shantung, signed February 4, 1922. The Japanese agreed to withdraw from Shantung and sell the formerly German-owned railroad. As the protector of Russian interests at the conference, Hughes also secured a Japanese promise to evacuate Russian Siberia and Northern Sakhalin. On the question of Manchuria, however, Hughes gained only minor concessions. The Japanese agreed to open their railway-loan options to the International Consortium and to withdraw the more noxious of their arrangements with China, including the use of military advisors in South Manchuria.

Hughes's achievements at Washington were far less significant than they first appeared. Although the U.S. delegation claimed victory for the Open Door in China, no such thing had actually occurred. In the Nine Power Pact Hughes did not secure any international commitment to oversee the spheres of influence already created. None of the powers with concessions in China were eager to have their affairs examined. Moreover, the abstract commitment to the territorial integrity of China did not include any substantial agreements to end those constraints on the exercise of China's fiscal and judicial functions which undermined its independence. The Nine Power Treaty did permit an increase in the Chinese treaty tariff and called for a special conference to abolish international transit taxes in China. Other resolutions called for the abolition of foreign post offices and for restrictions on foreign-owned radio stations in China. But the post offices to be abolished did not include those operating with China's consent or in leased territories. All Chinese proposals for concrete arrangements to end extraterritorial rights and the international control of the Chinese tariff were ignored. The United States itself would not relinquish its extraterritorial rights in China until World War II. Most important, the status quo agreed upon at Washington was not buttressed by any countervailing power which could guarantee its perpetuation over time. During the negotiation of the Four Power Pact Hughes insisted that the Anglo-Japanese alliance would not be expanded into a tripartite alliance. Thus the Four Power Treaty carried no commitments for the United States or Britain to fight should

Japan expand contrary to the status quo agreed upon in that treaty.

Finally, the 5:3 naval ratio, added to the non-fortification of the western Pacific, froze Japan's naval supremacy in the western Pacific. Although the Five Power Treaty would perpetuate U.S. control over the approaches to North America and the Panama Canal, it left Japan in virtual control of the Pacific west of Hawaii and as far south as the equator. As Admiral H. S. Knapp declared shortly after the closing of the Washington Conference, Article 19 "fatally impairs for the United States the 5 to 3 ratio of floating strength with Japan insofar as the western Pacific is concerned. The United States had yielded the possibility of naval equality in that region."[73]

Such criticisms that the United States gave away naval superiority to Japan overlooked the realistic alternatives open to the United States in 1922. No agreement would have been possible had the United States insisted on better terms for itself. As Hughes pointed out, it would have been "impossible to terminate competition in naval armaments if the Powers were to condition their agreement upon the advantages they hoped to gain in the competition itself."[74] Even the non-fortification agreement was no give-away, given the attitude of Congress. "Fortunately," Hughes noted; "at the Washington Conference the American delegation had among its members leaders of both parties in the Senate who could, and did, advise with confidence that Congress would not consent to the fortification of the Philippines and Guam."[75] Subsequently the United States, contrary to Hughes's advice, failed to build its naval strength to the level permitted by the Washington treaties. Between 1922 and 1929 the United States built or provided for only eleven ships as contrasted to 74 for Britain, 125 for Japan, and 119 for France.

Thus the only apparent guarantees of the status quo were the relatively specific terms of the treaties and the international cordiality which the Washington arrangements created. As Hughes stated in his official report of the conference, the Open Door and the territorial integrity of China had not been properly guaranteed in the past by binding international agreement.[76] The value of the Nine Power Treaty, as he said in a later address, was that it took the postulates of American foreign policy out of the unsatisfactory form of diplomatic notes and incorporated them into a solemn international engagement, signed by the nine powers especially interested in the Far East.[77] The major guarantee behind such specific obligations was to be found in the concern of most countries for their reputations as law abiding members of the community of nations.[78]

For the moment the Washington Conference seemed a huge success. The Senate approved the treaties, with one exception, either unanimously or with only one dissenting vote. It approved the Four Power Treaty by a vote of 67 to 27, four votes over the two-thirds needed. In Japan, after the ratification, a moderate government headed by Baron Kato followed through on its commitments. It scrapped capital ships and withdrew Japanese troops from Shantung and Siberia. Even the negative potential of Japanese exclusion under the U.S. Immigration Act of 1924 became muted as Baron Shidehara, the Japanese Foreign Minister, worked with Hughes to limit the effect.[79] Hughes could not have done more. He could not have perpetuated the moderate government of Japan through international agreement, and Congress would not have supported the measures required to curtail Japanese ambitions in the Pacific.

VIII

When Hughes came to office in 1921 American marines were stationed in Nicaragua, Haiti, and Santo Domingo—the consequence of earlier interventions under Presidents William Howard Taft and Woodrow Wilson. Although Hughes justified such interventions in the Caribbean, he believed that they should end as soon as their purposes had been served. As secretary of state he negotiated agreements with Santo Domingo and Nicaragua for the withdrawal of U.S. forces from their soil. But withdrawal from Haiti, he said, would be the occasion for revolution and bloodshed. To protect the property rights of American citizens in Mexico, Hughes did not even consider military intervention. Wilson's military incursions into that country had shown the limits of such action against large countries caught up in nationalistic and revolutionary fervor. But Hughes did take a rigid stance in his use of U.S. recognition policies to secure his ends. General Alvaro Obregon, who had secured the presidency of Mexico in 1920, made some informal overtures to the new Harding administration by setting aside some of the more objectionable land decrees and promising that Mexico would not apply the confiscatory clause regarding sub-soil rights in the 1917 constitution retroactively. Hughes insisted that guarantees for the protection of American property rights would need to be embodied in a treaty. So Obregon, who would have undermined himself politically by such an arrangement, cultivated business and congressional leaders in the United States through a series of private intermediaries. Finally, through the efforts of an oil man based in Mexico and President Harding himself, the State Department agreed to send a commission to Mexico City to negotiate a settlement.[80] The Bucareli Agreements, signed on August 13, 1924, gave the United States most of the assurances Hughes had sought earlier. In accord with Obregon's wishes, they took the form of an executive agreement rather than a treaty.[81]

Outside the Caribbean and Central America, Hughes turned to the Monroe Doctrine and Pan American principles for policy guidance. It was not always clear, however, how these principles fit the exigencies of his time. Several Latin America republics had joined the League of Nations by 1921. As soon as the League was in business, Peru, Bolivia, and Panama asked for assistance in the settlement of inter-American disputes. The Monroe Doctrine had never prevented European powers from offering their services on behalf of peaceful settlements in the New World. But U.S. sensitivities to such offers had been intensified by the recent debates over the League. Hughes himself had offered a special reservation to U.S. adherence to the Covenant which would have exempted the American system from the political jurisdiction of the League under Article XIX, providing for the peaceful settlement of disputes. Under pressure the League backed off from dealing with inter-American affairs. It rejected the appeals of Panama, Peru, and Bolivia.

As an alternative to League action Hughes offered the good offices of the United States in solving these inter-American disputes. On his second day in the State Department he called upon Panama and Costa Rica to cease their fight in the Coto district, and dispatched two warships to the area to emphasize his request. When Panama continued to remain in the disputed territory, in opposition to earlier arbitral awards, Hughes warned Panama that the United States might take steps necessary to implement the awards.[82] Panama retreated under this threat of force. Later Hughes's services helped to resolve disputes among Honduras, Nicaragua, and El Salvador in 1922 and among Brazil, Colombia, and Peru in 1925.

In the Peru-Chile controversy over the desert provinces of Tacna-Arica Hughes play a central, if somewhat less productive role. On

July 29, 1922, at a meeting in Washington that Hughes had initiated, the two countries agreed to permit the President of the United States to arbitrate the disagreement. The award emerged finally on March 4, 1925, Hughes's last day in the State Department. Hughes, in the name of the President, decided that the Treaty of Ancon (1883), which had provided for a plebiscite after ten years, had set no outside time limits. Hughes favored a plebiscite and, to administer it, gained a plebiscitary commission. The elections were never held; the commission's chairman reported in 1926 that suitable conditions for the election did not exist. The issue was finally resolved through a political compromise initiated by the parties to the controversy themselves. Chile and Peru suggested to President Herbert Hoover in 1929 that Tacna-Arica be divided between them. Peru would obtain the northern-most province of Tacna where most of its citizens resided. Chile would retain Arica to which most of its nationals had migrated. With the good offices of the United States the two countries that year worked out details of the partition.[83] Hughes had made the mistake of trying to arbitrate a controversy that required a political resolution.

To promote the peaceful settlement of conflicts in the Americas Hughes not only attempted to keep Europe out of the American sphere but also sought to breathe life into the principles of hemispheric unity which he associated with Pan Americanism. On several occasions Hughes went out of his way to act on these principles. In September, 1923, he attended the centennary celebration of Brazil's independence at Rio de Janeiro. He helped to secure passage in 1921 of the treaty negotiated by Wilson to pay Colombia $25 million for the Panama Canal Zone which Theodore Roosevelt had appropriated in 1903.[84] Hughes demonstrated his goodwill toward Cuba when he brushed off the Isle of Pines Treaty which had been pigeonholed for years. The treaty, which formally renounced all American claims to the island despite the property interests of U.S. citizens, was formally approved in March, 1924.

Overall, Hughes's resort to the traditional policies of the United States in the New World created no major problems. Except for the task of defining Latin America's relationship to the League, the American system remained much as it had been prior to the Great War. The traditional policies seemed to serve U.S. interests very well. Washington restricted its military intervention to the Caribbean where U.S. concerns were paramount and its capacity to influence high. For the stronger, more remote republics of South America, the general principles of the Monroe Doctrine and Pan

Americanism would suffice. Emphasizing the promotion of peace and stability through the good offices of third parties, the United States often furthered the ideals of Pan American cooperation even as it maintained a high level of political stability in the Western Hemisphere.

Perhaps Hughes's approach to Latin America bred too much complacency. The predominance of the United States in the hemisphere shielded it from the many disabilities of the Latin American states, the ultimate sources of regional turmoil and tension. In its determination to resolve Latin American disputes to its satisfaction the United States faced no equal competitors. The Pan American Union enabled the country to exercise its influence in accordance with legal forms. In short, the United States secured its goals in the Western Hemisphere without political alliances, the risk of major wars, or defiance of international law. Yet for Hughes the peace of the hemisphere resulted not from the hegemony of the United States but from its commitment to peace, order, and other aspects of the common good.

IX

Hughes's attitude toward Mexico's Obregon government demonstrated his rigidity when protecting property rights. Again his posture toward the new Soviet government in Russia helped to freeze the United States into a position which eliminated any formal dealings with that foreign power for over a decade. At a cabinet meeting on March 25, 1921, Hughes, along with Hoover and Treasury Secretary Andrew Mellon, argued that the administration should reject the recent appeal from the Soviet Union calling for trade relations. Later that afternoon Hughes announced that the United States would consider recognition of the Bolshevik regime when it recognized the rights of private property, free labor, and the sanctity of contract. In 1922 he dismissed out of hand the Soviet government's suggestion at the Geneva Conference that it was willing to recognize the principles of the United States but without any general guarantees. In a letter to Samuel Gompers on July 19, 1923, Hughes explained that the Soviet government, in repudiating Russia's public debt and confiscating the property of American citizens, had rejected those standards which made official intercourse possible. His most important concern, however, was the "conclusive evidence" that the Russians had "not given up their original purpose of destroying existing governments wherever they can do so throughout the world."[85]

In his refusal to deal with the Soviet government Hughes was more inflexible than others in his political milieu. On May 12, 1922, Borah introduced a resolution in the Senate which favored U.S. recognition of the Soviet Union. Hoover, as a result of his relief work in Russia and his close contacts with American business leaders who wanted access to the Russian market, sought to encourage trade with the Soviet Union.[86] Even Harding was more open than Hughes. Shortly before his death in the summer of 1923, the President had made arrangements to send former secretary of the interior Albert Fall (who would come to favor recognition) and liberal banker Raymond Robins (who already favored trade and recognition) to Russia to investigate conditions there. Indeed, as biographer Robert Murray states, Harding might have followed Hoover's lead on Soviet matters had he lived. In all probability, however, he would have retained U.S. nonrecognition policy because of Hughes's irrevocable commitment to it.[87]

Again Hughes's rigidity was evident in his use of the open door policy in the Middle East where he tried to open up the oil fields to American companies. London and Paris at the end of the war had divided the former territory of the Ottoman Turks between themselves and at the San Remo Conference seemed to be creating an oil monopoly in the form of the Turkish Petroleum Company. This would close access to the Mesopotamian oil fields. Hughes protested the San Remo agreements as contrary to the principle of the open door. He rejected subsequent attempts by the British at the First and Second Lausanne conferences to win U.S. recognition of the Turkish Petroleum Company in return for limited participation of American companies. But American oil companies were more interested in securing entree to the Middle Eastern oil fields than in upholding the principle of the open door. By the fall of 1923 they had worked out an arrangement which would give them a share of the Turkish Petroleum Company and open up some lots to competitive bids for all outsiders. Hughes, whose intransigence at the Second Lausanne Conference had disrupted an earlier agreement with the American oil companies, realized that he would need to give way or the American companies might drop out altogether and leave the fields to the British and French. He dropped his insistence on the full recognition of the open door principle and informed the American group that he would provide diplomatic support for the arrangements they had completed.[88] Hughes's lack of flexibility in these areas of policy reflected his views about the nature of justice and the world order. For him these conflicts were covered by rules which had behind them the reason, sentiment, and the common interest of all civilized nations. He saw revolutionary tactics or selfish interests as transient violations of a historical trend which would enhance over time the respect for private property on which trade, commerce, investment, and the wellbeing of the world was based.

Hughes's views of world order, as the foregoing suggests, led him to some policies which realistically promoted U.S. national interests, to some which did not. He never shared the enthusiasms of many of his peers for the development of collective security or the outlawry of war because he realized that fundamental national interests often conflicted and that self help was the ultimate means for protecting basic interests. He fostered projects of international adjudication, arbitration, and the codification of international law which amounted to little at the end. He was motivated by a simple faith that history guaranteed the progressive development of the world's peace sentiment and its embodiment in new legal forms.

Looking to tradition for the definition of American national interests, he was on relatively safe ground where the objective situation of the United States had not succumbed to the impact of the Great War. In Latin America, for example, the traditional hegemony of the United States still held. But the decline of British power had revolutionized the objective situation of the United States vis-a-vis Europe. Hughes knew that the country had to deal with Europe to protect its loans and exports and to promote its humanitarian interests; he fashioned programs that would paper over Europe's challenges for a time. Yet like many others of his generation he did not see that U.S. security rested on the European balance of power and that the nation could not choose to be interested or not, depending on how well the European powers behaved. In the Far East he combined the traditional American commitment to the Open Door and the territorial integrity of China with an instinctive appreciation of the need to check Japan. He demonstrated some skill and initiative in negotiating an overall agreement for the Far East; he could neither explain the need for nor fashion a military balance in the Pacific which could check a more expansionist Japanese government.

Hughes failed to see the extent to which order was based on power. Always equating the predominance of the United States in the New World with a commitment to reason and perceived common interests, Hughes contributed to the arrogance which created problems between the United States and the rest of the world. Refusing to recognize the national interest as the consequence, at least in part, of the power setting in which a nation might find itself, Hughes never questioned the validity of the traditional definitions of that interest. Because he assumed that all rational change takes place slowly, he did not realize that basic changes in technology, politics, and interests may require radical changes in policy. This is not to say that Hughes could have initiated a substantially different course of action in most regions of the world. Indeed, it required great political skill for him to accomplish as much as he did, given the attitudes of the irreconcilables in the Senate and the general state of American opinion. Because his world view was so in tune with the convictions of most of his contemporaries, he seldom faced the problem of being too advanced for his day. To understand Hughes is to understand the United States as it attempted to discover its proper post-Versailles role as the world's leading power.

NOTES

1. For a description of the free security system see C. Vann Woodward, "The Age of Reinterpretation," *American Historical Review,* LXVI (October 1960), pp. 1-8.
2. Harding quoted by Charles Michelson in the *New York World,* February 20, 1921; New York *Call,* February 20, 1921. See also Betty Glad, *Charles Evans Hughes and the Illusions of Innocence: A Study in American Diplomacy* (Urbana, Ill., 1966), pp. 132-33.
3. Hughes, Biographical Notes, pp. 253a, 253b, Charles Evens Hughes Papers, Library of Congress. Cited hereafter as Hughes, Notes.
4. Herbert Hoover, *Memoirs* (New York, 1952), II, 36; Francis Russell, *The Shadow of Blooming Grove: Warren G. Harding in His Times* (New York, 1968), pp. 447-49.
5. Hughes, Notes, p. 254.
6. *Ibid.,* p. 134.
7. For a more extensive treatment of Hughes's education and social philosophy see Glad, *Charles Evans Hughes,* pp. 21-47, 87-95.
8. "The Monroe Doctrine—A Review: Its Relations to American Foreign Policy in the Twentieth Century," *Pathway of Peace: Representative Addresses Delivered During His Term as Secretary of State, 1921-1925* (New York, 1925), p. 142. Article cited hereafter as "The Monroe Doctrine"; the book as *Pathway.*

9. *Ibid.,* pp. 142-43, 151-52.
10. Quoted in Henry C. Beerits, "The Separate Peace with Germany, the League, and the Permanent Court of International Justice," p. 45, in Hughes Papers. This paper is part of a series prepared in 1933-1934 under Hughes's supervision which summarize his career and provide a guide to his Papers. They are scattered through Hughes's papers (Boxes 165-180). They will be cited hereafter as Beerits, with title of the particular memorandum following.
11. "A Better Understanding—Support of the Dawes Plan," *Pathway,* p. 106.
12. "The Monroe Doctrine," *ibid.,* pp. 143, 153; "Observations on the Monroe Doctrine," *ibid.,* 140.
13. "The Monroe Doctrine," *ibid.,* pp. 153-54.
14. "Observations on the Monroe Doctrine, *ibid.,* pp. 120-24.
15. *Ibid.,* p. 124; Charles Evans Hughes, *Our Relations to the Nations of the Western Hemisphere* (Princeton, N.J., 1928), p. 81.
16. "Observations on the Monroe Doctrine," *Pathway,* pp. 120-21.
17. *Ibid.,* pp. 122-27; Hughes, *Our Relations to the Nations of the Western Hemisphere,* pp. 53, 81.
18. *Ibid.,* pp. 81, 83; "The Monroe Doctrine," *Pathway,* p. 162.
19. "Observations on the Monroe Doctrine," *ibid.,* pp. 128-37; "Latin American Relations," *ibid.,* 164-65.
20. *Ibid.,* 165.
21. "The Outlook for Pan-Americanism," American Society of International Law, *Proceedings,* XXII (1928), pp. 2-3.
22. *Ibid.,* p. 2; "On the Codification of International Law," *Pathway,* p. 170.
23. *Ibid.,* 170; see also "Latin American Relations," *ibid.,* p. 168.
24. Abstract of Statement of Charles Evans Hughes, Secretary of State, Before the Committee on Foreign Relations of the Senate in Relation to Pending Commercial Treaty with Germany, Hughes Papers, Box 172. For a discussion of Hughes's recognition policies in historical context see Eugene P. Trani and David L. Wilson, *The Presidency of Warren G. Harding* (Lawrence, Kansas, 1977), pp. 113-15; also "Russia," *Pathway,* p. 62; "Some Aspects of the Work of the Department of State," *ibid.,* pp. 254-55.
25. "The Monroe Doctrine," *ibid.,* 142.
26. "The Development of International Law," American Society of International Law, *Proceedings,* XIX (1925), p. 35. See also "Pathway to Peace," *Pathway,* p. 3.
27. "The Development of International Law," pp. 4-5; "Pathway to Peace," *Pathway,* pp. 6-7.
28. *Ibid.,* pp. 6-8.
29. *Ibid.,* pp. 11-14.
30. "Some Observations on Recent Events," American Society of Inter-

national Law, *Proceedings,* XX (1926), pp. 6, 14; "The Development of International Law," p. 1.

31. "Pan American Peace," *Yale Review,* XVIII (June 1929), pp. 646-48.
32. "Some Observations on Recent Events," pp. 6-9; Hughes, *Our Relations to the Nations of the Western Hemisphere,* pp. 91-112.
33. J. L. Brierly, *The Law of Nations* (4th ed., Oxford, 1949), pp. 268-69.
34. "The Development of International Law," pp. 5-8. See also "The Future of International Law," Academy of Political Science in the City of New York, *Proceedings,* VII (May 28, 1917), pp. 2-3, 6-7; "Institutions of Peace," American Society of International Law, *Proceedings,* XXIII (1929), pp. 2-3.
35. "Some Observations on Recent Events," p. 13.
36. "Possible Gains," American Society of International Law, *Proceedings,* XXI (1927), pp. 8, 11.
37. *Ibid.,* pp. 9-13
38. For differences between Hughes and Hoover see Trani and Wilson, *Presidency of Harding,* pp. 115-16, 124-25, 137; Joan Hoff Wilson, *American Business and Foreign Policy, 1920-1933* (Lexington, 1971), p. 163.
39. Penrose quoted in the *New York World,* February 22, 1921. See also Glad, *Charles Evans Hughes,* p. 140.
40. For Hughes's political naivete as governor see Robert T. Wesser, *Charles Evans Hughes: Politics and Reform in New York, 1905-10* (Ithaca, N.Y., 1967), p. 343. See also Glad, *Charles Evans Hughes,* pp. 66-86; Clinton Gilbert, *The Mirrors of Washington* (New York, 1921), pp. 82-83.
41. Hughes to George Wickersham, March 28, 1923, quoted in Beerits, "The Separate Peace," pp. 18-18a.
42. Hughes to A. Lawrence Lowell, July 20, 1922, Hughes Papers.
43. Hughes to George Wickersham, March 28, 1923, Beerits, "The Separate Peace," pp. 18-18a.
44. Glad, *Charles Evans Hughes,* pp. 167-72.
45. *New York Times,* March 30, 1919.
46. Hughes to Senator Hale, July 24, 1919, Hughes Papers.
47. *New York Times,* April 13, 1924.
48. Thomas A. Bailey, *A Diplomatic History of the American People* (3rd ed., New York, 1944), p. 682.
49. *New York Times,* April 16, 1924.
50. Hughes, Notes, p. 310. See also Glad, *Charles Evans Hughes,* pp. 180-81.
51. Hughes to Warren Harding, February 17, 24, 1923, *Foreign Relations of the United States, 1923,* I (Washington 1938), pp. 14, 17-18.
52. Hughes to Calvin Coolidge, November 5, 1925, Hughes Papers.
53. "Some Observations on Recent Events," pp. 11-12.
54. "Pan American Peace," pp. 653-59.

55. Beerits, "The Separate Peace," pp. 20, 22.
56. *Ibid.,* 20a.
57. *New York Times,* August 3, 1922.
58. "Some Aspects of our Foreign Policy," *Pathway,* pp. 54-55.
59. Beerits, "The Dawes Plan," p. 9.
60. See Glad, *Charles Evans Hughes,* pp. 226-29.
61. Quoted in *ibid.,* p. 235.
62. Hughes, Notes, p. 367.
63. "A Better Understanding—Support of the Dawes Plan," *Pathway,* p. 108.
64. Beerits, "Treaty for the Limitation of Naval Armament," pp. 1, 7-8.
65. "Limitation of Naval Armament," *Pathway,* pp. 26-27.
66. Beerits, "Treaty for the Limitation of Naval Armament," pp. 4-5.
67. "Limitation of Naval Armament," *Pathway,* p. 25; Bailey, *Diplomatic History of the American People,* p. 691.
68. *New York Times,* November 13, 15, 1921.
69. "Possible Gains," p. 11.
70. Hughes memorandum of interview with Auckland Geddes, June 23, 1921, *Foreign Relations, 1921,* II (Washington 1936), pp. 314-16.
71. U.S. Congress, Senate, *Conference on the Limitation of Armaments, 67th Cong., 2d Sess., Senate Document 126,* p. 621. Hereafter cited as *Conference.*
72. For details on Japan's involvement in the Shantung Peninsula, Manchuria, and Siberia see Yamato Ichihashi, *The Washington Conference and After* (Stanford, Cal., 1928).
73. Quote taken from American Society of International Law, *Proceedings,* XVI (1922), p. 19.
74. *Conference,* pp. 798-99.
75. "Possible Gains," p. 10. For a view that the United States suffered later in the Far East primarily because of a lack of follow-up on the processes started at the Washington Conference see Thomas H. Buckley, *The United States and the Washington Conference, 1921-1922* (Knoxville, Tenn., 1970), p. 100. For an analysis of the popular press and the evidence that there was still some expectation of war between Japan and the United States in the 1920s see Shöichi Saeki in Akira Iriye, ed., *Mutual Images: Essays in American-Japanese Relations* (Cambridge, Mass., 1975), p. 108.
76. *Conference,* p. 820.
77. "The Monroe Doctrine," *Pathway,* p. 148.
78. "Possible Gains," p. 6.
79. Foster Rhea Dulles, *Forty Years of American-Japanese Relations* (New York, 1937), p. 183.
80. "Some Observations on the Monroe Doctrine," *Pathway,* pp. 128-37, passim. For details of American influence in the Caribbean during the early 1920s see Glad, *Charles Evans Hughes,* pp. 38-49. Hughes

also blocked U.S. loans to Mexico in an attempt to force the Mexicans to sign the treaty he wanted. See Trani and Wilson, *Presidency of Harding,* p. 130. For Harding's role in the negotiations with Mexico see Kenneth J. Grieb, *The Latin American Policy of Warren G. Harding* (Fort Worth, Texas, 1976), pp. 132-38; Robert K. Murray, *The Harding Era: Warren G. Harding and His Administration* (Minneapolis, 1969), pp. 328-31. For Harding's instructions to the delegates see Trani and Wilson, *Presidency of Harding,* p. 132.

81. Murray, *The Harding Era,* p. 329.
82. Beerits, "Latin American Boundary Disputes," pp. 1-27.
83. For details on the Tacna-Arica arbitration see Glad, *Charles Evans Hughes,* pp. 203-05.
84. The push to approve the treaty with Colombia was motivated to a great extent by the desire to open the rich Colombian oil fields to American investors, as Senator Lodge argued in defense of the treaty. See John D. Hicks, *Republican Ascendancy, 1921-1933* (New York, 1960), p. 30.
85. Hughes to Samuel Gompers, July 19, 1923, *Foreign Relations, 1923,* II (Washington 1938), pp. 760-64. For an overview of Hughes's recognition policies vis-a-vis Russia see Trani and Wilson, *Presidency of Harding,* p. 120; Murray, *The Harding Era,* pp. 349-54.
86. For the disagreements between Hughes and Hoover on trading with the Russians see Trani and Wilson, *Presidency of Harding,* pp. 121, 124-25; Murray, *The Harding Era,* p. 353.
87. Trani and Wilson, *Presidency of Harding,* p. 126; Murray, *The Harding Era,* p. 354.
88. For an overall view of Hughes's use of the open door policy to open up the Middle Eastern oil fields see Wilson, *American Business and Foreign Policy,* pp. 188-97; Murray, *The Harding Era,* pp. 354-60; Glad, *Charles Evans Hughes,* pp. 308-11.

6

CORDELL HULL AND AMERICAN INTERWAR INTERNATIONALISM

Richard Dean Burns

"I was vain enough to believe I was not a novice in foreign affairs when I entered the State Department," Cordell Hull reflected in his *Memoirs*. "I had some definite ideas on what our foreign policy should be in the vital fields." Then he added, "I believed I had in mind the methods to make these ideas work."[1] Hull would discover, however, that establishing goals was much easier than developing the means for accomplishing them. On February 24, 1933, three days after President-elect Franklin D. Roosevelt announced his appointment as secretary of state, Hull outlined his views on the general state of world affairs:

> There has been . . . a general letting down since the war of moral and political standards by both peoples and governments. There should be no laxity on the part of this nation or any other nation in the observation of both the letter and spirit of treaties and international good faith.
>
> There should be sane and realistic international co-operation, keeping in mind our traditions and our Constitution, to aid in preserving the peace of the world. This policy is vital. . . .
>
> The success of the principal foreign policies of the incoming administration, therefore, will be determined

> by the extent of its aid in restoring world commerce . . . and its aid in maintaining world peace under the fundamental policy of right and justice.[2]

As this statement suggests, Hull would attempt to resolve the burgeoning challenges of world affairs by building an international consensus which favored Wilsonian internationalism, with its emphasis on peaceful change and unhampered world trade. In practice he would attempt to maintain the peace by inviting all nations to follow the treaty-abiding principles of the United States.

Lacking diplomatic experience, Hull brought to the State Department philosophical convictions garnered from his legal training and rural Tennessee background, and political instincts honed by his years as a jurist and legislator. He liked to view himself, politically and economically, as a Gladstone liberal, and he accepted without reservation the principles of Jefferson and Jackson, to which he added, selectively, those of Locke, Milton, Pitt, and Burke. This intellectual "melting pot" emphasized the typical nineteenth century belief in the dignity and freedom of the individual to follow the bent of self-interest within the framework of a natural, self-regulating society. "I believed that the final achievement of the five hundred years' struggle for Anglo-Saxon liberty," Hull wrote in his *Memoirs,* "was written in these axioms and principles [of Jefferson and Jackson]. . . . They were to carry a strong appeal to me during my years in Congress and in the State Department."[3] Hull's exposure during World War I to Wilsonian internationalism gave form to his ideals and led to his view that international organization, ethics, and law were essential for attaining and maintaining world peace.

In true Wilsonian spirit, Hull railed against any diplomacy which defined policy in terms of national self-interest and which employed the traditional balance of power approach to resolve international disputes. "I had formed the firm conclusion," he noted in his *Memoirs,*

> that the balance of power had to be replaced by an association of nations. Federations of nations had been organized in Europe ostensibly to protect themselves against other federations, but in reality, in the case of Germany, to advance their military principles of aggression. If felt that these federations, otherwise known as alliances, and their basic idea of balance of power had

> to give way in favor of a confederation of nations that would maintain the peace.

As early as World War I Hull came to reject the use of force in support of foreign policy objectives. He favored the limitation and reduction of *all* military forces, but he did not oppose American rearmament during the 1930s in the face of German, Italian, and Japanese aggression. He recognized "the necessity for maintaining armed forces adequate for national security," while, as a matter of principle, he emphasized noninterventionism and self-restraint.[4]

Again and again, as secretary of state, Hull stressed his conviction that the world was a community of nations which, in order to live together in peace, must recognize and respect international standards of conduct. "No nation," he told the American Society of International Law in April, 1933,

> was sufficient unto itself. The normal life of a nation, no less than that of an individual, is one of association with others. If the nations must depend, one upon the other, in the normal development of their social, intellectual, financial, and political well-being, they, of necessity, must do so in accordance with certain standards of conduct which we may term international ethics. By this we mean honesty of purpose, frankness of expression, and a proper regard for the rights of others as members of the great family of nations.[5]

Hull insisted on using his secretaryship as a pulpit from which to preach this view of the worth of international law and ethics in shaping a peaceful, thriving world. At the heart of these principles, he noted on July 16, 1937, in direct response to the Japanese assault on China following the Marco Polo Bridge incident, lay

> national and international self-restraint; abstinence by all nations from use of force in pursuit of policy and from interference in the internal affairs of other nations; adjustment of international problems by peaceful negotiations and agreement; faithful observance of international agreements; modification of treaties, when necessary, by orderly processes in a spirit of mutual helpfulness and accommodation; respect by all nations for the rights of others and performance of established obligations; revitalizing and strengthening of international law; eco-

> nomic security and stability the world over; . . . [and] limitation and reduction of armaments.[6]

Hull constantly reiterated these principles in his meetings with diplomatic representatives from recalitrant nations, especially Germany, Japan, and the Soviet Union. His memorandums of these meetings frequently began: "Today I preached to the Soviet ambassador" or "the Japanese ambassador," or "I gave him a sermon he won't forget."[7] When the Portuguese government objected to this "habit of entrusting the solution of grave problems to vague formulae," Hull was peeved. "I never lost an opportunity, in fact, to state and restate these principles in public speeches, statements, diplomatic notes, and conversations with foreign diplomats and visiting statesmen," he proudly wrote. "To me there was nothing vague about them. They were solid, living, all-essential rules. If the world followed them, the world could live at peace forever. If the world ignored them, war would be eternal."[8] Hull never understood that the challenge of his office lay essentially in dealing with governments that did not follow his rules.

Hull entered the State Department certain that a modest amount of American economic and moral initiative could arrest international instability and shore up the fading peaceful climate. Yet by 1933 control of events was passing into other hands which were not interested in a revival of international ethics and law, but rather tended to define their foreign policy issues in terms of national self-interest. Hull's difficulty in adjusting to these new circumstances resulted largely from his addiction to abstract principles and to his prediliction for preaching. As a State Department associate noted in a contemporary opinion of the Secretary:[9]

> [Hull has] . . . a ruminative mind which has pondered long on the economic and political history of the U.S. and on international economics. But one which is unclear outside of this sphere, which had stopped taking ideas from others, and which when confronted with obstacles and difficulties to his good intentions does not analyze them and figure out ways and means of licking them—but preaches merely against them.

Hull's approach, however, reflected more than the tenets of Wilsonian internationalism; his views and policy statements repeatedly stressed a *universalist* focus. That is, he not only rejected American isolationism but also regionalism, bilaterialism, spheres of influence, as well as any special interest or national particularism. Yet if he philosophically and emotionally favored a universalist approach to international settlements, Hull often had to settle for less. Domestic isolationism, New Deal economic nationalism, and the contrary practices of other nations would see to that.

II

In Hull's opinion, prosperity and peace went hand in hand. During the World War, he had pressed for the removal of all economic barriers to achieve "an equality of trade conditions." On February 21, 1919, he directed his fellow Congressmen's attention to the third of President Wilson's Fourteen Points which he believed had been prompted by his suggestions. To achieve permanent peace and friendship of nations, Hull urged that the United States take positive, prompt action on a four-point agenda: (1) steps toward the permanent preservation of the principles of unconditional most-favored-nation treatment; (2) discussion of the maritime rights of noncontraband commerce; (3) discussion of trade barriers and discrimination of various types between nations; and (4) development of treaties incorporating agreements on international trade, finance, [and] industry.[10] European wars of the recent decades, he argued, were attributable chiefly to economic strife, the struggle for trade, colonies, protectorates, and concessions in underdeveloped countries. The elimination of trade discriminations and other barriers, and the unconditional adoption of most-favored-nation agreements in commercial treaties were the first steps toward economic peace and thus political stability. Later he deplored the "failure of the Paris Peace Conference to achieve an international agreement to abandon the more vicious trade practices."[11]

Although Hull entered Congress with a typical Southern Democrat's adversion to protective tariffs, he did not stress the economic foundations of international political stability and world peace during his legislative years. Although he did on several occasions indicate his belief that the major causes of war were economic in nature, his tariff views in 1932 were basically the ones he had held when he entered Congress in 1907.[12] Indeed, in lobbying Congress for passage of the Reciprocal Trade Agreements Program during 1934, Hull largely ignored the foreign policy potential of the program. Before the House committee examining the trade act, he noted that its enactment would not only aid natural restoration of worldwide prosperity, but also would be "the greatest civilizer and peace-maker" ever experienced by the human race. However, when pressed on this point, Hull quickly agreed that the general purpose of the bill was "the welfare of our own people." Asked if the President considered the bill "absolutely necessary as a part of the recovery program," the Secretary replied—employing considerable license—that if Roosevelt did not, "I do not think there would have been the slightest disposition to propose such a measure."[13]

Still, within a year or two after passage of the Trade Program, Hull fervently asserted the Program's potential as a means of perserving world peace. Its scope was enlarged to include the twin objectives of economic well-being and peace. In an interview over the Columbia Broadcasting System on March 9, 1935, Hull told his audience that "on the program of Trade agreements, together with the maintenance of the 'open door' policy which is synonymous with commercial fair play, rests my hope of restoration of world trade and, to a measurable extent, of world peace."[14] On the occasion of affirming the United States-Canadian Trade Agreement, the secretary pointed with pleasure to the fact that while the rest of the world was devoting its major efforts to constructing engines of war, the Americas were showing "the way to a more far-seeing, constructive basis for prosperity and for peace." He saw the treaty as a step in the direction of economic sanity: "It sets an example of what must be done to establish a solid foundation upon which to rebuild a suitable structure of world peace."[15]

The promotion of peace was to Hull the primary objective of American foreign policy. To further this purpose, the secretary insisted that the Trade Agreements Program was "an indispensable part of our broad and comprehensive program designed not only to promote for our nation stable and sustained economic prosperity but also to assure for our nation a condition of durable peace." As he would often state: "Prosperity and peace go hand in hand. To promote one is to promote the other." If the United States desired peace and prosperity, Hull argued, it "should be governed, in [its] relations with other nations, by those fundamental principles of justice, morality, good-will, and friendliness which, in civilized international relationships, underlie order under law *with economic security as its chief foundation.*"[16]

There was, as Professor William Allen has pointed out, "an element of plausibility in Hull's sweeping dicta pertaining to economic forces and the conditions as the motivating influences in most political and social activity." Yet, few scholars would care to endorse these same theories with the assurance that was the secretary's. They would rather accept his conclusion that there had often been, or were, "economic causes" of war, and that by freeing international trade, the United States could make a contribution to the maintenance of peace. To Hull's insistence that foreign trade carried with it civilizing qualities, Professor Allen concluded that if such qualities existed, they surely must be applauded and encouraged; however, "probably few today put much reliance on trade's bringing out the 'goodness' of people." Nor did Allen accept the one-way casual relationship between peace and free trade. He concluded that "it can be convincingly argued that peace is as much a condition for a system of substantially free trade, as the freedom of trade is a necessary condition of peace." But Hull stressed only the latter relationship."[17]

Other critics, especially those from the left, have been less kind. Charles A. Beard, William Appleman Williams, Gabriel Kolko, and Dick Steward have all pointed to the Trade Program's failures in the underdeveloped countries.[18] Hull, they argue, did not understand that the principles of self-determination, mutual gain, and equality of sovereignty would succumb to the vast economic prowess of the American business system. The initial trade agreement negotiated after the passage of the new Trade Program was with Cuba. It was signed on August 24, 1934, but much to Hull's displeasure did not contain the most-favored-nation clause. However, the twenty-seven other agreements—mostly with small nations and nations located in the Western Hemisphere—did include this vital provision. Eventually in the late 1930s England and France joined this fraternity; but Nazi Germany, Italy, and Japan never accepted the Trade Program.[19] Ultimately the program had little influence on the course of international relations in the 1930s.

III

The thunderheads of war building over Europe presented Hull with serious foreign policy dilemmas not to be resolved by preaching or reciprocal trade agreements. The World Disarmament Conference sitting at Geneva was floundering, Adolf Hitler was preparing to rearm and launch a new round of German expanionism, and Benito Mussolini was readying Italy's bid for international respect and empire. At home, congressional isolationists offered little assistance as they pressed ahead with neutrality legislation designed to limit presidential initiatives in foreign affairs and to restrict American involvement in crises abroad.

Hull viewed the collapsing disarmament conference at Geneva with special alarm. He had long considered disarmament to be an indispensable element of peace. Three considerations shaped his approach to the issue: (1) disarmament would prevent arms races and "the exhaustion of nations' material resources"; (2) unrestricted arms buildups "as a rule resulted in war"; and (3) disarmament must be universal.[20] Republican leadership in the 1920s had failed to accomplish much in this direction, he believed, because they had shunned the League of Nations and had bowed to domestic isolationism. Ironically, Hull condemned the Washington naval treaty system—one of the most significant arms control agreements of the century—because it was regional and not universal!

Disarmament aspirations were being thwarted by the quest for security. France's reluctance to accept any significant limits on its army was dictated by a fear of a rearmed Germany. Although French leaders detected considerable domestic dislike for "the burdens of armament," Ambassador Norman H. Davis, the Department's diplomatic trouble-shooter and Hull's long-time friend, noted that they would not agree to an arms reduction treaty without the machinery in place "for collective action if Germany runs amuck." Hitler, meanwhile, had made it quite clear to Davis that Germany would not remain "defenseless" while France and Poland had "a crushing superiority" in armaments. The Chancellor demanded that Versailles treaty restrictions on manpower and weaponary give way to equality.[21]

Isolationist pressures persuaded the Roosevelt administration not to offer any concrete proposals which might allievate France's fears about its security. Nevertheless, Hull announced in February, 1935, that he considered four pillars of a sound "peace" structure to be: "First, the renunciation of war as an instrument of national policy; second, a promise of non-aggression; third, consultation in the event of a threat to peace; and, fourth, noninterference on our part with such measures of constraint as may be brought against a deliberate violator of peace."[22] Already the slim opportunity for stemming the rush to arms had passed. A few weeks later, on March 15, 1935, Hitler renounced the military clauses of the Versailles treaty and began rearming.

Hull saw little that he could do regarding Hitler's decision to rearm Germany, except to preach. While America was not a signatory to the Versailles treaty, he told the press:

> Everybody knows that the United States has always believed that treaties must constitute the foundation on

> which any stable peace structure must rest. All who believe in peaceful settlement of international problems of all kinds have felt increasing concern over the tendency to fail to live up to the letter and spirit of treaties. I believe that the moral influence of the United States and its people must always encourage living up to treaties.[23]

Newspaper headlines lifted Wal Wal, an obscure East African watering hole, to world prominence in early December 1934, when fighting broke out there between Ethiopian and Italian troops. Hull promptly decided that the United States should steer clear of the entire conflict. He cabled the American Chargé in Addis-Ababa "to refrain scrupulously from encouraging" any request from Emperor Haile Selassie for American mediation. The Ethiopian crisis was a League of Nations issue, in Hull's view, and ought to be kept solely in its hands. When the League failed to deal with Ethiopia's plea for assistance and the American government refused to invoke the Kellogg-Briand Pact, some colleagues suggested to Hull that the Pact was dead. This remark prompted an immediate public response from the secretary:

> The Pact of Paris is no less binding now than when it was entered into by the 63 nations that are parties to it. By form and designation it constitutes a treaty by and among those nations. It is a declaration by the governments of the world that they condemn recourse to war for the solution of international controversies, and renounce it as an instrument of national policy in their relations with one another. Furthermore, it is an agreement and a solemn obligation that the settlement or solution of all disputes or conflicts among nations, of whatever nature or of whatever origin shall never be sought except by pacific means.
>
> The United States and the other nations are interested in the maintenance of the pact and the sanctity of the international commitments assumed thereby for the promotion and maintenance of peace among the nations of the world.[24]

These considerations did not prevent Mussolini from ordering Italian troops to move against Ethiopia on October 2, 1935, in an act of open aggression.

At this point FDR quizzed Hull about the "exact language"

under which the Kellogg-Briand Pact could be "invoked," Hull replied that there were "no provisions and no language prescribing any method of its invocation." The Pact "simply outlaws war . . . and renounces it as an instrument of national policy." His predecessors were unofficially of the opinion, Hull continued, that the Pact implied consultation and "it is our view that consultation" now could "not contemplate anything more than a concerted or simultaneous appeal by all of the signatories to the belligerent countries to abide by their legal and moral obligations by desisting from further hostilities and returning to a state of peace."[25] Hull would accept no answer to aggression, even in a time of crisis, that would demand more of the United States than simple declarations that all nations should practice self-restraint under the principles of the Kellogg-Briand Pact.

While the League swiftly declared Italy an "aggressor" nation, the economic sanctions it vowed against Italy proved to be quite mild and did not hamper Italian importation of essentials such as oil and coal. Hull, meanwhile, had been evolving the idea of a moral embargo. He believed "that a line should be drawn at normal exports and the exports to a belligerent above that line should be discouraged as strenuously as a Government could do so which had no authority by legislation to forbid them." On October 30, Hull and FDR issued statements appealing to the American people, and especially commercial agents, to forego the additional commerce and its profits with belligerents which could well prolong the conflict.

When the Italian Ambassador complained that, since the United States had little or no trade with Ethiopia, the effect of the neutrality act and moral embargo approached that of a "sanction," the Secretary exploded in indignation. Mussolini had ignored both his and the President's pleas not to go to war, Hull replied, "and now seems to expect us to furnish him with war supplies while he prosecutes the war ad libitum." Also, the Secretary noted, he had almost worn himself "out physically in an effort to aid in world-economic rehabilitation" to provide Italy and other countries with an adequate amount of international trade to meet their needs. "You can imagine the deep disappointment I feel," he concluded, "at the effort to renew the practice that all nations have recently undertaken to abandon—that of military aggression by any and all countries at any and all times. Of course, if one country is to be allowed to violate this new policy of the pacific settlement of disputes, then every country may do so with consequences that one shudders to contemplate."[26]

Italy's conquest of Ethiopia ended with United States policy toward Europe intact. The nation had refrained from entangling itself or being "dragged" into the conflict. Hull had successfully kept the problem in the League's hands and, apparently, could find no vital American interest at stake. His objections to Italy's action was simply that it had gone to war. But war, he told the graduating class at Brown University, "exacts too high a price to be conducive to human welfare . . . War is sometimes described as the last resort of the statesman. I should rather say that recourse to war as a means of obtaining the aims of national policy is an unmistakable symbol of bankrupt statesmanship."[27]

During the critical years from 1936 to 1938, Hull refused to deviate from his inherited policy of nonentanglement in European affairs, but he attempted to educate public opinion at home and abroad toward the "right" internationalism. In the continental crises, Hull and FDR faced increasing difficulties arising from the rigidity of their policy of involvement. This was especially true in the Spanish civil war and the Czechoslovakian crisis. Hull believed that France and England should take the lead in seeking solutions to continental issues. Still his insistence that they make their actions conform to his principles of international ethics frequently eliminated any consideration or sympathy in Washington for their dilemmas and the burdens which they carried.

Thus Hull refused to endorse Prime Minister Neville Chamberlain's attempts to appease Hitler and Mussolini. This was especially true when appeasement seemed to require the violation of the principle that change to be legitimate needed also to be peaceful. When Chamberlain early in 1938 suggested that he might surrender the principle of nonrecognition of change emanating from force and recognize the Italian conquest of Ethiopia in return for concessions from Italy, Hull immediately upbraided the Prime Minister. The nonrecognition principle, he declared, "had been very carefully kept alive by this and certain other governments during recent years. . . . [I]f any important country like Great Britain suddenly should abandon that principle, to the extent of recognizing the Italian conquest of Ethiopia, . . . desperado nations [would herald such action] as a virtual ratification of the opposing policy of outright treaty violation, and treaty wrecking. . . . [28] British officials reminded Washington that they faced a world of dictators and had no choice but to seek some peaceful understanding with them.

Hull continued to oppose any resort to force or negotiation in dealing with aggressors. Hitler's annexation of Austria in March, 1938, inaugurated Germany's open assault on the territorial arrangements of the Versailles Treaty. Hull's reaction conformed to his established formula. "It is our profound conviction," he said, "that the most effective contribution we, as a nation sincerely devoted to peace, can make . . . is to have this country respected throughout the world for integrity, justice, goodwill, strength, and unswerving loyalty to principles." Shortly before the Munich crisis of September, 1938, Hull acknowledged the need to place some restraint on aggression. He remarked to Joseph Davies: "In Tennessee . . . and in the West, when outlaws ran amuck, disturbed the peace and the safety of peace-loving citizens, all law-abiding men set their hands against them and put them in jail or made them incapable of disturbing the peace."[29] The secretary, however, could translate neither this homily nor his growing criticism of appeasement into any recommendation for a precise course of action aimed at altering the dangerous trends in international politics.

Germany's seizure of Czechoslovakia in March, 1939, threatened the whole Versailles settlement for Eastern Europe with disaster. Hull condemned the new German aggression but again suggested only that Germany accept the status quo in accordance with the Wilsonian principle of peaceful change. The State Department's official pronouncement on Hitler's elimination of the Czech nation differed little from Hull's response to the Austrian *Anschluss:* "The position of the government of the United States has been made consistently clear. It has emphasized the need for respect for the sanctity of treaties and the pledged word, and for non-intervention by any nation in the domestic affairs of other nations; and it has . . . expressed its condemnation of a policy of military aggression." Hull informed the press that the United States would continue to strive, as it had in the past, "to strengthen the threatened structure of world peace by fostering in every possible way the rule of law." Such words, demanding Germany's acceptance of the status quo (except as the Berlin government might alter it through peaceful procedures), had no effect whatever on the course of German policy. Showing no restraint, Hitler sent his dreaded Panzer divisions into Poland on September 1. Europe was now at war.

IV

While a tradition of non-entanglement governed America's attitude toward Europe in 1933, Hull inherited a Far Eastern policy enmeshed in moral and security commitments accruing from previous decades. This policy, moreover, was currently being challenged by Japan's aggressive search for empire. If Hull was uncertain as to the threat Hitler and Mussolini posed to American interests in Europe, he apparently had no such hesitation in evaluating the significance of Japanese ambitions in the Western Pacific. To Hull, Japan was "a highway robber." When he entered the State Department, Hull has written, he "had two points on the Far East firmly in mind. One was the definite interest the United States had in maintaining the independence of China and in preventing Japan from gaining overlordship of the entire Far East. The other was an equally definite conviction that Japan had no intention whatever of abiding by treaties but would regulate her conduct by the opportunities of the moment."[30]

Nonrecognition was one of the planks of Hull's inherited Far Eastern policy. It stemmed from the Hoover administration's refusal to admit the "legality" of Japan's 1931-1932 occupation of Manchuria and North China. President Herbert Hoover explained that he was "inflexibly opposed to the imposition of any kind of sanctions except purely public opinion." This sanction, he argued, if continuously applied under the nonrecognition doctrine, would "ultimately be triumphant. The whole doctrine of non-recognition is not alone a method of invoking world opinion but it is equally important in the phase that it avoids precipitant action and allows time to work out proper solutions." Hull added his endorsement to the nonrecognition doctrine. Rejecting a League of Nations' proposal that the puppet government in Manchuria be included in the international effort to control narcotics, Hull declared that "adherance to and observance of the principle of non-recognition . . . is more vital and important" than regulating the shipment of drugs.[32] As with Hoover, however, the secretary was unwilling to put any teeth in the doctrine.

Disarmament negotiations shifted during 1934 and 1935 from the hopelessly deadlocked Geneva talks to discussions on renewal of the London naval limitation pact of 1930. Anticipating difficulties with Germany and Japan, the British made it clear that they were likely to need more, not less, naval strength; however, if the United States and England "could agree upon a policy of co-operation in the Far East—which they would like very much to do—our differences on technical naval questions would automatically solve themselves." The British effort to explain the political realities of Europe and Asia in the context of naval power escaped the Roosevelt administration. "The whole British approach to these conversations both political and technical," Hull complained, "has been intensely disappointing." The President and he agreed, he continued, that United States policy did not "represent a bargaining position but a deep conviction that only on the basis of further reduction or at the very least extension of the present treaties" could a valid, useful naval limitation agreement be reached. The American position was shattered by the end of November, 1934, when word came from Tokyo that Japan was planning to abrogate the Washington naval system and agree to a new treaty only if granted full naval parity with Great Britain and the United States.[33]

Hull's official response to the outbreak of the Sino-Japanese War in 1937 was a reiteration of his litany of international principles. The July 16 statement—elaborated above—called for all nations to abstain from the use of force, to uphold treaties, to abide by international law, to seek relief of their domestic needs through increased economic resciprocity, and to search for means of achieving disarmament. Principles alone did not satisfy Chinese leaders. When the Chinese Ambassador at Washington asked Hull to define the United States position relative to China under the Nine Power Treaty, the Secretary refused to answer directly. He asked the Ambassador if he did not think that the Secretary's July 16 statement of principles more than covered the situation. The Ambassador agreed that it did, "so far as principles were concerned, but what his government was now seeking was action."[34]

Three days later, Hull informed the press that his statement of July 16 had "a direct and fundamental" bearing on America's policies toward the Sino-Japanese conflict. "This Government," he noted on August 23,

> is firmly of the opinion that the principles summarized in that statement should effectively govern international relationships. . . . Without attempting to pass judgment regarding the merits of the controversy, we appeal to the parties to refrain from resort to war. We urge that they settle their differences in accordance with principles, which, in the opinion not alone of our people but of most

> peoples of the world, should govern in international relationships.
>
> This Government is endeavoring to see kept alive, strengthened, and revitalized, in reference to the Pacific area and to all the world, these fundamental principles.[35]

As American diplomats, particularly Nelson T. Johnson, Joseph Grew, and Stanley K. Hornbeck, joined the cry for a more substantive basis on which to ground the East Asian policies of the United States, Hull argued that his policies had been motivated by a desire to encourage both the Japanese and Chinese "to develop attitudes of real co-operativeness toward each other and toward the rest of the world." The Secretary readily admitted that little hope of success remained because the Japanese particularly refused to reciprocate. Yet, Hull continued, "the administration has endeavored in the current crisis to follow a course of absolute impartiality. We realize that manifestations of disapprobation on legal or moral grounds are not likely to bring the hostilities to an end." However, he noted,

> My statement of July 16 made clear the principles which are guiding this Government, principles in general support of which more than 50 States of the world have expressed themselves affirmatively. My subsequent statement on August 23 makes it clear that we regard these principles as applicable to the Pacific area. We consider those principles fundamental to a well-ordered existence of and in the society of nations. It is evident that neither Japan nor China in their present courses of action are acting in accordance with those principles and that the course which Japan is pursuing is in direct conflict with many of them.

The only course of action that Hull could recommend was that the American Ambassador in Tokyo "overlook no opportunity to impress upon Japanese officialdom the importance which we attach to the principles laid down in my statement of July 16 and the significance of my statement of August 23, and to suggest to them that by the course she is pursuing Japan is destroying the world's good will. . . . "[36]

Although pressure mounted during the ensuing months for the United States to take some positive action to curtail Japan's aggressive advances, Hull remained unmoved. He resisted efforts of the delegates to the Brussels Conference of November, 1937, which condemned Japan's violations of the Nine Power Pact, to initiate any embargoes of Japan or aid programs for China. While ultimately Hull would reluctantly agree to both, he constantly urged caution to avoid provoking Japanese retaliation or exciting American public opinion.

When the U.S. announced in mid-1939 it would not renew its 1911 Commercial treaty with Japan, Japanese diplomats pressed to find out what would happen after the treaty expired on January 26, 1940. Hull was deliberately vague, but he did reject Japanese pleas to open negotiations for a new treaty. The secretary did not believe that Japan enjoyed the freedom to demand negotiations with the United States. The Tokyo government, he later wrote, "had no more right to make demands upon us than an individual gangster had to make demands upon his intended victim."[37] Hull rejected the need, even the legitimacy, of any diplomatic effort to come to terms with expansionist countries. Throughout the later 1930s and early 1940s, Hull constantly pointed back to his July 16 statement of principles and his August 23 elaboration as the core of United States policy toward East Asia. Before Japan could expect serious negotiations with the United States, Tokyo authorities must acknowledge the validity of these principles in words and, especially, in deeds.

Nowhere was the hopelessness of Hull's (and Roosevelt's) diplomacy more clearly demonstrated than in its futile attempts from 1938 to 1941 both to halt Japan's empire-building and to keep the United States out of war. It failed in both objectives; yet, it could hardly have done otherwise, for if Hull was adept at argumentation, the Japanese refused to limit the quarrel to logic. Perhaps the gravest charge to be levied against Hull's handling of Far Eastern affairs was his failure to formulate and clearly present to the American people the issues at stake—to define vital American interests in East Asia. He was not alone, however, for there was little desire among political leaders to face the harsh realities of American isolationism and Japanese aggression squarely and openly. The temptation was strong to substitute words for action, and to seek success without cost. In the ensuing drift, especially after the embargo of late July, 1941, the Japanese ran out of time. Facing the choice of capitulation or war, they opted for the latter. The result was the attack on Pearl Harbor.

V

Although during World War II President Roosevelt undertook personal direction of American foreign affairs, Hull's views would help shape major policy decisions. In particular, the Secretary continued to seek reductions of trade barriers in the postwar world, objected to secret allied territorial arrangements that appeared to introduce regionalism, and actively worked to establish a universally recognized international organization. Thus Hull enthusiastically greeted the Atlantic Charter's statement of post-World War II goals when it appeared on August 14, 1941, as a "statement of basic principles and fundamental ideas and policies that are universal in their practical application." His *Memoirs,* however, reveal his profound unhappiness with Article Four, in which Britain and America stated that they would "endeavor, with due respect for their existing obligations, to further the enjoyment by all states . . . of access, on equal terms, to the trade and raw materials of the world . . . " He put his disappointment thusly: "Unfortunately the phrase 'with due respect for their existing obligations' deprived the article of virtually all significance since it meant that Britain would continue to retain her Empire tariff preferences against which I had been fighting for eight years."

Even after the United States entered the war, disagreements over commercial policies, Hull complained, continued to be "one of our most delicate meeting grounds with the British." When Britain reluctantly signed the Lend-Lease Agreement of 1942, Article VII contained a provision which pledged Britain to give up its preferential trade arrangements after the war. Hull, however, was convinced that Prime Minister Winston Churchill, despite this pledge, would search for ways to continue the imperial tariff preference. One such opportunity arose at the Quebec conference in September, 1944, when Roosevelt agreed to a Treasury Department proposal extending six and a half billion dollars of credits to Britain without any quid pro quo. The President argued that it was essential that the United States not attach any conditions on Lend-Lease supplies destined for Britain that would hinder the recovery of its export trade. "This struck me amidships," Hull later noted. "It tended to shatter negotiations we had been conducting with the British for three years." Additionally, it tended to nullify the 1942 British pledge to end imperial tariff preferences; however, broader policy considerations were to carry the day.[37]

During December, 1941, and again in the spring of 1942, Hull prevailed upon FDR to resist British pleas to accept the Soviet Union claims to Poland east of the Curzon Line, the Baltic States, and parts of Rumania and Finland. In a December 5, 1941, telegram to Ambassador John Winant at London, Hull urged that all diplomatic efforts be aimed at winning the war and not arranging for a "victors peace" replete with secret agreements and territorial delineations. Hull wanted Winant to remind British Foreign Secretary Anthony Eden, preparing to journey to Moscow, that the United States was willing to provide material aid to the Soviet Union. It would, however, view any secret agreements to be in conflict with the Atlantic Charter.

In February, Hull sought to alert FDR to Soviet efforts to develop a secret political treaty which would reassign Central and Eastern European territories after the defeat of Hitler. Such adjustments, he noted would make the Russians "the dominating power of Eastern Europe if not the whole continent." The British should be informed that making any agreements with the Soviets, which recognized the latter's territorial claims, would becloud the postwar peacemaking efforts, violate the Atlantic Charter, and open the way for a deluge of further Soviet demands for concessions. Hull believed that the Soviets had substantial ambitions in Europe which sooner or later the United States and Great Britain would need to oppose. To meet the Soviet challenge, Hull argued, the United States and Britain should not "agree in advance" to such demands; rather, they should take a firm stand now rather than "to retreat and to be compelled to take a firm attitude later when our position had been weakened by the abandonment of the general principles referred to in the Atlantic Charter."[38]

Hull consistently resisted the tendencies of America's allies to fall back on the old traditions of spheres of influence and power politics. Internal State Department documents suggest, nonetheless, that he was aware that his earlier assessment of Soviet ambitions were squaring with the emerging postwar realities. In late 1943, he half-jokingly told Alfred M. Landon that he might journey to Moscow to urge the independence of the Baltic States and Poland's pre-1939 borders, but that if he hoped for success "he ought to take some of the U.S. Army and Navy with him."[39]

Not surprisingly, then, Hull was aroused by a 1944 proposal for a British-Russian agreement under which the former would assume primary influence over Greece and later over Rumania. "I was, in fact," he later wrote,

> flatly opposed to any division of Europe or sections of Europe into sphere of influence. I had argued against this strongly at the Moscow Conference . . .
>
> I was not, and am not, a believer in the idea of balance of power or spheres of influence as a means of keeping the peace. During the First World War I had made an intensive study of the system of sphere of influence and balance of power, and I was grounded to the taproots in their iniquitious consequences. The conclusions I then formed in total opposition to this system stayed with me.[40]

When Churchill, a few days later, expanded the proposal to give Russia primacy in Bulgaria and Britain in Yugoslavia, the Secretary was unmoved in his opposition to "this dangerous proposal."

Roosevelt's decision—not discovered by Hull until later—to give the agreement a three months' trial prompted a rare acknowledgement by Hull of a policy difference with the President. "When I left office in November, 1944," he later wrote,

> we had agreed to no Russian acquisition of Territory by reason of war. We had unfortunately agreed, through the President and over the opposition of the State Department, to a temporary delineation of military sphere of influence in the Balkans between Russia and Britain, proposed by the latter.

Hull believed that his strong opposition to any British-Russian territorial arrangements in the spring of 1942 had been the wiser course: "Had we made such a determined fight against the Anglo-Russian agreement as we had made successfully against the proposed territorial clauses of the Anglo-Russian alliance in May, 1942, it is possible that some of our later difficulties in the Balkans might not have arisen."[41]

Hull had stoutly resisted spheres of influence because they smacked of regionalism, while he believed that the hope for a peaceful world lay with a United Nations organization that was truely universal in scope and application. Once, however, a pattern of alliances and arrangements outside the United Nations was established, the organization was doomed as an effective instrument for keeping the peace and providing a solid foundation for international cooperation. This objective was not achieved without struggle for even within Hull's own Advisory Committee on Postwar Foreign Policy Sumner Welles was a "convinced advocate of regional organization." More significantly,

> . . . Welles echoed the ideas of President Roosevelt and Prime Minister Churchill. In the spring of 1943 both the President and Prime Minister were convinced that after the war the world should be organized on a regional basis. The nations in certain geographical regions would band together to maintain the peace in those areas. There might be an international organization, but it would do little more than coordinate the work of the regional organizations.[42]

Hull's journey to Moscow in the fall of 1943 resulted in Stalin's formal endorsement of a new world organization that would be supreme over any regional one. In the Four Nation Declaration issued at Moscow, the United States, Great Britain, the Soviet Union, and China recognized "the necessity of establishing at the earliest practicable date a general international organization, based on the principle of the sovereign equality of all peace-loving states, and open to membership by all such states, large and small . . . for the maintenance of international peace and security."[43] Hull's commitment to his Wilsonian vision at Moscow was not deflected by contemporary political issues. When Ambassador Averell Harriman urged him to press the Soviets about their plans for Poland, the Secretary brusquely informed Harriman: "I don't want to deal with these piddling little things. We must deal with the main issues."[44]

The agreement of these four great nations on the principle of self-determination and on the establishment of the United Nations made 1943 seem to Hull a turning point in world history. International security could now be managed on the collective basis envisioned by Woodrow Wilson more than two decades earlier. As he told an enthusiastically cheering joint session of Congress on November 18, 1943: "As the provisions of the four-nation declaration are carried into effect, there will no longer be need for spheres of influence, for alliances, for balance of power, or any other of the special arrangements through which, in the unhappy past, the nations strove to safeguard their security or to promote their interests."[45]

VI

Hull's *Memoirs* dwell on his personal conviction that he had piloted American foreign policy to some exceedingly positive accomplishments and steered it away from many dangerous situations. He could point to certain substantial contributions: (1) the development of the Reciprocal Trade Programs; (2) the improvement of Inter-American relations; and (3) the initiation of postwar planning, especially the early development of the United Nations Charter. However, as with many self-appraisals, Hull's assessment was too generous and lacked self-criticism. Perhaps a more balanced view is that Professor Richard N. Kottman who has written:

> When he proclaimed to the world the benefits of rehabilitated international commerce or preached moral sermons regarding international political behavior, he perhaps had no equal. When questions became less academic and more practical, he revealed his indecision. Hull was not a strong, persevering individual who, convinced that he had an answer to the world's ills, fought unswervingly for its acceptance. He persevered in homilies, thinking that verbal endorsements had moral force, but he faltered when he had to make decisions.[46]

If Hull tended to think in clichés and to speak in moral absolutes, he came to realize the difficulties in persuading others to accede to his principles. Long before the outbreak of World War II, the pressure of events forced Hull to admit that controlling the forces of nationalism and expansionism demanded stronger measures than the lowering of trade barriers and the lessening of economic selfishness. In opposing the expansionism of Germany, Italy, Japan, and Russia, Hull often boasted that he never compromised his principles. To the end he behaved as if those principles were the controlling elements in the international politics of his secretarial years. In practice Hull's response to aggression enabled him to escape the necessity of creating policies that faced the issues of war and peace. Throughout his years in the State Department he scarcely contemplated the means required to match his objective of limiting all change in international life to mutual agreement alone. His focus on attitudes, on the determination, shared by Americans generally, to avoid war even while passing firm judgment on the behavior of others, sustained his influence, indeed his popularity, in Washington. Unfortunately it eliminated his influence where it mattered—in the capitals of those powers bent on tearing up the unwanted provisions of the Versailles treaty structure.

NOTES

1. Cordell Hull, *The Memoirs of Cordell Hull,* 2 vols. (New York, 1948), I, 163. Hereafter referred as *Memoirs.*
2. *Ibid.,* p. 159.
3. *Ibid.,* pp. 24-25.
4. *Ibid.,* pp. 86, 536.
5. U.S. Department of State, *Press Release, 1933,* April 29, 1933, p. 299.
6. *Memoirs,* I, 533-34; *Foreign Relations of the United States, 1937,* I (Washington, 1954), pp. 699-700.
7. Edward M. Bennett, "Cordell Hull and Soviet-American Relations: The Diplomacy of a Moralist," unpublished manuscript.
8. *Memoirs,* I, 536.
9. Arthur M. Schlesinger, Jr. *The Coming of the New Deal* (Boston, 1958), pp. 207-208.
10. *Congressional Record,* 65th Cong., 3rd Sess., Feb. 21, 1919, pp. 3955-60.
11. *Ibid.,* (Dec. 9, 1919), p. 8743.
12. William R. Allen, "The International Trade Philosophy of Cordell Hull, 1907-1933," *American Economic Review* 43 (March 1953), p. 105.
13. *U.S. House, Committee on Ways and Means, Hearings; Reciprocal Trade Agreements, 73rd Cong., 2d. Sess., March 8, 1934,* p. 11.
14. U.S. Department of State, *Press Release, 1935,* March 9, 1935, p. 164.
15. *Ibid.,* November 16, 1935, pp. 380-381.
16. Cordell Hull, "Foreign Trade, Farm Prosperity and Peace," Department of State, *Commercial Policy Series,* No. 44 (Washington, Feb. 19, 1938), pp. 14-15. Italics added.
17. William R. Allen, "Cordell Hull and the Defense of the Trade Agreements Program, 1934-1940," in Alexander DeConde, ed., *Isolation and Security* (Durham, N.C., 1957), pp. 130-31.
18. Charles A. Beard and G. H. E. Smith, *The Open Door at Home* (New York, 1935), p. vii; William A. Williams, *The Tragedy of American Diplomacy* (New York, 1959), p. 133; Gabriel Kolko, *The Politics of War: The World and United States Foreign Policy, 1943-1945* (New York, 1968), p. 244; and Dick Steward, *Trade and Hemisphere: The Good Neighbor Policy and Reciprocal Trade* (Columbia, Mo., 1975), ch. 10.
19. A brief summary of these agreements may be found in Julius W. Pratt, *Cordell Hull,* 2 vols. (New York, 1964), I, 107-38.

20. *Memoirs,* I, 222.
21. *Foreign Relations, 1933,* I, pp. 85, 89, 91.
22. *Memoirs,* I, 234.
23. *Ibid.,* 243.
24. U.S. Department of State, *Press Releases, 1935,* July 13, 1935, pp. 53-54.
25. *Foreign Relations, 1935,* I, 773-74.
26. *Ibid.,* pp. 830-32; *Memoirs,* I, 434-39.
27. *Memoirs,* I, 473.
28. *Foreign Relations, 1938,* I, 133-34.
29. Joseph Davies, *Mission to Moscow, 1936-1938* (New York, 1941) p. 371.
30. *Memoirs,* I, 270; Hull stated in November, 1940, that "Japan only understands force," Fred L. Israel, ed., *War Diary of Breckinridge Long* (Lincoln, 1966), p. 129.
31. *Foreign Relations, 1933,* III, 209-10; for the formulation of the Non-Recognition Doctrine, see Richard N. Current, "The Stimson Doctrine and the Hoover Doctrine," *American Historical Review* 59 (April 1954), pp. 513-42.
32. *Foreign Relations, 1933,* III, 306.
33. *Ibid., 1934,* I, 279-80, 284, 329.
34. *Ibid., 1937,* I, 699-700; *ibid.,* IV, 5; *Memoirs* I, 533-34.
35. U.S. Department of State, *Press Releases, 1937,* August 22, 1937, p. 166.
36. *Foreign Relations, 1937,* III, 506-08.
37. *Memoirs,* II, 976, 1476, 1613-14.
38. Telegram and memorandum, Hull to Winant, December 5, 1941, Papers of Harry L. Hopkins, Box 304, Franklin D. Roosevelt Library, Hyde Park, cited in Edward M. Bennett, "Cordell Hull and Soviet-American Relations: The Diplomacy of a Moralist," unpublished manuscript.
39. Eduard Mark, "American Policy Toward Eastern Europe and the Origins of the Cold War, 1941-1946: An Alternative Interpretation," *Journal of American History* 68 (September 1981), pp. 315-16.
40. *Memoirs,* II, 1452-53.
41. *Ibid.,* 1459, 1640.
42. *Ibid.,* 1640.
43. *Foreign Relations, 1943,* I, 756.
44. W. Averell Harriman and Elie Abel, *Special Envoy to Churchill and Stalin, 1941-1946* (New York, 1975), p. 236.
45. Department of State *Bulletin, IX* (November 20, 1943), p. 343.
46. Richard N. Kottman, *Reciprocity and the North Atlantic Triangle, 1932-1938* (Ithaca, N.Y., 1968), p. 279.

7

FRANKLIN D. ROOSEVELT AND THE WARTIME STRATEGY FOR PEACE

Whittle Johnston

In studies of the Presidency of Franklin D. Roosevelt uncertainty persists in many areas, but consensus seems firm on one: its pragmatic character. In Richard Hofstadter's view, "The New Deal will never be understood by anyone who looks for a single thread of policy, a far-reaching, far-seeing plan. It was a series of improvisations, many adopted very suddenly, many contradictory."[1] Eric Goldman, in anecdotal fashion, affirmed his agreement with Hofstadter. He recorded this exchange at a White House dinner:

> "What are you going to say when they ask you the political philosophy behind the TVA?" Senator Norris laughed.
>
> "I'll tell them it's neither fish nor fowl," Roosevelt laughed back, "but, whatever it is, it will taste awful good to the people of the Tennessee Valley."[2]

In 1938 Reinhold Niebuhr, exasperated by the contrast between Roosevelt's "whirligig reform" and the "clear-cut logic of socialism," exclaimed: "If that man could only make up his mind to cross the Rubicon!" Arthur Schlesinger, Jr. added this perceptive rejoinder: "For Roosevelt, of course, the problem was not to cross the Rubicon but to navigate up it."[3]

Roosevelt's pragmatism was born from "the crisis of the old

order" that had brought him to the White House. Schlesinger noted the intellectual dilemma that confronted the new President:

> In February 1933, the Senate Finance Committee summoned a procession of business leaders to solicit their ideas on the crisis. Said John W. Davis, the leader of the American bar, "I have nothing to offer, either of fact or theory." . . . [B]ankruptcy of ideas seemed almost as complete among the intellectuals. "My heartbreak at liberalism," wrote William Allen White, "is that it has sounded no note of hope, made no plans for the future, offered no program. . . . Others, in their despair, could only yearn for a savior. Hamilton Fish, the New York congressman, spoke for millions when he wrote to Roosevelt late in February that in the crisis we must "give you any power that you may need."[4]

The orthodox wisdom, particularly in economics, seemed to have proved wrong in practice. As the President put it, "All this is perfectly terrible because it is all pure theory, when you come down to it."[5] His use of the word "theory" was clearly pejorative—roughly equivalent to idle speculation without practical relevance. Roosevelt's skepticism of established dogmas served, simultaneously, to justify his emphasis on creative experimentation.

Roosevelt's faith in the possibilities of experimentation was also an expression of his own remarkable personality. All through his life he displayed insouciant assurance in his ability to find common ground among all manner of persons and philosophies, however incompatible their relations might seem to others. When confronted with two wholly divergent recommendations on tariff policy, he once left Raymond Moley speechless by instructing him to "weave the two together." Another defining trait of Roosevelt's personality—driving political ambition intensified by the power of family example—worked toward the same end. Robert Dallek, in a major study of Roosevelt's foreign policy, observed:

> Sometime during these years, Franklin decided to duplicate Theodore's career. By 1907 at least, he was telling his fellow law clerks at Carter, Ledyard, and Milburn that "he wasn't going to practice law forever, that he intended to run for office at the first opportunity, and that he wanted to be and thought he had a very real chance to be President.[6]

To Roosevelt the very essence of the political art was discovery of common ground among apparently diverse constituencies. He became the commanding political figure of the nation through the exercise of his dazzling talent in coalition-building—the life blood of the democratic political process. The unity of Roosevelt's presidency lies in political strategy far more than in philosophical doctrine.[7]

Personal factors of another dimension helped shape the character of Roosevelt's leadership. In his heroic recovery from crippling illness he proved to himself that through hope, spirit, and will, one could overcome contradictions that devastated the merely rational faculties. Throughout his presidency Roosevelt gave the sense of towering over dilemmas, in part because they seemed small in comparison with those he had already surmounted. Faith in the triumph of hope over fear was a central theme in the first message of his administration, as it was in the last. In the opening sentences of his first inaugural address, he spoke these famous lines:

> This great Nation will endure as it has endured, will revive and will prosper. So, first of all, let me assert my firm belief that the only thing we have to fear is fear itself—nameless, unreasoning, unjustified terror which paralyzes needed efforts to convert retreat into advance.[8]

The closing lines of his draft for a Jefferson Day address on April 13, 1945, (which he never lived to deliver) were, "The only limit to our realization of tomorrow will be our doubts of today. Let us move forward with a strong and active faith."[9] In a centennial remembrance, Joseph Alsop concluded that "Hope was in fact Franklin Roosevelt's greatest gift to his fellow Americans."[10] For Roosevelt there had, indeed, been a sunrise at Campobello.

II

Pragmatism was as definitive an explanation of Roosevelt's foreign policy as of his domestic, and it derived from the same basic sources: the interplay of the President's conviction that the traditional wisdom had been tried and found wanting and high confidence in his ability to discover novel and creative means to accomplish necessary ends. He was, from the first, an internationalist who vigorously supported "cousin Ted's" emphasis on the importance of naval power and shared his admiration for the strategic wisdom of Admiral Mahan. The invitation to serve as assistant secretary of the navy in the Wilson Administration suited him, he said, "better than anything in the world."[11] Because of conversations with Wilson on a return voyage from Europe on the *George Washington* in 1919 and the enormous popular acclaim that greeted Wilson as peacemaker, Roosevelt came to share much of Wilson's own enthusiasm for the League of Nations. When he ran as the Democratic candidate for Vice President in the 1920 campaign, he fought vigorously for Wilson's policies. In the early 1920s he prepared an elaborate plan for a Society of Nations which he felt would preserve the best features of the League of Nations while it cast off the most objectionable ones. However, as the movement away from Wilsonism gained momentum, Roosevelt was very much a part of it. His defection came to a climax in his quest for the presidency in 1932. Hearst demanded of all presidential aspirants, as a condition of his support, that they "repudiate Woodrow Wilson and his 'visionary policies of intermeddling in European conflicts.'" Roosevelt yielded to these pressures. In February, 1932, he avowed publicly that the League of Nations was "not in accord with 'fundamental American ideals,'" and added, "I do not favor American participation."[12]

Roosevelt's relation to Wilson in foreign policy was not unlike his relation to Hoover in domestic. Through imaginative pragmatism Roosevelt was determined to succeed domestically where Hoover, a man of fixed principle, had been a costly failure. Through similar creativity he would also succeed internationally where Wilson, another man of firm principle, had failed disastrously. Roosevelt did not start as a Wilsonian nor did he end as one. Wilsonism had a strong grip on his thought for only the relatively brief period, from the latter part of World War I into the early 1920s. Roosevelt was, at heart, an *instrumental* Wilsonian. Given the hold the Wilsonian tradition had on important groups in the public (to say nothing of those within the Roosevelt administration itself), the President was perfectly willing to portray his purposes in Wilsonian terms when he felt this politically expedient for the furtherance of his own very different policies. The complexity of his partnership with Cordell Hull (an authentic Wilsonian) bespoke the clouded nature of his relation to the Wilsonian tradition as a whole.

When Roosevelt broke with Wilsonism and aligned himself with the dominant isolationist trend of the interwar years, did he become an isolationist of conviction or an isolationist of convenience? Robert Divine argues the case for the former interpretation:

> If we accept Roosevelt's own public statements at their face value, then we can dismiss the concept of two Roosevelts, one the public figure saying what the people wanted to hear, the other the private man with an entirely different set of beliefs. Equally important, we no longer have to explain Roosevelt's conduct on the basis of a devious political expedience. Instead, we can state simply that Roosevelt pursued an isolationist policy out of genuine conviction.[13]

Divine thinks the strongest basis of Roosevelt's isolationism stemmed from his abhorrence of war and his heartfelt longing for peace. These emotions were most vividly expressed in his address at Chautauqua in the 1936 campaign: "I have seen war. I have seen war on land and sea. I have seen blood running from the wounded. . . . I have seen the dead in the mud. I have seen cities destroyed. . . . I have seen the agony of mothers and wives. I hate war. I have passed unnumbered hours, I shall pass unnumbered hours, thinking and planning how war may be kept from this nation."[14]

Roosevelt's commitment to political pragmatism provides, once again, an invaluable clue to his actions. His allegiance to isolationism was as complex and tentative as had been his earlier allegiance to Wilsonism. Even when isolationist pressures were at their most powerful, Roosevelt followed events abroad with intense attentiveness and always with an eye to how he might bring his influence to bear most effectively to aid the prospects of peace—despite the multiple constraints under which he labored. Although he understood that some form of neutrality legislation was politically inevitable, he opposed an "impartial law" (the preference of the isolationists) and worked persistently for legislation that would leave maximum discretion in the President's hands. As he had taken into account internal and external changes in the 1920s and moved away from his allegiance to Wilsonism, when he witnessed the increase in international anarchy and the ineffectuality of American isolationism to arrest the drift toward war in the later 1930s, he sought to maneuver his nation in an ever more internationalist direction.

The most important public expression of Roosevelt's search for new directions was his famous Quarantine Speech on October 5, 1937:

> There is a solidarity, an interdependence about the modern world, both technically and morally, which makes

> it impossible for any nation completely to isolate itself from political and economic upheavals in the rest of the world. . . . There can be no stability either within nations or between nations except under laws and moral standards adhered to by all.[15]

Ruthless aggressors, driven by the greed for power, were destroying the freedom of innocent nations and threatening the foundations of civilization itself. If these trends continued, he warned, "let no one imagine that America will escape . . . that this Western Hemisphere will not be attacked." The famous analogy which gave the speech its title pictured the world as a single community which must act jointly to meet the common threat:

> It seems to be unfortunately true that the epidemic of world lawlessness is spreading.
>
> And mark this well! When an epidemic of physical disease starts to spread, the community approves and joins in a quarantine of the patients in order to protect the health of the community against the spread of the disease.[16]

Despite the vigor with which Roosevelt sounded the alarm, he was still groping his way uneasily over uncertain terrain. As Robert Divine observes:

> At this point, his listeners must have been leaning forward, straining to hear how he proposed to quarantine the lawbreakers. If so, they were disappointed, because Roosevelt then retreated into generalities. . . . Indeed, he reiterated his determination "to adopt every practicable measure to avoid involvement in war."[17]

In Norman Graebner's view, "Roosevelt . . . required a formula that would convey the administration's deep concern for Europe's stability, even while it permitted the United States to escape all responsibility for its preservation." Roosevelt's failure to outline a more specific course of action in the Quarantine Address reflected deep uncertainties, as Dorothy Borg has pointed out.[18] For he was still pulled between a tendency to seek peace through the attempted containment of aggressor states, and an inclination to seek peace through compromise with them.

Roosevelt's dilemmas would have been less perplexing had he felt able to turn for guidance to alternative models of effective international behavior. But Wilson's League, by that late hour, seemed clearly to have passed the point of no return. Europe's traditional statecraft hardly provided a more adequate mould. Neville Chamberlain was then the most influential voice of the democratic powers in Europe. The governing principle of his diplomacy was the quest for a general settlement to be achieved through a "redress of legitimate grievances."[19] Its fulfillment in practice came with the Munich settlement in the fall of 1938. As Norman Graebner has shown, Roosevelt initially "saw in the Munich agreement not simply a costly and fragile peace, but also the possibilities for a more principled future. The President confided to Ambassador William Phillips in Rome: 'I want you to know that I am not a bit upset over the final result.' " He sent the following congratulatory message to Chamberlain:

> I fully share your hope and belief that there exists today the greatest opportunity in years for the establishment of a new order based on justice and law. Now that you have established personal contact with Chancellor Hitler, I know that you will be taking up with him from time to time many of the problems which must be resolved in order to bring about that new and better order.[20]

But Roosevelt was soon to realize (as was Chamberlain) that Munich did not make peace more certain but war more likely.

Under the clouds of the "gathering storm," into which America would soon be swept, Wilson's heirs gained new strength. The course of events, they argued, vindicated their convictions. Because America had repudiated Wilson's vision and rejected membership in his League, the scourge of war had once again befallen mankind. They cast this vast drama in dualistic terms: Wilsonism as protagonist and isolationism as antagonist. Through tireless preaching and organizing they would drive home the hard lessons of experience; Wilsonism would prevail over isolationism; the world would, at last, be set aright. Americans United, which sought to put the internationalist movement solidly behind a new international organization, took as its slogan Santayana's maxim, "Those who do not remember the past are condemned to repeat it." Doubts about exactly what "lessons" the past taught turned on matters of detail alone; advocates were convinced that the fundamental requirements of international society stood out with unquestionable clarity. Hidden in the recurrence of tragedy the Wilsonians found great hope. As one of their favored slogans ran: "Once in a great while mankind gets a second chance. This is such a time."[21]

Roosevelt did not, emphatically, live in this two-dimensional world of the American internationalists. The starting point for his policy—domestic no less than foreign—lay in his pervasive intuition that old worlds had fallen and that the way to future ones could not be found through a vain attempt to make workable in present difficulties the formulas of the past. The skepticism toward the received wisdom that stamped his domestic policy, and spurred his confidence to chart new courses was, if anything, more pronounced in his foreign policy. The ingenuity with which Roosevelt masterminded the destroyers-for-bases deal in 1940 (which he himself stated, if mismanaged, would "raise hell with Congress") illustrates his unique approach. In the end he was highly successful. "You can't attack a deal like that," one Senator declared. "If you jump on the destroyer transfer, you're jumping on the acquisition of defense bases in the Western Hemisphere."[22] The Lend-Lease program of early 1941 provided an even more revealing illustration of Roosevelt's creative pragmatism, for here he consciously set out to meet Britain's urgent need for financial support but in a way to avoid a replay of the previous quarrel over war debts. While Roosevelt and others had discussed this scheme during the fifteen months since the war began, the overall plan and timing were strictly the President's.[23]

III

This consideration of fragmentary aspects of Roosevelt's foreign policy is important for the light it casts on the larger pattern of his behavior. He sought to bring to bear on his foreign policy as a whole the same creative pragmatism he displayed in these specific actions. He was the "master innovator of a great design" that corresponded to no traditional patterns—neither Wilsonian, isolationist, or realist. Roosevelt defied categorization. Given the novelty of his views, and the fact that they did not fit into any established framework, Roosevelt played his hand cautiously, cards close to his chest, and relied on the course of the play itself to bring home to others the nature of the game and the merit of his strategy. Since he felt his plans for peace entailed departures from mainstream American opinion, he could only lead through subtle indirection and wait on major events (some of which he would help contrive) to bring the public into phase with him. In the interval he kept the lines of policy fluid. Goals, when defined at all, were done so in highly abstract terms; means were usually refined behind the scenes and, when presented to the public, disguised in traditionalist garb. Too much discussion, too soon, on specific substantive issues risked a crystallization of positions that would constrict the maneuverability Roosevelt felt essential to advance his own design.

In the Quarantine Address Roosevelt had voiced concern that the spread of world lawlessness threatened the peace of America, but he had been unable to convert this generalized anxiety into specific policies that would fend off the mounting danger. In the war years he persistently strove for the most cogent formulation of the two great goals he felt policy must serve: defeat of the Axis and a durable settlement after victory to preserve the peace. At the same time, his determination to move beyond the ineffectuality of pre-war policy led him to an untiring quest for means to make real the goals of victory and peace.

One of his most memorable formulations of the goals he felt should guide policy was given in his Annual Message to Congress on January 6, 1941:

> In the future days, which we seek to make secure, we look forward to a world founded upon four essential human freedoms.
>
> The first is freedom of speech and expression—everywhere in the world.
>
> The second is freedom of every person to worship God in his own way—everywhere in the world.
>
> The third is freedom from want. . . . everywhere in the world.
>
> The fourth is freedom from fear—which, translated into world terms, means a world-wide reduction of armaments to such a point and in such thorough fashion that no nation will be in a position to commit an act of physical aggression against any neighbor—anywhere in the world.
>
> That is no vision of a distant millennium. It is a definite basis for a kind of world attainable in our own time and generation.[24]

In the Atlantic Charter, drafted jointly with Churchill in August, 1941, the two statesmen based "their hopes for a better future for the world" on their commitments to seek: no aggrandizement or territorial changes not in accord with the freely-expressed popular will; the right of people to self-government and equal economic opportunity; the furtherance of international economic collaboration, and protection of freedom of the seas; freedom from fear and want; and, finally, disarmament.[25]

After the United States became an official belligerent in December, 1941, Roosevelt cast the contrast between the goals of the two warring coalitions in Biblical terms: "Our enemies are guided by a brutal cynicism, by unholy contempt for the human race. We are inspired by a faith that goes back through all the years to the first chapter of the Book of Genesis: 'God created man in His own image.' We on our side are striving to be true to that divine heritage. We are fighting as our fathers have fought, to uphold the doctrine that all men are equal in the sight of God."[26] The sharp distinction between the virtue of the one side and the evil of the other found policy expression in the doctrine of unconditional surrender, proclaimed by Roosevelt in a seemingly off-the-cuff manner in a press conference at Casablanca in January, 1943:

> Another point. I think we have all had it in our hearts and our heads before, but I don't think that it has ever been put down on paper by the Prime Minister and myself, and that is the determination that peace can come to the world only by the total elimination of German and Japanese war power.
>
> . . . The elimination of German, Japanese and Italian war power means the unconditional surrender by Germany, Italy, and Japan. That means a reasonable assurance of future world peace. It does not mean the destruction of the population of Germany, Italy, or Japan, but it does mean the destruction of the philosophies in those countries which are based on conquest and the subjugation of other people.[27]

In his Annual Message to Congress on January 11, 1944, Roosevelt echoed themes from the "four freedoms" address three years earlier, but now with a very different emphasis. Clear priority was now assigned to freedom from fear and, in the aftermath of conferences at Moscow, Cairo, and Teheran, to the assumed commitment of the major Allies to its achievement: "We are united in determination that this war shall not be followed by another interim which leads to new disaster. . . . The one supreme objective for the future, which we discussed for each nation individually, and for all the United Nations, can be summed up in one word: Security."[28]

Finally, in the Declaration on Liberated Europe, at Yalta, Roosevelt, Churchill, and Stalin jointly reaffirmed their allegiance to the Atlantic Charter, and vowed to

> assist the people in any European liberated state or former Axis satellite state in Europe . . . to form interim governmental authorities broadly representative of all democratic elements in the population and pledged to the earliest possible establishment through free elections of governments responsive to the will of the people; and to facilitate where necessary the holding of such elections.[29]

IV

Roosevelt began to shape the means through which he sought to give effect to these goals under the relentless advance of Axis military power. His speech at the University of Virginia in June, 1940, was cast against the backdrop of Nazi Germany's devastating victory in western Europe that spring.[30] While his indictment of the follies of isolationism was far more outspoken than in the Quarantine Address, the larger significance of the speech lay in the boldness of Roosevelt's proposals to bring America's power into the struggle against aggression:

> In our American unity, we will pursue two obvious and simultaneous courses: we will extend to the opponents of force the material resources of this nation and, at the same time, we will harness and speed up the uses of those resources in order that we ourselves in the Americas may have equipment and training equal to the task of any emergency and every defense.[31]

In the months that followed, Roosevelt's conception of the effective means to achieve desired goals continued to be shaped by the unrelenting pressures of military necessity—the collapse of France, the threatened collapse of the Soviet Union and China, the growing intensity of the Battle of the Atlantic, the rapid Axis advances in North Africa. He came, ever more openly, to stress the critical significance of strategic factors, as in these passages from an address of September 11, 1941: "We are not becoming hysterical or losing our sense of proportion. . . . Instead, we Americans are taking a long-range point of view in regard to certain fundamentals—a point of view in regard to a series of events on land and on sea which must be conceived as a whole—as part of a world pattern." It was simple arithmetic that the American Navy could provide invincible protection only if the British Navy survived. "For if the world outside of the Americas falls under Axis domination," he said, "the shipbuilding facilities which the Axis powers would then possess . . . would be much greater than all the shipbuilding facilities and potentialities of all the Americas—not only greater, but two or three times greater, enough to win."[32] In this passage one sees Roosevelt's basic strategy for future peace, as well as for current victory, beginning to take shape: only if America and Britain act together as international enforcers of the peace can the far-reaching forces of aggression be contained. The inexorable realities Roosevelt faced as war leader profoundly shaped his conception of the necessary conditions of a durable peace.

With America openly in the war, strategic universalism became the governing conception of Roosevelt's military policy. He stated this universalist perspective vividly in his Washington's Birthday Address of 1942:

> The present great struggle has taught us increasingly that freedom of person and security of property anywhere in the world depend upon the security of the rights and obligations of liberty and justice everywhere in the world.
>
> This war is a new kind of war. It is different from all other wars of the past, not only in its methods and weapons but also in its geography. It is warfare in terms of every continent, every island, every sea, every airlane in the world.[33]

He saw the policy of the Axis as one of divide and conquer—to separate the United States, Britain, China, and the Soviet Union, to isolate them from one another, so that each could be surrounded and cut off from sources of supplies and reinforcements. This threat mandated the United Nations response: "In the partnership of our common enterprise, we must share in a unified plan in which all of us must play our several parts, each of us being equally indispensable and dependent on the other."[34] He stressed the same point in the news conference at Casablanca where he had proclaimed the doctrine of unconditional surrender: "[T]hese conferences have discussed, I think for the first time in history, the whole global picture. It isn't just one front, just one ocean, or one continent—it is literally the whole world."[35]

As the scale of the war expanded, so did Roosevelt's conception of the scale of cooperation necessary for victory now and peace in the future. The notion of "two policemen," implicit in his earlier definition of United States relations with Britain, grew to four, as the Soviet Union and China became major allies. During Soviet Foreign Minister V. M. Molotov's visit to Washington in the spring of 1942, Roosevelt elaborated his proposals, and felt that he had gained Soviet acceptance of them:

> In reply Mr. Molotov declared that he had considered and reported to Moscow the President's earlier proposals as to post-war organization. He had received an answer from Mr. Stalin, who was in full accord with the President's ideas on disarmament, inspection, and policing with the participation of at least Great Britain, the United States, the Soviet Union, and possibly China.[36]

In development of the same theme in the spring of 1943, Roosevelt put particular weight on the importance of China's role (to a somewhat skeptical Anthony Eden): "The President told Eden he thought that China might become a very useful power in the Far East to help police Japan and that he wanted to strengthen China in every way possible."[37] The following month Forrest Davis, Washington editor of *The Saturday Evening Post,* published an article entitled "Roosevelt's World Blue print." This article was of far more than ordinary importance because it was based on a confidential interview with Roosevelt, who had then read and approved the manuscript in advance of publication. Roosevelt built on his "quarantine" theme of five years earlier, but now with far stronger views on how to make effective the restraints on the aggressors. The first step would be to establish a total blockade of the offender; if this proved insufficient, an ultimatum would be issued, to conclude with this stark question: "Do you wish your strategic centers bombed to destruction?" The President had already arrived at that clear order of priorities, with his emphasis on security, which later found expression in his Annual Message of 1944:

> Mr. Roosevelt's first concern is for security—"freedom from fear." When he announced the Four Freedoms to Congress in January of 1941, he did not rank them as to importance. They now have taken on hierarchical order

> in his mind. Without the prospect of a 'durable peace,' without agreement by the great powers on administering and policing a peace, he feels that international economic understandings will be hard to reach. No 'moral imperialist,' he has no thought of imposing the freedoms of speech and worship on other countries, hoping that in a world free of fear of aggression those values can be propagated by example and moral suasion.[38]

The President was concerned to distinguish his approach from the "welfare politics" of Wallace and Willkie, the structural procedures of Hoover and Stassen, and his own previous articulation of the aspirations for a better world in the Four Freedoms or the Atlantic Charter. He was determined, instead, to underscore the centrality of the "cold, realistic techniques, or instruments, needed to make those aspirations work."[39] The center of Roosevelt's concern, in short, had become power politics: security was taken to be the overriding goal of foreign policy, and preservation of a strong alliance the essential means to achieve that goal.

V

At the conferences, which included the Big Four, at Cairo and Teheran in the late fall of 1943, by which time the threat of German victory had significantly receded, discussions of the strategy for the next phase of the war became increasingly intertwined with considerations of the bases of peace. Roosevelt made it ever more explicit that the controlling component in his strategy for peace was to project into the post-war era, on a durable basis, the great power cooperation that was making possible the defeat of the Axis. In his Fireside Chat of December 24, 1943, he explained to the American public the significance of Cairo and Teheran, and gave this emphatic formulation: "Britain, Russia, China, and the United States and their allies represent more than three-quarters of the total population of the earth. As long as these four Nations with great military power stick together in determination to keep the peace there will be no possibility of an aggressor Nation arising to start another world war."[40]

In May, 1944, Forrest Davis published a two-part article entitled "What Really Happened at Teheran." It was, like his earlier piece, of special importance. It, too, was based on direct interviews with the President and approved in advance by the White House.

Davis gave the public a fresh look at the current contours of Roosevelt's overall policy and how the events of the past year or so might have influenced it.

> [T]he President's "great design" rests on two sweeping assumptions. First he accepts the prevalent view that the Soviet Union will be able to organize effectively its manpower and resources in peace as well as war, thus becoming permanently a great power. He further assumes that the interests of a victorious Russian state can be reconciled to those of the Atlantic powers, China and the small nations of Europe and America.[41]

The discussion of problems in Poland, Finland, the Danube area, the Balkans, and Germany "hinged on Stalin. Hence the Administration's Russian policy became the cornerstone of its approach to the whole complex of postwar Europe." As Lincoln had not allowed abolitionist critics to deflect him from the great goal of preservation of the Union, the President would not allow his detractors to throw him off course with the Soviet Union; he would play out "the string of conciliation to the end."[42]

Roosevelt would pursue his goal of postwar cooperation through direct contact with Stalin "with its opportunity for exchange of reassurances." These direct exchanges would enable Roosevelt "to assure the Russian of his own complete good faith." This reciprocal spirit of confidence was more important than specific compacts, and hence the President attached particular importance to the closing sentences in the Teheran Declaration: "We came here with hope and determination. We leave here, friends in fact, in spirit and in purpose."[43] Rather than lay out specific terms of settlement in this highly fluid situation, it was wiser, wrote Davis, "to extemporize in harmony with developing events."[44] In contrast to those who were fearful that Russia would violate the trust he was placing in it, Roosevelt had been "betting that the Soviet Union needs peace and is willing to pay for it by collaboration with the west." Roosevelt believed that the alternative, in any case, gave him little choice, for was the United States to exclude Russia, drive her in upon herself, and "prepare for the inevitable war of continents?"[45]

Roosevelt explicitly set apart his "great design" from Wilson's. Wilson had tried to organize a world structure based on law, but Roosevelt faced the problem of bringing the Soviet Union back into the family of nations as a condition which would precede a world organization. Davis wrote:

> Whereas Wilson could lead forthrightly from strength, the President's objective, as he sees it, calls for finesse, a skillful statecraft that cannot always be exposed to view. In the interest of his objective, Mr. Roosevelt has avoided the slightest cause of offense to the Kremlin. Pursuing a soft policy instead of the firm line urged by certain advisers, he has followed the Biblical injunction to walk the second mile.[46]

Roosevelt, unlike Wilson, recognized the role of great powers in world affairs. The President had long made unmistakable his opposition to an attempted revival of the League of Nations, but nevertheless felt certain of its instrumentalities could play a constructive role in the coming peace. Among these was the mandate principle, which he wanted to enlarge and expand into "something he called trusteeship."[47] While this might, at first glance, seem to establish a direct tie with Wilson, in truth it merely gave a Wilsonian guise to Roosevelt's preference for great-power management of security problems. For Roosevelt was convinced that in the future "only countries with an abundance of manpower and resources plus huge industrial plants can engage in the complex business of war." Small powers in the shadow of great ones could not possibly "enforce their will" in military terms and would have to rely on the self-restraint of their powerful neighbors, and "the moderating influence of an organized world society for security."[48] As a safeguard against possible abuse by the Soviet Union of its great power predominance, Roosevelt dutifully directed a seminar at Teheran, for Stalin's benefit, in the good-neighbor policy.[49] Roosevelt was far more concerned, however, to protect the peace against the revival of German and Japanese aggression, and to convince Stalin that the "four policemen" arrangement would be effective to that end. On the future status of the Kiel Canal, for example, Roosevelt proposed that it be internationalized, administered by a tiny "Kiel free state" whose policy, in turn, "should either be assimilated to that of a great power or managed by the United Nations." Roosevelt's "ad-lib" suggestions fascinated Stalin. He lumbered around the table and gravely shook hands with the President, saying, "That is the solution; the right thing to do." Churchill was less convinced.[50]

Rooseveltian trusteeship was also directly tied to America's postwar military role, for the President assumed that the United States would "naturally be selected as the trustee power" inasmuch as it had wrested control through force of the Japanese mandated islands. In future, while the United Nations flag might fly over the islands as a whole, the Stars and Stripes would fly over the bases.[51] For Roosevelt, then, trusteeships were to be a means to win political acceptance for the management of global security problems by the "four policemen" through presentation of their condominium. Roosevelt's anti-imperialism also had less to do with a Wilsonian faith in the prospects for a worldwide growth of self-government than it did with giving the Big Four unchallengeable positions of strength. Stalin's push for "strong physical points" matched the security strategy behind Roosevelt's espousal of trusteeships and anti-colonialism. As Robert Dallek was to make clear (a third-of-a-century after Davis's articles), the two rulers also came together in a shared view of France's post-war role:

> Stalin's strong expression of opposition to restoration of France's colonial empire particularly gratified him [Roosevelt]. . . . Roosevelt agreed and urged that Indochina, New Caledonia, which represented a threat to Australia and New Zealand, and Dakar, which, "in unsure hands," posed a direct threat to the Americas should be brought under trusteeship. Mindful of the need to couple the realistic with the idealistic, he insisted that these strategic points come under United Nations control. By this means, considerations of power politics, which would offend American opinion, would be submerged under a "new" system of collective rule.
>
> Roosevelt envisaged satisfying specific Soviet interests by the same means.[52]

When the brilliant success of the Anglo-American invasion of Western Europe was coupled with the relentless pressure by Soviet armies on the Eastern Front, it seemed only a matter of time before Nazi Germany would collapse. The strategic situation in Asia, by contrast, was far more uncertain. In Dallek's words, "Of all the doubts about the future that concerned Roosevelt during 1944, none weighed on him more heavily than China.[53] His recall of Stilwell in October, 1944, and acceptance of Marshall's advice that he not place another American officer in command of China's armies, indicated that the administration had essentially dropped its goal of pushing the Chinese into effective military action.[54] Roosevelt now put increased emphasis on the effort to bring about (through his emissary, Patrick Hurley) an accord between the

Nationalists and the Communists that, he hoped, would head off a civil war and preserve his plan that China play a leading role in upholding the peace. This, too, came to naught. As Gaddis Smith explained:

> Any hopes Roosevelt had that Hurley could work a change in Chinese affairs evaporated in the last six weeks of 1944. . . . Consequently, by mid-December, Roosevelt began seeking a settlement in China through an agreement with Stalin. If he could persuade Moscow to accept a coalition regime, Roosevelt believed that the Chinese Communists would also accept it, that a civil war would be averted, and that a weak, but relatively stable China would be able to lend the United States political support in postwar Pacific and even world affairs. . . . Though Stalin's remarks gave little encouragement to Roosevelt's plan, FDR believed that he could exchange territorial concessions in the Far East for Soviet support of a coalition in China.[55]

The foundation was thereby laid in Roosevelt's mind for the "bargain" that was to be consummated in the agreement concluded with Stalin at Yalta the following February. As Herbert Feis has pointed out, "the arrangement seems to have been worked out almost entirely just between Roosevelt and Stalin; and the consultation with China seems to have been incidental."[56] When Stalin sought clarification of the political terms under which the Soviet Union would enter the war against Japan, Roosevelt said "he saw no difficulty in regard to turning over to Russia at the end of the war the Kurile Islands and the southern half of the island of Sakhalin." With reference to Stalin's desire for a warm-water port in the Far East, Roosevelt recalled his suggestion at Teheran that the Soviet Union be given "the use of a warm-water port at the end of the Manchurian railway, possibly at Dairen." In Feis's words, Roosevelt's instinct, "it may be surmised, was to try by this show of free and ready assent to make it a little harder for the Russians to press for more."[57] Stalin declared that he wanted use of the Manchurian railways as well. Roosevelt accepted Stalin's claims on both the ports and the railways, along with a guarantee that "the preeminent interests of the Soviet Union shall be safeguarded." It was acknowledged that these agreements on ports and railways (as well as preservation of the status quo in Outer Mongolia) would require the concurrence of Generalissmo Chiang Kai-shek.

Roosevelt agreed to seek this concurrence while Stalin, for his part, expressed readiness to conclude a pact of friendship and alliance with Chiang to free China from the "Japanese yoke."[58]

These accords at Yalta were of momentous significance—not only because of their impact on the future of East Asia, but also for the entire structure of Roosevelt's "great design." Roosevelt assigned importance to the Soviet Union, in both his strategy for victory and his strategy for peace. In consequence of the course of strategic-diplomatic events, particularly in the Far East, the Soviet role in Roosevelt's great design had now become doubly decisive. Not only did Roosevelt rely on Soviet cooperation militarily, as perhaps the strongest of the four policemen, for final victory over Japan; he had now come to depend on Soviet cooperation politically as the condition for the effective reconstruction of Europe. Without these assurances of Soviet cooperation, Roosevelt had no design for the postwar world.

The last major address of Roosevelt's life was his personal report to Congress on the outcome of the Yalta Conference, delivered on March 1, 1945. Great success, he declared, was achieved in both of the main purposes of the Conference: to defeat Germany at the earliest possible date with the lowest cost in manpower, and to build the basis of a lasting peace. He assured the nation: "Never before have the major Allies been more closely united—not only in their war aims but also in their peace aims. And they are determined to continue to be united with each other—and with all peace-loving Nations—so that the ideal of lasting peace will become a reality. . . . "[59] The Conference, he said, "ought to spell the end of the system of unilateral action, the exclusive alliances, the spheres of influence, the balances of power, and all the other expedients that have been tried for centuries—and have always failed." In their stead he now proposed a "universal organization in which all peace-loving Nations will finally have a chance to join." Problems arose, to be sure, over Poland, or over Yugoslavia. "But at the end, on every point," he continued, "unanimous agreement was reached. And more important even than the agreement of words, I may say we achieved a unity of thought and a way of getting along together." As for Asian matters, the conference had concerned itself only with the European war and with the political problems of Europe, and not with the Pacific war. "It is still a long, tough road to Tokyo," the President admitted, "it is longer to go to Tokyo than it is to Berlin, in every sense of the word. The defeat of Germany will not mean the end of the war against Japan. On the contrary, we must be prepared for a long and costly struggle in the Pacific."[60] Roosevelt did not mention the detailed agreements with Stalin on Asia.

While many difficulties arose over the implementation of the Yalta provisions—most flagrantly those on the structure of the Polish government—Roosevelt remained hopeful that they could be resolved and refused to bring more forceful pressures to bear on Stalin. Soon after Yalta he told State Department Officer Adolf Berle, "I didn't say the result was good. I said it was the best I could do." Because the Joint Chiefs were insisting on the redeployment of American forces from Europe to Asia, the United States would be unable to send troops into the Russian area of control.[61] The United States had no choice but to rely on the Russian word; Roosevelt had no plan to confront Soviet power in Eastern Europe.[62] In a cable to Churchill on April 10, the President admitted the need (with reference to Poland) to "consider most carefully the implications of Stalin's attitude and what is to be our next step." At the same time he sought to dissuade Churchill from stressing in public the extent of the divergences. Two days later the President died.

VI

How are we to evaluate Roosevelt's policies in the Second World War from the standpoint of ethical principles? Roosevelt was a life-long politician who thought the very essence of his craft was to seek common ground among many diverse groups for the furtherance of worthy purposes. He had solid cause for the conviction that his purposes were worthy. For in both the depression and the war he saw himself facing a largely black and white world: poverty against prosperity, prejudice against opportunity, tyranny against freedom, war against peace. Confronted with the two monstrous threats of economic breakdown and rampant aggression, he felt his foremost task as a political leader was to build the broadest possible coalitions to throw back these perils. Given the nature of these threats, he believed this achievement would, in itself, constitute an enormous service to democratic and humane values.

Roosevelt's effort to forge a global coalition to defeat the Axis, and to sustain it into the future as the basis for a durable peace, bore significant similarities with the way he had shaped coalitions in domestic politics. He sought to suffuse both vast enterprises with the same hopeful spirit. As he had endeavored to convert the crisis of the depression into an opportunity to build a better America, he hoped to transform the destructiveness of the war into an opportunity to build a better world. The democratic humanitarianism of his domestic programs carried over, in their way, into his foreign policies. In behalf of his "great design" Roosevelt sought repeatedly to emphasize the democratic character—or at least the democratic potential—of the Grand Alliance. The Allies, after all, represented a majority of the world's peoples. All had been victims of aggressive assault, and millions of their peoples, especially in Russia and China, were the needy poor.

Any attempt to evaluate Roosevelt's policies should also maintain awareness of the conflict between his convictions and the prevailing trends in American opinion. Roosevelt was convinced that the United States confronted threats to its security that could not be addressed effectively unless America played a major, long-term role in the world. At the same time, he understood all too well that this conviction brought him into conflict with the deep-seated concern among his countrymen that such involvement would exact an unwarranted toll on national resources, as well as imperil their national tradition of isolation from European politics. Roosevelt's outlook was shaped by Wilson's failure to carry his hopes for American world leadership into the 1920s. He recalled as well the unending tactical ingenuity he needed in the 1930s to advance even the most modest foreign policy goals in the face of public opposition. Any effort to weigh the toll of Roosevelt's pragmatism upon ethical principles must, then, reach far beyond the President himself, and be directed to the virtues and failings of the people over whom he sought to exert leadership. Nor can the question of evaluation be answered in the abstract. What may strike one critic as evidence of immoral manipulation may seem, from a different perspective, the determination of a leader who bore responsibility for the security of his state to take the steps necessary for its protection. Many components of Roosevelt's pragmatism reflected his ever-present awareness that policy, if it would be effective, needed to circumvent its potential domestic detractors.

One illustration of the impact of circumstance upon content was Roosevelt's conviction that China should be one of the four major powers in the postwar peace structure.[63] This conviction derived in part from Roosevelt's sense of China's enormous latent potential, in part from his presumption of a special bond with China based on family ties, in part from America's long tradition of friendship with that land. But it also derived from Roosevelt's political calculation that the inclusion of China as a principal pillar of the post-war structure would help him legitimize his proposals with the dreaded isolationist opposition. As Selig Adler has pointed out, "American isolationism and an exaggerated concern for Asia bear a close historical relationship."[64]

Another element in Roosevelt's concern was the need to keep down American casualties in the war, because these casualties were intimately related to his assessment of whether America would sustain foreign commitments after the war. "If the sacrifices involved became too great . . . ," John Gaddis has written, "then pressures for reversion to a 'fortress America' concept, if not outright isolationism, might still prevail. Letting allies bear the brunt of casualties was a way of ensuring internationalism for the future."[65] Roosevelt's preoccupation with "squaring the political circle," matching the role he felt America *had* to play with the role it would be *willing* to play, accounts for his optimistic projections about the future effectiveness of the Big Four. Those hopeful assumptions greatly reduced the prospect that America would be asked to bear heavy military burdens as a keeper of the peace. The relative power of the four policemen would be further increased when coupled with the unconditional surrender of the three aggressors and the disarmament of such intermediary powers as France. Risks would be even further lessened because the United States would be concerned primarily with the Western Hemisphere, using chiefly naval and air power—both in accord with old strands in the national tradition.

It was not strange that Roosevelt, in his desire to sustain a major American role in world affairs, emphasized the high ideals of his wartime agreements at Teheran and elsewhere.[66] Despite the radical divergence between his own and Wilson's views, he kept the Wilsonian Cordell Hull as his secretary of state throughout most of his presidency and tried to dissuade him from resigning because of ill health in late 1944. At Dumbarton Oaks Roosevelt's great power condominium was incorporated into Hull's organizational universalism, and the end result proclaimed as a triumph of Wilsonianism. In Robert Divine's words:

> Though the Four Policemen disappeared in substance, the grant of veto power to the permanent members of the Security Council continued Roosevelt's insistence on great-power control over the enforcement of peace.

> . . . in place of the Four Policemen, the member nations were to provide stand-by military forces through separate agreements with the Security Council, which could then employ them in a crisis.[67]

A week before his death, however, Roosevelt gave a glimpse of the reality behind the appearances when, in reply to reporters' questions about the grant of three seats to the Soviet Union in the General Assembly, he answered: "It is not really of any great importance. It is an investigatory body only. . . . This business about the number of votes in the Assembly does not make a great deal of difference.[68]

VII

The divergence between Roosevelt's international strategy and Wilson's was, in truth, a matter of the greatest importance. Roosevelt's notion of the "four policemen" differed fundamentally from Wilson's approach to the security problem. While Wilson's collective security was meant to *free* states from specific alliances, Roosevelt's whole strategy hinged on the *perpetuation* of the Grand Alliance.[69] Beyond this, Roosevelt advocated a severely hierarchical management of security problems, with effective power concentrated in the hands of the Big Four (and very little left to others), while Wilson had called for a "community of power" under which all states would enjoy equal rights and for the maintenance of which all states would enjoy equal rights and for the maintenance of which all states would share common responsibilities. Most important of all, Roosevelt's conception of the bases of peace differed radically from that of Wilson. The order of priorities Roosevelt had made public among his Four Freedoms provides a valuable clue. Provision of freedom from fear—i.e. direct protection against the use of force—was to be the first order of business in peacemaking; furtherance of such other freedoms as those of expression or religion or from want—i.e. longer-term efforts to address the injustices from which the will to use force might derive—were to be strictly derivative. Roosevelt assumed that if the foundations of order could be firmly laid through the effective management of the security problem, then, through the power of example and friendly persuasion, justice would flow from it. Wilson had, by contrast, seen the will to force as a *derivative* issue and had, in consequence, given exacting attention to the *substantive* terms of the prospective peace. The striking incongruity between Wilson's meticulous exchanges with the German Chancellor on the terms of an armistice in the fall of 1918 and Roosevelt's astonishing irresolution on German policy to the very end is a case in point. Of far vaster consequence was the gulf between Wilson's quest for a management of the security problem that would deny to any state rationalization for the claim that its security needs necessitated violation of the integrity of other states, and Roosevelt's approach which, by providing justification for Big Power preponderance, pointed in precisely the opposite direction.[70]

Roosevelt's world, of course, was far different from Wilson's. The multiple difficulties he encountered in foreign policy were vastly compounded by the degenerative character of the historic era during which he tried to lead the nation, for the "crisis of the old order" was far deeper internationally than it was domestically. In his search for the right relation between America and the world Roosevelt felt compelled to improvise, since he saw at hand no traditional models which could give him effective guidance. Beyond this, while "Wilson could lead forthrightly from strength" as head of the rising American colossus in a world overshadowed by the Atlantic powers, Roosevelt felt that at the end of the War the relative strength of America and Britain would have declined, and both would have to come to terms with the enormous increase in the power of the Soviet Union.[71]

A few years after the war's end, George Kennan sought to put the constraints under which democratic statesmen had operated in the Second World War in historic perspective. The range of choices open to the Western democracies at the onset of the war, Kennan argued, was severely constricted by their military weakness in relation to the power of the totalitarian states. Germany and Russia together, he said,

> . . . could not be defeated at all. Individually, either of them could be defeated only if the democracies had the collaboration of the other.
>
> But such collaboration, if permitted to proceed to the point of complete victory, would mean the relative strengthening of the collaborating power and its eventual appearance as a greedy and implacable claimant at the peace table.

The democratic powers could not expect to avoid paying the price of their military weakness: "Theirs were no longer the choices of strength. The cards were so stacked against them that any complete, unsullied democratic victory in a new world war was practically impossible to foresee."[72]

The constraints Kennan highlighted were still powerfully operative, albeit in a rather different configuration, at the time America was drawn into the war. Judgment of Roosevelt's policies must always bear in mind the uncertainties under which he was then compelled to act, not the outcomes some may now accept as if preordained. At the center of Roosevelt's uncertainties lay the possibility of Axis victory. For all the President's buoyancy of spirit the danger could not be brushed aside, for it was inherent in the indeterminacy of reality itself. In June, 1942, Roosevelt told his chief advisors that his main concern "was to do something in 1942 that would help the Russians. 'If the Russians held until December, he would give odds that we would win the War,' while if they 'folded up,' he thought the Allies would have less than an even chance."[73] A similar logic shaped Roosevelt's strategy in the Pacific. In February, 1943, he made clear that he had no intention

> to bring Japan to final defeat merely by inching our way forward from island to island across the vast expansion of the Pacific. "If we took one island, in the advance from the south, once a month . . . ," he told reporters, "I figured out it would take about fifty years before we got to Japan." The way to defeat Japan, he added, was to use China as a base of operations.[74]

A moment's reflection brings starkly to mind how the costs to America would have soared had the Eastern Front collapsed, and Germany been able to concentrate its strength in the West. Operation Overlord, a high risk venture under the best of circumstances, might then have proved impossible altogether.

To the charge, then, that his emphasis on Big Power unity involved a needless sacrifice of principle to political expediency, Roosevelt could plausibly answer that it was, on the contrary, in accord with the most elemental necessities of national survival. To retain one's perspective on this matter it is useful to recall that Churchill, doughty champion of Europe's liberties, also—and more than once—yielded to the compulsions of *raison d'etat.* Although Churchill had originally resisted Stalin's demands for acceptance of the Soviet 1941 boundaries as the condition for conclusion of an alliance with Britain, he later changed because he doubted that the Western powers could make such demands on a nation that alone was engaged in fighting the Germans.[75] British leaders argued, moreover, that Russia, in signing the Atlantic Charter, had assumed that it could keep the areas that it had acquired in the Nazi-Soviet Pact of August, 1939. In consequence, on March 7, 1942, Churchill informed Roosevelt that "The increasing gravity of the war has led me to feel that the principles of the Atlantic Charter ought not to be construed so as to deny Russia the frontiers she occupied when Germany attacked her."[76] Although Roosevelt himself weakly tried to "square the circle" through the proposed addition of a clause to the treaty that affected nationals of these states be allowed to leave with their belongings, Hull stood firm against this "Baltic Munich." Under Roosevelt's promise of a second front the Soviets relented. In London Molotov signed a twenty-year alliance treaty with Britain, put forward by Eden, which made no reference to frontiers.[77]

Recognition that *some* form of unity with the Soviet Union at *some* stage for *some* purposes in the war against the Axis was defensible gives no automatic justification to the actual *mode* of unity Roosevelt sought. In a profound formulation of the relation of ethics to politics, Reinhold Niebuhr stated: "There are fixed principles and norms in the political realm, but there is no fixed principle for relating the norms to each other."[78] Given this diversity of norms, and the absence of a fixed principle for the resolution of tensions among them, the first requirement of a statesmanship that seeks to be responsible ethically is to acknowledge this tension explicitly and bring to bear the most exacting analysis possible on the modes for its mitigation. A statesman who would act dutifully cannot make the pursuit of the "larger whole" a good in itself. Roosevelt's single-minded devotion to the preservation of Big Power unity became an *idee fixe* that corrupted the foundations of his statesmanship. This single-mindedness contributed to grave errors of judgment on the sources, the processes, the durability, and the effects of the unity he sought. The problem focuses on Roosevelt's errors of judgment in his relations with the Soviet Union, not because it is here alone that they are to be found, but because it is here that he confronted the most intractable barriers to his expectations, and here that his misjudgments proved most detrimental to future prospects in international politics.

VIII

The primary source of Roosevelt's commitment to the preservation of unity among the Big Four was his genuine abhorrence of war. Although he had failed in his efforts to prevent the breakdown of peace in the 1930s, he reaffirmed the commitment to peace as the main goal of America's war effort. The ordering of priorities among the Four Freedoms to assign primacy to freedom from fear made this explicit. His concern to advance the cause of peace dominated Roosevelt's last major address:

> I am confident that the Congress and the American people will accept the results of this Conference [Yalta] as the beginnings of a permanent structure of peace upon which we can begin to build, under God, that better world in which our children and grandchildren—yours and mine, the children and grandchildren of the whole world—must live, and can live.[79]

His own convictions were reenforced, politically, by the fact that they blended genuinely with the deep hopes of his own people for peace.

Roosevelt was also confident a common interest in peace was shared by America's major allies, for they had suffered more grievous wounds in war than had America. To skeptics who stressed the high risks in his great design, Roosevelt answered, through Davis, that "he was willing to settle for the lowest common denominator—what he conceived to be the overpowering need and desire for peace among the great powers—as the foundation for a world society."[80] His commitment to peace also stemmed from deep apprehension that the alternatives were too dreadful to contemplate—an apprehension perhaps intensified by his singular premonitions of the destructiveness of things to come.[81] In the spring of 1944 he told Davis that unless the great powers "can be brought into a sincere compact" that goes beyond an "uncertain balance of power," a war of continents would come which would bring down western civilization itself.[82]

Roosevelt assumed the goals of the other policemen corresponded to his own. It was essentially a matter of making explicit the multiple advantages of cooperative behavior, and laying to rest the insecurities which, in his view, were largely behind the impulses of his allies to "go it alone." If the American people had come to learn the superior benefits of international cooperation as opposed to those of narrow-minded isolationism, so could any other people. Roosevelt's more immediate task, then, was so to conduct relations within the Grand Alliance that its latent potential for unity could be fully actualized. All the more specific tactics he pursued in his dealings with the Soviet Union were undertaken with an eye to overcoming barriers he thought stood in the way of the preservation and strengthening of that unity—most notably in his ceaseless prodding for the establishment of a second front, his persistent quest for personal rapport with Stalin, the unconditional surrender policy, the grant of an economic generosity through Lend Lease to the Soviet Union, his support for the destruction of German unity, and his recurrent subordination of boundary claims (most lamentably in the case of Poland) to the presumed security needs of the Soviet Union.[83]

If Roosevelt's assumptions of the existence of a common interest in unity between the United States and the Soviet Union were accurate, and his means to further that unity were effective, the Alliance should have grown in cohesion as the war neared its end. More nearly the opposite, in truth, was the case. For despite Roosevelt's efforts at Allied unity he never conceded the principle of political self-determination. At the time of Roosevelt's death divergences between the United States and the Soviet Union on all the great issues of the peace were unresolved—the status of Germany, the status of Eastern and Danubian Europe, the terms of economic settlement, to mention but the most obvious. The special intimacy Roosevelt fancied he had established with "Uncle Joe" proved insufficient to prevent acerbic exchanges between them over clashes of policy. Roosevelt himself by late 1944 was at last coming to question the prudence of unreciprocated economic largesse. The destruction of German power was having no detectable effect on Soviet aggressiveness. The successful establishment of the Second Front—which should, by Roosevelt's analysis, have laid to rest Soviet unilateral actions incompatible with Alliance unity—had, instead, brutally magnified them. In the spring of 1942, when the Soviet Union was under mortal danger from Nazi force, Stalin had backed off from his insistence on the termination of the independence of the Baltic states as the condition of alliance with Britain. In the late summer of 1944, with German armies driven from Soviet territory, Stalin made savagely clear his contempt for the Atlantic Charter. Ambassador Kennan analyzed the Soviet reaction to the Warsaw uprising:

> This, more than anything that had occurred to that point, brought the Western governments face to face with what they were up against in Stalin's Polish policy. For if the inactivity of the Red army forces as they sat,

> passive, on the other side of the river and watched the slaughter by the Germans of the Polish heroes of the rebellion was not yet eloquent enough as an expression of the Soviet attitude, then the insolent denial by Stalin and Molotov to Ambassador Harriman of permission for use of the American shuttle base in the Ukraine to facilitate the dropping of arms and supplies to the beleaguered Poles, and the significant demand, expressed on the same occasion, that we withdraw the shuttle bases entirely, left no room for misunderstanding.[84]

Kennan felt that no further justification could be given for failure to clarify the terms on which the Alliance rested:

> It has been my opinion, ever since, that this was the moment when, if ever, there should have been a full-fledged and realistic political showdown with the Soviet leaders: when they should have been confronted with the choice between changing their policy completely and agreeing to collaborate in the establishment of truly independent countries in Eastern Europe or forefeiting Western-Allied support and sponsorship for the remaining phases of their war effort.[85]

If projections on the course and duration of American relations with the Soviet Union, based on Roosevelt's assumptions, proved faulty, this poses, at the least, questions on the accuracy of Roosevelt's understanding of the *source* of the unity, and on the efficacy of the means he prescribed for its furtherance.

On the *effects* of his *idee fixe* the evidence seems more clear-cut. An understanding of why Roosevelt's projections collapsed in Germany provides a clue to the reasons for the collapse of his grand design as a whole. From a meeting with Roosevelt in the fall of 1944, Robert Murphy recounts the importance the President attached to the preservation of cooperation with the Soviet Union, not only as a general guide to United States policy, but as the basis for the approach that the United States should take on specific issues:

> His topic that day was the future of Soviet-American relations. He declared we must arrange the German occupation in a manner which would convince the Russians that Americans really desired to cooperate with them. . . . He urged me to bear in mind that our primary postwar

> objective was Soviet-American cooperation—without which world peace would be impossible—and that Germany would be the proving ground for such cooperation. That was my parting word from the President before I returned to Europe, and I considered it the equivalent of an oral directive.[86]

President Truman may be seen as acting in accord with Roosevelt's goals in his agreement to the political and economic principles of the Potsdam Conference in August, 1945, e.g. Number 14: "During the period of occupation Germany shall be treated as a single economic unit. . . . " And Ambassador Murphy may still have had Roosevelt's directive in the back of his mind when, in the months after Potsdam, the American Government confronted countless obstacles in its efforts to implement the principles of Potsdam. Murphy argued that "Centralized German economic agencies would have at least partially broken down zonal boundaries . . . making it difficult for the Russians to continue running their zone on a unilateral basis." George Kennan, however, sharply disagreed and warned "that German economic unity would not necessarily weaken the Soviet position: the Russians would agree to central agencies only if they thought they could control them, and this could lead to the eventual communization of the entire country." Kennan saw the real alternatives as two:

> (1) to leave [the] remainder of Germany nominally united but extensively vulnerable to Soviet political penetration and influence or (2) to carry to its logical conclusion the process of partition which was begun in the east and to endeavor to rescue [the] western zones of Germany by walling them off against eastern penetration and integrating them into [the] international pattern of western Europe rather than into a united Germany.[87]

The options the United States faced in its confrontation with the Soviet Union over the specific problem of Germany also provide the paradigm for the options it faced in its encounters with the Soviet Union in the world as a whole. The preferred outcome for President Roosevelt—and, initially, for President Truman—was the conclusion of general accords with the Soviet Union that would serve the presumptive common interest in peace, in such areas as a peace settlement in Germany or control over atomic power. However, the Truman administration became increasingly determined to resist agreement with the Soviet Union—in Germany or Japan, in the United Nations, or over atomic power—in which it felt the cost of agreement *as such* outweighed the *substantive* gains. Truman began to break with the essence of Roosevelt's strategy as he came to judge the costs from the attempted preservation of unity to be higher than the costs from the breach of it.

The paralysis of the provisions for Big Four management of security problems under the auspices of the United Nations may be taken as symbolic of the paralysis of Roosevelt's great design as a whole. Those provisions which rested on assumed accord among the Four Policemen foundered on the persistence of conflict among them—conflict with the Soviet Union in particular. Articles 43 and 45, as instances, remained dead letters. The very eccentric centrality that came to be assigned to the peacekeeping function was itself demonstration that such contribution as the United Nations could discover for itself in the security area was on a trial-and-error basis, widely at odds with the role prescribed for it in the formal clauses of the Charter. In Raymond Aron's words,

> the Charter had a double face. Veto right, legitimate defense, and action against ex-enemies constituted the traditional face and made possible the classical interplay of power politics. The authority of the Security Council to impose peace represented the other face and was to have created a world order. The conflict of the two superpowers has paralyzed the Security Council and today the traditional face alone appears, in a harsh light.[88]

The United Nations never proved able to turn its Rooseveltian face to the world; the face it turned was that from which Roosevelt's strategy was meant to turn the world away. As the policies derivative from the Rooseveltian implications of the Charter atrophied, the United States came to put ever greater weight on policies derivative from the traditionalist implications of Article 51, most notably in the Rio Pact of 1947, the North Atlantic Treaty of 1949, and the American-Japanese Mutual Security Treaty of 1951.

IX

Although the assumption that a common interest in peace was strong enough to lay to rest the multiple divergences that mark the relations of states with one another has persisted over the centuries, it has never proved true. There is, indeed, an implausible paradox in the argument that the insecurities which result from the clash of purposes among states themselves provide the means to resolve the very clashes that generated them. While Stalin did, in a sense, seek peace, nothing in Marxist doctrine or Soviet experience led him to define that sense in a fashion coincident with Roosevelt's. From the fact that they seemed largely to have resolved their own inner debate on the importance of, and the means to, peace, many Americans came to assume the problem *itself* had been resolved. But the terms of the debate within the United States were largely irrelevant to its terms in other lands—and certainly in the Soviet Union.

There was even less empirical ground for Roosevelt's conviction that perpetuation of the Grand Alliance was the most effective means to peace than for his belief in a common interest in peace itself. The long historic record pointed to a very different outcome: that the bonds of alliance would weaken as did the threat that had brought it into being. So it had been with the alliances that threw back Hapsburg power in 1648, Bourbon in 1713, Napoleonic in 1815. For those who based statesmanship on the behavior of states, it could occasion little surprise that the second front proved more vexatious to the unity of the Alliance after its establishment than before; Stalin's dependency on Allied unity—and the price he was willing to pay for it—varied in proportion to the gravity of the Nazi threat to Soviet survival. That the outcome of the Grand Alliance would follow the general historic pattern was made all the more probable by the specific impact of Soviet ideology on the course of events. In February, 1946, Stalin made public the authoritative Soviet interpretation of the causes and effects of the Second World War: "It would be wrong to think that the Second World War was a casual occurrence or the result of mistakes of any particular statesmen. . . . Actually, the war was the inevitable result of the development of world economic and political forces on the basis of modern monopoly capitalism."[89] While wars might be avoided if it were possible for capitalists to redistribute economic goods peacefully, said Stalin, "that is impossible to do under present capitalist conditions of the development of world economy." For Stalin the Grand Alliance had been strictly a temporary marriage of convenience during an interlude when it served Soviet interests "to profit by the division within the capitalist world, and thus to utilize the power of one segment of that world against its own interests."[90] Yet it was one member of that capitalist world that had unleashed the forces of destruction and change.

It would be wrong to infer from these considerations that Soviet policy was governed by ideological determinism. The cunning of Stalin's own calculations, to say nothing of the indeterminacy of the circumstances he faced, make such an interpretation inadequate.[91] But while Stalin's ideological beliefs did not in themselves determine outcomes, they gave a very significant indication of what his dispositions would be, given opportune circumstances. While Roosevelt directed his main energies to the preservation and strengthening of Allied unity, Stalin saw that unity as but one instrument—and by no means the most important one—for the furtherance of his purposes. He was willing to utilize the Grand Alliance when it advanced his interests, ignore it when it had no bearing on his interests, defy it when it blocked his interests. He proved a far more worldly practitioner of pragmatism than did Roosevelt.

The major factor that determined the course of relations within the Grand Alliance was the course of the strategic-diplomatic struggle against the Axis. We have noted earlier that Roosevelt's concern to keep in being the Eastern and Far Eastern fronts was justified, at a certain stage in the conflict, by elemental strategic prudence. But as the course of the war changed, so did its nature—from one to prevent an Axis victory, to one to determine the mode of Axis defeat and lay the foundations for a postwar order. Throughout all these momentous transformations, however, Roosevelt continued to convey to Stalin the impression that preservation of unity with the Soviet Union was more important than the *terms* on which that unity was to rest. Any party who proceeds on this assumption automatically becomes vulnerable to the danger that the other party will define, unilaterally, the terms of the relationship. A statesman who would be true to ethical obligations must be clear in his own mind on the substantive standards which are to be met if the loss in the pursuit of unity is not to outweigh the gain from it. Long after unreciprocated concessions to the Soviet Union ceased to be justifiable as a means to stave off Axis victory, Roosevelt continued to make them because his strategy for peace was a logical extension of his strategy for victory. The inadequacy of Roosevelt's policy toward the Soviet Union was compounded by his insufficient attention to the importance of *means:* those he was willing to use often proved ineffective; those that might have proved effective he was usually unwilling to use. The freedom of action of America—already under objective constraint to turn from victory in Europe to the war with Japan—was further compromised by Roosevelt's failure to appreciate the critical importance in statecraft of *timing* and *means*. In the end, Roosevelt could neither satisfy the security concerns of Russia nor preserve the historic liberties of Europe. When the free world renewed its struggle with totalitarianism, it was under handicaps, both strategic and moral, that need not have been.

Criticism of Roosevelt's wartime diplomacy is not an easy indulgence in *ex post facto* moralism. During the war itself Churchill had a profound insight into the objective conditions that would have to be met if the liberties of Europe were to be preserved. Another great contemporary of Roosevelt's has given us a classic object lesson in how a commitment to principle and the courage to act can widen, even in highly constrictive circumstances, the realm of freedom in history. When General de Gaulle went to Moscow in December of 1944 to discuss the terms of a Franco-Soviet pact, he confronted unrelenting pressure that, as the condition for its conclusion, he give recognition to the Lublin Committee as the government of Poland. This the General refused to do (in agreement with Roosevelt and Churchill), rightly recognizing the Committee as but a front for Communist domination of Poland. When the Soviets proved unyielding, de Gaulle described his response: "[I]t is useless and will become disadvantageous to continue the negotiation. I shall therefore bring it to an end.' At midnight, the film over and the lights on again, I stood up and said to Stalin: 'I am now making my farewells. Soon the train will be taking me back to France.' "[92]

Before the evening was out, Stalin reversed course and concluded the pact, with no further insistence that France recognize Lublin. De Gaulle also left an account of Stalin's reaction after the signing: "In a low voice, he complimented me: 'You have played well! Well done! I like dealing with someone who knows what he wants, even if he doesn't share my views.' "[93] Then de Gaulle recorded an eloquent insight on the role of principle in politics:

> . . . however little weight France's attitude might have at the moment, it could later be important that she had adopted it at that particular moment. The future lasts a long time. All things are possible, even the fact that an action in accord with honor and honesty ultimately appears to be a prudent political investment.[94]

In the history of statecraft Roosevelt's "great design" was an idiosyncratic interlude. Deeply rooted in no prior body of experience, it gave no durable guidance to experiences soon to come. Churchill's somber judgment stands as the controlling judgment; triumph in war was followed by the tragedy of hopes unfulfilled. Roosevelt's triumph came as a soldier of victory; his tragedy, as a soldier of freedom.

NOTES

1. The statement by Richard Hofstadter is found in *The American Political Tradition* (New York, 1958), pp. 331-32.
2. Quoted in Eric F. Goldman, *Rendezvous with Destiny* (New York, 1953), p. 339.
3. C. Kegley and R. Bretall, eds., *Reinhold Niebuhr: His Religious, Social, and Political Thought* (new York, 1956), pp. 142-43.
4. Arthur M. Schlesinger, Jr., *The Crisis of the Old Order* (Cambridge, Mass., 1957), pp. 4-5.
5. William E. Leuchtenberg, *Franklin Roosevelt and the New Deal, 1932-1940* (New York, 1963), p. 344.
6. Robert Dallek, *Franklin Roosevelt and American Foreign Policy, 1932-1945* (New York, 1981), p. 6.
7. This is also emphasized in Hofstadter's study.
8. Basil Rauch, ed., *Franklin D. Roosevelt: Selected Speeches, Messages, Press Conferences, and Letters* (New York, 1957), p. 90.
9. *Ibid.*, p. 391.
10. Joseph Alsop, "A Centenary Remembrance of FDR," *Smithsonian*, 12 (January 1982), p. 48.
11. Dallek, *Roosevelt and American Foreign Policy*, p. 7.
12. Robert Divine, *Roosevelt and World War II* (Baltimore, 1969), p. 55.
13. *Ibid.*, p. 7.
14. Cited in *ibid.*, p. 9.
15. Rauch, *Selected Speeches*, pp. 189-190.
16. *Ibid.*, p. 191.
17. Divine, *Roosevelt and World War II*, p. 17.
18. Professor Graebner develops his thesis in *Roosevelt and the Search for a European Policy* (Oxford, 1980), p. 6, *passim*. Professor Borg's argument is presented in "Notes on Roosevelt's 'Quarantine' Speech," *Political Science Quarterly*, 72 (September 1957), pp. 405-33.
19. Arnold Wolfers, *Britain and France Between Two Wars* (New York, 1966), Ch. 12.
20. Quoted in Graebner, *Roosevelt and the Search for a European Policy*, p. 35.
21. Robert Divine, *Second Chance: The Triumph of Internationalism in America during World War II* (New York, 1971), p. 249.

22. Dallek, *Roosevelt and American Foreign Policy,* p. 247.
23. *Ibid.,* p. 255.
24. Rauch, *Selected Speeches,* pp. 274-75.
25. T. Brockway, ed., *Basic Documents in United States Foreign Policy* (Princeton, N.J., 1957), pp. 126-27.
26. This speech may be found in Norman A. Graebner, ed., *Ideas and Diplomacy* (New York, 1964), pp. 650-51.
27. *Ibid.,* pp. 656-57.
28. Rauch, *Selected Speeches,* pp. 338-349.
29. *Foreign Relations of the United States: The Conferences at Malta and Yalta* (Washington, 1955), p. 972.
30. Divine, *Roosevelt and World War II,* p. 31.
31. Rauch, *Selected Speeches,* pp. 252-54.
32. *Ibid.,* pp. 284-86.
33. *Ibid.,* p. 304.
34. *Ibid.,* p. 307.
35. Graebner, *Ideas and Diplomacy,* p. 656.
36. Robert E. Sherwood, *Roosevelt and Hopkins: An Intimate History* (New York, 1948), p. 573.
37. *Ibid.,* p. 716.
38. Forrest Davis, "Roosevelt's World Blueprint," *Saturday Evening Post,* 215, Pt 4 (April 10, 1943), p. 109.
39. *Ibid.,* p. 20.
40. Graebner, *Ideas and Diplomacy,* p. 659.
41. Forrest Davis, "What Really Happened at Teheran," *Saturday Evening Post,* 216, Pt 4 (May 13, 1944), p. 37.
42. *Ibid.,* p. 39.
43. *Foreign Relations of the United States: Conferences at Cairo and Teheran* (Washington, 19•1), pp. 640-41.
44. Davis, "What Really Happened at Teheran, II," *Saturday Evening Post,* 216, Pt 4 (May 20, 1944), p. 23.
45. Davis, "What Really Happened at Teheran," p. 37.
46. *Ibid.*
47. Davis, "What Really Happened at Teheran, II," p. 44.
48. Davis, "What Really Happened at Teheran," p. 37.
49. *Ibid.,* p. 13.
50. Davis, "What Really Happened at Teheran, II," p. 44.
51. *Ibid.,* p. 48.
52. Dallek, *Roosevelt and American Foreign Policy,* p. 435. A helpful analysis of Roosevelt's policies toward the colonial world may be found in Gaddis Smith, *American Diplomacy During the Second World War, 1941-1945* (New York, 1965), pp. 81-98.
53. Dallek, *Roosevelt and American Foreign Policy,* p. 485.
54. *Ibid.,* p. 498.
55. *Ibid.,* p. 501.

56. Herbert Feis, *The China Tangle* (Princeton, 1953), p. 241.
57. *Ibid.*, p. 242.
58. *Ibid.*, p. 244-45.
59. Rauch, *Selected Speeches*, p. 384.
60. *Ibid.*, p. 387.
61. Dallek, *Roosevelt and American Foreign Policy*, p. 521.
62. *Ibid.*
63. Barbara W. Tuchman, *Stilwell and the American Experience in China, 1911-1945* (New York, 1971), p. 451.
64. Selig Adler, *The Isolationist Impulse: Its Twentieth Century Reaction* (New York, 1961), p. 25.
65. John Lewis Gaddis, *Strategies of Containment* (New York, 1982), p. 7.
66. Dallek, *Roosevelt and American Foreign Policy*, p. 438.
67. Divine, *Roosevelt and World War II*, pp. 66-67.
68. Cited in Divine, *Second Chance*, p. 276.
69. Inis L. Claude, Jr., *Power and International Relations* (New York, 1962), pp. 144-45, and following.
70. For a fuller discussion of Wilson's strategy of peace see my essay, "Reflections on Wilson and the Problems of World Peace," in Arthur Link, ed., *Woodrow Wilson and a Revolutionary World, 1913-1921* (Chapel Hill, 1982). Arthur Walworth gives an excellent discussion of the details of of Wilson's policies in *America's Moment: 1918* (New York, 1977). For observations of Wilson's German policy see my review essay, "Wilson the Peacemaker," of Walworth's book in *The Virginia Quarterly Review*, 54 (Spring 1978), pp. 361-67.
71. Davis, "What Really Happened at Teheran," p. 37.
72. George F. Kennan, *American Diplomacy, 1900-1950* (Chicago, 1951), p. 75.
73. Dallek, *Roosevelt and American Foreign Policy*, P. 345.
74. *Ibid.*, pp. 388-89.
75. Winston Churchill, *The Hinge of Fate* (Boston, 1950), p. 327. For a thoughtful discussion of the issue in Churchill's policy see Kenneth W. Thompson, *Winston Churchill's World View: Statesmanship and Power* (Baton Rouge, La., 1983).
76. Churchill, *Hinge of Fate*, p. 327.
77. Divine, *Roosevelt and World War II*, p. 89.
78. H. Davis and R. Good, eds., *Reinhold Niebuhr on Politics* (New York, 1960), p. 177. For a more extended discussion of the relation of ethical principles to foreign policy see my essay in C. Griffith, ed., *Christianity and Politics* (Washington, 1981).
79. Rauch, *Selected Speeches*, p. 388.
80. Davis, "What Really Happened in Teheran, II," p. 46.
81. It would be of much value to know in what measure Roosevelt's views of the centrality of peace were shaped by his awareness of the

destructiveness of nuclear power. I have found no material that casts significant light on this.

82. Davis, "What Really Happened at Teheran, II," p. 48.
83. John Lewis Gaddis, *The United States and the Origins of the Cold War, 1941-1947* (New York, 1972), p. 82. In his meticulous account, Gaddis lists the perpetuation of the Grand Alliance as but one among the several goals of Roosevelt's policy. It is my contention that it was the primary one, and that the other goals which Gaddis discusses can be understood more clearly as aspects of this primary one.
84. George F. Kennan, *Memoirs: 1925-1950* (Boston, 1967), p. 210.
85. *Ibid.,* p. 211.
86. Robert Murphy, *Diplomat among Warriors* (Garden City, N.Y., 1964), p. 227.
87. Gaddis, *Origins of the Cold War,* p. 328.
88. Raymond Aron, *Peace and War* (New York, 1966), p. 716.
89. Excerpts from the text may be found in Alvin Rubinstein, ed., *The Foreign Policy of the Soviet Union* (New York, 1960), p. 221.
90. Gordon Wright, *The Ordeal of Total War, 1939-1945* (New York, 1968), p. 204.
91. For an excellent discussion of Stalin's wartime policy see Vojtech Mastny, *Russia's Road to the Cold War* (New York, 1979).
92. Charles de Gaulle, *The Complete War Memoirs* (New York, 1955), p. 754.
93. *Ibid.,* p. 756.
94. *Ibid.,* p. 750.